P9-DMH-243

CANADIAN STUDIES IN CRIMINOLOGY

EDITED BY J. LL. J. EDWARDS

1 Sentencing as a Human Process

BY JOHN HOGARTH

2 Men Released from Prison

BY IRVIN WALLER

Men Released from Prison

Irvin Waller

Published by the University of Toronto Press
in association with the Centre of Criminology
University of Toronto

Toronto and Buffalo

Printed in Canada

ISBN 0-8020-2105-0

LC 73-85690

This book has been published with
the help of a grant from the
Social Science Research Council of Canada,
using funds provided by the
Canada Council.

Foreword

Parole and its precursor, ticket-of-leave, have been integral parts of Canada's penal system as correctional measures since the turn of this century. The national parole organization was introduced in 1959, so that we now have fifteen years of experience upon which to draw in evaluating its worth and importance. Federal penitentiaries have been part of the penal scene for very much longer, the first being built in Kingston, Ontario, in 1835. Over the years many reports have emanated from royal commissions, parliamentary committees, and governmental task forces seeking to describe and rectify conditions inside penal institutions and they have gradually moved towards a rehabilitative philosophy as the cornerstone of Canada's present-day penal network.

Until now, however, there has been a notable lack of empirical information as to what happens to the prison inmates when they are eventually discharged back into free society. Up to the time when the research reported upon in this book was undertaken the penitentiary population fell into two principal categories: first, those released on the expiry of their sentence without any form of supervision or assistance other than that available to them on a voluntary basis by such independent bodies as the Salvation Army and the John Howard Society; and, secondly, those who were released before their sentences had expired and who were subject to parole supervision and control. Dr Waller's book is concerned with both of these groups and represents the first major effort in Canada to examine, in depth, the life experience, over a period of twelve months, of a large group of men released from prison either conditionally or absolutely. On a less intensive scale the post-release criminal record of the same ex-prisoners has been followed for a total span of two years from the day of their release back into society.

A word of explanation is called for at this point. In 1972, after the collection of the data for this study had been completed, legislation became effective introducing a scheme whereby mandatory supervision is made available even for those who do not apply for, or who have not been granted, parole before release. The effects of this latest innovation in the federal government's correctional policies were not studied empirically as part of the present research project. Nevertheless, based on the findings from his study, Dr Waller has some trenchant observations to make on the probable consequences of the new law and particularly on the predicted future burgeoning of the penitentiary population. Early indications suggest that insufficient regard may have been given to the possible negative aspects of mandatory supervision while the merits of supervised liberation have been correspondingly exaggerated.

This latest volume in the series 'Canadian Studies in Criminology' is essentially an evaluation of the effects of penitentiary sentences and of the parole experience upon a representative sample of 423 inmates who were released from Ontario penitentiaries in 1968. To those unidentified men who voluntarily participated in the research project, the sincere thanks of the Centre of Criminology are publicly extended. Total participation over the entire study period was an unrealizable goal from the beginning but the following report indicates the high level of response sustained despite the inevitable difficulties of keeping in touch with former prisoners bent on invisibility in the outside world. Dr Waller succeeds in drawing together the broad set of experiences and reference points – moving beyond the re-arrest and reconviction of the parolee or former inmate – upon which the relative success or failure of existing correctional principles and practices in this area can be determined. The author is surely right to attempt, before making any evaluative judgments, to know and record the levels of adjustment attained by the former inmates in such areas as marital and family relationships, employment opportunities, and work experience – social habits in the broadest sense of that term – as well as brushes or confrontations with the law enforcement authorities following his release.

The depressing picture to be drawn from this study includes the following findings:

- within six months of release from penitentiary, one out of every three men not on parole was re-arrested and subsequently convicted of an indictable offence;
- within a period of two years following release, two out of every three men not on parole were re-arrested and convicted of an indictable offence;
- within the same period of two years, slightly less than one out of every two men released on parole were similarly re-arrested and convicted or had their parole revoked;
- within a period of three years, the above proportions were expected to have increased still further;

– the length of sentence bears no relationship to the probability of reconviction following release, whether on parole or not;
– the threat of revocation of parole affects the behaviour of parolees only marginally;
– parole makes little difference to the actual employability of the ex-prisoner;
– employment, family, and friends are among the most important aspects of life on the outside for the ex-prisoner – if maintained, they significantly lower the likelihood of re-arrest and conviction of further crimes;
– another crucial factor in the same context is drinking habits.

Such findings, it is suggested, must direct public attention, less to the high levels of recidivism that flow in the wake of a penitentiary sentence, with or without parole supervision, and more to the analysis of why such a high failure rate persists, in what amounts to recycling the same basic group of individuals who populate our prisons at such high costs to the state. The conclusions reached by Dr Waller cast doubt on the repeated claims that the rehabilitative successes derived from parole are in sharp contrast with the failures attributable to release from penitentiary without any form of outside supervision. But it would be unwise to jump too readily to the conclusion that parole has failed as a correctional practice. It is difficult, in any case, to ignore the economic implications drawn by Dr Waller in comparing the costs that attach to incarceration and parole, respectively.

The author's research findings do not indicate in any way the necessity for considering the removal of parole from the statute book. What this study does reveal in impressive detail is the near futility of our present system of parole supervision which tackles, all too often, the form, but not the substance, of the inmate's real problems on the outside. The dire and inevitable results that accompany such an approach are now a matter of public record. The directness of the author's criticisms cannot easily be blunted and will be set aside only at the expense of seeing an increasing erosion in the confidence of members of probation and parole services, as well as after-care agencies, to discharge their difficult tasks. What is called for is a major realignment of the time and energies of those engaged in the fields of correction and related organizations towards the alleviation of those problems associated with employment, family and community relationships, and alcoholism which are at the root of most failures following release.

Despite all the advances in the social and behavioural sciences, our knowledge of how to modify human behaviour and individual attitudes is regrettably unimpressive. Expectations of what can be achieved from the sentences imposed by judges and the efforts of correctional institutions, which attempt with difficulty to combine the edicts of both the judicial and executive branches of government, continue to be wholly unrealistic. The danger of disillusionment with our penal methods is very real and must not be underestimated. In large measure, this strange mixture of uncritical confidence and growing disenchantment is traceable to the implicit faith which we accord to the principles of deterrence and rehabilitation. Both concepts have innate weaknesses and it is to Dr Waller's credit that these are exposed and explained to a wider public than those standing close to the system itself, who sometimes prefer to remain silent.

Any stance reflecting negativism and despair is unhelpful unless accompanied by suggestions of fresh approaches designed to overcome existing faults. In this respect the author, from empirical data, has made substantial contributions to the rejection of some old theories of crime and corrections and has generated the beginnings of testable alternative theories. In another capacity, as a member of the Hugessen Task Force on Parole whose report was recently tabled in Parliament, Dr Waller has made a noted contribution to the development of future policy with regard to the national parole system. If implemented, time will demonstrate whether the changes recommended have been beneficial. At this stage, I would only express the strong belief that research studies of the kind reflected in the present work are an essential part of any enlightened system of criminal justice. New policies, when carried into practice, should be subjected to the same kind of evaluative testing as that described in this book.

Such an approach, it must be emphasized, is slow, often tedious, and dependent on painstaking attention to myriad details. There are no short cuts to the finish line. It calls for the combined efforts of a research team whose several contributions are all essential to the successful completion of the project. The Centre of Criminology has been especially fortunate in this regard and I gladly acknowledge the dedication of those colleagues listed in the author's preface. Special mention is also due to the members of the Penitentiary Service and the National Parole Service who made it possible, in many ways and on many occasions, for the research staff to fulfil their tasks and to collect the data essential to the study. Finally, the Centre of Criminology gratefully records the financial support extended to the project by the Federal Department of the Solicitor General, the University of Toronto, and the Ford Foundation. I am confident that this volume will amply confirm the many acts of co-operation, financial and otherwise, which eased the project towards its final accountability, the publication of the research findings.

Centre of Criminology
University of Toronto

J. LL. J. EDWARDS

Acknowledgements

This monograph is based on analysis undertaken as part of a research study into penitentiaries and parole in Canada carried out by the Centre of Criminology, University of Toronto, with financial support from the Federal Department of the Solicitor General, the Ford Foundation, and the University of Toronto. The Laidlaw Foundation awarded a research fellowship, thus enabling me to work away from the problems of data collection for eight months, and view after-care in Belgium, Czechoslovakia, England, Holland, and Poland.

As the reader glances through the sections of this report he will soon realize that despite the magic powers of the computer, this study was only completed through the enthusiasm, assistance, and hard and sometimes boring work of many people.

The basis for this study is 213 men released at the expiration of sentence and 210 men released on parole, who allowed their lives to be followed in varying degrees of detail from a month before release from a penitentiary, until the end of their first twelve months in the community. Their full co-operation and their voluntary consent allowed information to be recorded about them from many different files and from their parole supervisors.

The original doors were opened to this project by Frank Miller, who had been a member of the Canadian National Parole Board and was at that time Executive Director of the National Parole Service. He and Roger Beames, Regional Director of the National Parole Service in Toronto, were particularly important in my initial introduction to parole in Canada and in arranging the necessary co-operation from those responsible in the National Parole Service. Parole supervisors across Canada, particularly those employed by the Ontario Probation Service, the John Howard Society of Ontario and the National Parole Service in Ontario, with few complaints, helped in the piloting phase of the study and completed more than 1400 questionnaires about the interpretations of their role and their details of the parole supervision experience for the 210 parolees involved in this study. Many of these questionnaires are the subject of detailed analysis in a later publication. There were many obstacles to this co-operation which often seemed insurmountable. Keith Couse and George MacFarlane played vital roles within their agencies to remove these obstacles, helped others to be surmounted and, more importantly to me, showed interest in ensuring that the project got under way and that it would be completed successfully. The credit that such a complete sample of questionnaires was available for analysis lies with all these people.

The co-operation of the wardens and staff of the federal penitentiaries in Ontario was essential to all of the pre-release and some of the post-release interviewing. The Regional Director of Classification for the Federal Penitentiary Service, Stan Farrell, was quick to arrange for the opening of doors and to interpret our aims to many of those in these institutions. Undoubtedly, the necessity of taking female interviewers into the institutions and the type of analysis in which we were engaged were felt as a threat and a nuisance by many of the institutional staff. However, many accepted our assurances which meant that interviewing could take place under appropriate circumstances, and that information could be taken from penitentiary files.

The governors of jails, superintendents of reformatories, the directors of half-way houses, and many others working with ex-prisoners allowed their premises to be used, or helped contact these ex-prisoners, or simply encouraged or gave constructive criticism in the course of this study. The police forces returned data on re-arrest and reconviction particularly efficiently.

Both at the Centre of Criminology, University of Toronto, and the Institute of Criminology, Cambridge, there have been several members of staff and students who have encouraged, criticized, or suggested as the research progressed. While it may make for invidious comparisons, some particular mentions must be made. John Edwards has made the research project possible not only by finding the funds but also by creating a research environment. Susan Binnie contributed much in the early stages of research design and helped sort out problems during my period of leave of absence in Cambridge. However, it is to Peter Macnaughton-Smith that I owe my special debt of thanks. His continued encouragement and support have made the task of the organization and interpretation of the results of this project much more pleasant. Many of the statistical techniques reported on or used during the course of the study were those which he suggested. In Cambridge, I am particularly grateful to Dr Donald West for his sound, concise and sympathetic guidance, and to Keith Hawkins who contributed much to my broader understanding of parole.

Among those directly employed on this project by the Centre, the enthusiasm and tenacity of Joan Buchanan must be specially recorded. Her ability to empathize with ex-prisoners, to listen for hours to the worries, concerns, or escapades of the men who co-operated with us, and to communicate these to me are just a few of her qualities. Without these, and especially her dedication and loyalty, this project would not have been completed. I am grateful also for the ideas contributed and the interviews carried out by Joanne Aimer and Muriel Johnson during the respective eighteen-month periods that they worked with me on this project. It was their responsibility to locate and ensure the co-operation of the subjects in the study as well as to handle the occasional difficult situation in a job where both support and supervision were minimal.

Kathy Catton worked for eight months programming many of the analyses carried out in the later sections of this report. She willingly and efficiently carried out an often depressing and soul-destroying task. There are many individuals who have assisted during the summer vacations with various items of coding and data processing and I am particularly grateful for the accuracy and competence with which they completed these tasks. Lynn Bailey worked as Research Secretarial Assistant on this project for a number of years and was responsible particularly for all the chasing-up and coding of the questionnaires returned by parole supervisors. In the closing stages of the project, Denise Rush took the responsibility of turning scruffy tables and notes into an interpretable and accurate manuscript.

Anna Mallin ably initiated the slow metamorphosis from the research report to monograph. Finally, the painful process of editing, shortening, and clarifying a long and technical report was enthusiastically undertaken by Elizabeth Maunsell.

The sacrifices made by my wife and children for this project can only be justified by rational assessed experimentation which leads to humane improvements in the ways in which we manage offenders.

Irvin Waller

Introduction

This is a study of men released from prison. It was designed to describe and contribute to the understanding of the experiences of these men, and investigate the impact of prison, parole, and after-care on their behaviour; as such it hopes to contribute to the field of penology. Since many of these men became reinvolved, re-arrested and reconvicted for criminal offences, it hopes also to make a contribution to the field of criminology.

The principal subjects are 423 men, who form a representative sample of ex-prisoners released from Ontario federal penitentiaries into Southern Ontario, Canada, during 1968. Of these, 210 were selected for early release on parole, 113 never applied for parole, and 100 did apply but were refused. The latter two classes combined form the group of 213 men who were unconditionally released at expiration of sentence.

While the men were still inmates, the investigation included group interviews, administration of several standard psychological tests, and the collection of data from the institutional files. The most important sections of the study were based on an intensive analysis of the progress of the ex-prisoners during their first twelve months in the community. This was based mainly on interviews carried out by female interviewers concerning the men's experiences in their first five weeks, six months, and twelve months from release and on questionnaires completed by the parole supervisor of each parolee at seven predetermined stages during those first twelve months. Standard data were also collected from the police, on arrests and convictions of the men during at least a full twenty-four-month follow-up period from each man's date of release.

Of the 213 men unconditionally released at expiration of sentence, 144, or 68 per cent, were re-arrested in connection with an indictable offence within two years from release. Of the 210 men selected for parole, 93, or 44 per cent, were similarly re-arrested or had their parole revoked within two years from their release. The man released from prison is involved in many events, both probable and unpredictable, before and after release, which may or may not be associated with re-arrest rates. After describing some of these events, this study isolates aspects of each man's penitentiary and parole experience that might be related to the large recidivism rates. Considerable emphasis is placed throughout the study on such items as the man's family circumstances, work adjustment, and general personal life, factors that are sometimes referred to as his 'integration into society.' Thus, the study concentrates on the extent to which the penitentiary experience alone, compared with the combined experience of penitentiary and parole, effects any increase or reduction in the likelihood of recidivism and the integration into society of the men released from prison. It is only from such understanding that one can say to what extent penitentiary or parole are effective in the protection of the public and rehabilitation of the released offender, and the extent to which money is being saved or squandered. Of course, these are not the only purposes or considerations of correctional administration; however, they are two of the more important ones and are often referred to as the goals of correction by government commissions, officials, and politicians. Whether or not they are explicitly stated, worked towards, or sought after by members of the criminal justice system, they are goals ascribed to it by most of those involved in that system.

An initial orientation of the study was also one of cost-benefit analysis. Systematic attempts were made to relate interventions within the machinery of justice and corrections, particularly certain ingredients of prison, release under the parole agreement, and compulsory community supervision, to various aspects of the post-release careers of ex-prisoners. As the reader delves deeper into this study, it will become apparent that, in general, any relationship between an intervention on the one hand, and a benefit to, or change in, the circumstances surrounding the ex-prisoner on the other, is usually incidental. As a result, the simple extension of the findings to financial analysis of cost and benefit would not have been justified, and was therefore abandoned.

Those financial costs are, however, not insignificant. Apart from vast capital expenditure in 1968, the Canadian Federal Penitentiary Service was spending on average more than $5000 a year on each of its approximately 7000 inmates without any knowledge of their progress after release, beyond the fact that some were sentenced to penitentiary again and some were not. Within the same federal department, the National Parole Service was spending an average of $500 to keep a man on parole. The Service is aware of the number of parole violators in any one year but does not know how many are reconvicted during a specified time or how many are reconvicted after parole.

The analysis of the data and of the questions which the data are used to answer is presented in four basic sections.

In the first section the various studies of the correctional effectiveness of both prison and parole are reviewed. This leaves unanswered a number of obvious but essential questions, such as how imprisonment is related to post-release behaviour, and, relative to unconditional release, what is the importance of the threat and use of revocation on parolees? In chapter 2 the use of parole and penitentiaries in Canada is discussed, highlighting the trend towards increased use of parole in the late 1960s that was associated with dramatic increases in the 'failure' rate. In chapter 3 the method of gathering the data and the extent to which they were obtained for this study are presented.

In the second section, the men on whom the study is based are described in chapter 4: who is the man released from prison and what have been his past experiences? Chapter 5 details the experience of release from prison together with the man's feelings and reactions to his situation. How long does it take to make the transition from prison to community? What is it like to be released? How is he treated by friends, employers, or police? How does he manage financially? Does his family wait for him? How have they changed? How often does he get drunk or just drink? Whom does he call a friend? Was he frightened by prison? Does he intend to commit new offences? In chapter 6 the details of parole surveillance and assistance are reviewed, and some essential changes in the life situation of the parolee are described. We answer such questions as: to what extent is the parolee watched by his supervisor? How is he controlled by the parole agreement? How is he helped by his supervisor? What does the parolee think of parole? What sort of relationship exists between parolee and supervisor?

The third section focuses on arrest and recidivism. In chapter 7 after-release arrest and time to arrest are related to variables such as previous arrest, parole selection statistics, and whether or not the man gets a job after release or goes back to his children. We will see many differences in arrest rates associated both with parole and with variables such as family or employment. However, we still do not know which of these provide us with new information. In chapter 8 we discuss the extent to which the variables combine to provide reliable or efficient equations predicting arrest. Particular attention is paid to equations based on data known before, as compared to data known after, release. In chapter 9 the same data are used to show the extent to which we can predict or account for particular levels of social functioning and the decision of the inmate to apply for parole or of the parole board to grant it.

In the fourth section, in chapter 10, the importance of the inmate's decision to apply for parole and parole selection by the board are contrasted with an assessment of the impact of prison and then parole on the ex-prisoner as global measures, and the differential effects of parole on parolees are briefly considered. In chapter 11 we summarize the findings before discussing what they contribute to our understanding of men released from prison, the impact of prison, and parole. We also review these findings in comparison with changes in parole legislation since the study was completed, such as mandatory supervision and short suspensions at the discretion of the parole supervisor. Finally, alternatives and changes in policy are suggested in chapter 12. We renew the search for innovations which, remaining within both economic and humanitarian constraints, seek to reduce the frequency of 'crime,' and find alternatives to our rejection of men sent to prison.

Two of the appendices help the reader to understand terms used in special ways in the text. First, a short glossary provides definitions of unfamiliar terms. Second, rather than define a variable such as 'penal record' each time it is used, we include an appendix giving specific definitions of the variables used frequently and in the prediction equations.

Contents

Tables

Figures

MEN RELEASED FROM PRISON

1

The Correctional Effectiveness of Prison and Parole: The State of Knowledge

Studies of the effect of prison and parole on the offender's reintegration into society are not new, and in this chapter we will take a critical look at some of them. Our tentative conclusions will be developed and tested more fully in this study.

Is Parole Effective?

While parole may function to relieve overcrowding in penitentiaries or to mitigate severe sentences, it has been primarily advocated as a means of 'rehabilitating' the prisoner in conjunction with providing 'protection' for society against the offender. The questions that concern us are these: 'Does it work? If so, why? If not, why not?' Apparently, at least as far as reported statistics indicate, it does seem to have some measure of success. This is generally attributed to the work of the parole supervisor or thought possibly to be the result of the deterrent effect of the threat of return to prison with extra time to serve. However, it seems clear from the present study, as we shall see later, that while parole does have effects on the ex-prisoner's life, it may not be very successful in terms of its primary objective: the reduction of the likelihood of future criminal behaviour.

There has been a great deal of research (mainly in California) on certain aspects of parole. It has concentrated heavily on the effects of variation in the size of parole officers' case-loads, with mainly inconclusive results. On the other hand, there seems to have been insufficient consideration of exactly how much of a 'deterrent' the threat of revocation is. Moreover, revocation can be subject to the discretion of the parole officer, and the exercise of this power does vary widely between parole systems and between parole offices and officers. Parole supervision could also be examined from the point of view of its constituent parts in order to see what is and what is not effective, but this is rarely done. Another neglected area is that of cost; often parole programmes are extended almost without regard for expense, in spite of the fact that they seem to yield relatively small returns.

Apart from research into the 'harder' facts of revocation rates (which, as we shall see later, are not directly comparable from jurisdiction to jurisdiction) such as case-load size and cost per parolee, the whole area of the parolee's subjective experience of parole has been neglected. In the first place, how does the parolee, selected to go to prison, differ from the offender who was not sent to prison?[1] What does the experience of being 'inside' do to him? What are the after effects of imprisonment? Is he affected by 'forced association with other criminals?' Finally what difficulties does he experience in the transition back to the free community, and does parole supervision provide assistance?

In this chapter we shall review the published research on parole. This comes mainly from experiments in California, the US federal system, and England, although studies from other countries support their conclusions. Results so far (Robison and Smith, 1971) indicate that variations in penal treatments bear only a slight relation to outcome. The success of these treatments is often illusory, mainly a result of magistrates selecting 'better' persons for probation, and parole boards, 'better' prisoners for parole. Obviously, then, cost-benefit analyses have favoured the cheapest forms of treatment (as do offenders themselves since fewer restrictions are involved). Parole or probation is cheaper than imprisonment, absolute discharge cheaper than parole, and some form of fine or restitution cheapest of all, at least in terms of providing a 'return' to either the victim or the state. Because so much of the research on parole has been done in California, it is important to note that the system of sentencing and granting parole there differs from that in Canada. For felonies, where the maximum sentence is over a year, the court in California places the offender in the custody of the Adult Authority for a period which is usually statutorily determined and depends on the offence. There are sometimes rules for the minima too. This means that the Adult Authority, which has responsibility for granting parole, almost always decides *when* an offender should receive parole rather than *if* he should be paroled. Few prisoners with such sentences are released without parole. On the other hand, after two years on parole, the Adult Authority may discharge from parole. However most failures occur within the first two years so that the Adult Authority has very little control over its failure rates in comparison to the Canadian parole board which has the power to screen out altogether those it considers unsuitable. In addition to this, in Canada there is a process of 'self-selection' by the prisoners, who can and do exclude themselves by not applying. It is easy to see that simple revocation rates are not directly comparable between jurisdictions. Indeed, we suggest that the process of self-selection, together with the parole board selection policy may have more effect on parole 'success' rates than many of the other factors to be considered.

The Parolee as an Ex-Prisoner

Does the ex-prisoner have any characteristics related to the likelihood of his post-release re-arrest and reconviction? Prediction studies indicate that the more serious the current offence, the older the prisoner, and the fewer his previous convictions, the less likely he is to be arrested after release (Hood and Sparks, 1970, chap. 6). However, even when many such variables are considered, their predictive power, while it may be greater than that of the presence or absence of the parole supervision variable, is still not very high.

What influence do the offender's prison experiences have on his behaviour after release? To date, this has rarely been touched on. Early studies did little more than get statistics on reconvictions from parole officers, or sometimes information about post-release adjustment (Martinson et al., 1964). More recently, particularly in California, parole administrators have begun to see the idea of 'treatment' as an integral part of the parole programme,[2] so that much research has concentrated on such variables as size of case-load, group therapy, and use of the nalline test for drug usage.[3] Even so, these studies do not explicitly relate pre-release experience to post-release behaviour.

We are not, however, completely ignorant of inmate society. Since the classic work of Clemmer,[4] sociologists such as Sykes, Morris and Morris, Mathieson, and others have studied maximum security institutions in North America, England, and Scandinavia;[5] Polsky (1962) and Street et al. (1966) have also looked at less custodial, more treatment-oriented institutions. Their findings indicate clearly differentiated role relationships in inmate society. We have a picture of the seemingly total power of the 'wheel' and the 'tobacco baron,' the degradation of a 'fish' raped by a 'wolf' (Huffman, 1961; Herbert, 1968); these in addition to the simple but vicious process of prisonization are believed to be detrimental to the prisoner.[6] But as yet we have no systematic research on, for example, the proportion of prisoners who do in fact experience incarceration in these terms, and whether they do or not, how the prison experience affects them after release.

Some research has focused on the relationship between conduct after release and the role played in prison. But as Glaser and Stratton (1958) point out, there are difficulties with this type of investigation because of a lack of clear definitions of inmate roles and of the significance attached to specific roles, and doubt about which role a given inmate has played. Irwin and Cressey (1962) have suggested that these roles, and inmate culture in general, are not caused by the institution per se, but are imported by the prisoners themselves. In an attempt to get some empirical grounding, Himelson and Tagaki gave a number of attitude tests to California prisoners about to be released on parole.[7] They deduced the type of inmate role played by each prisoner from his expressed attitudes to staff and fellow prisoners. Although they did find that the inmate role was related to whether or not a prisoner went on to complete his parole period successfully, they also found that knowledge of inmate roles did not increase the predictability of parole outcome. That is, knowing the inmate role told them nothing more about the prisoner's chances of completing parole than they already knew from his history and characteristics on entry into the prison.

Daniel Glaser's (1964) extensive studies of the US Federal Prison and Parole System seem to refute the theory that inmates develop strong ties with other prisoners that are maintained after release. His findings in a post-release follow-up study were that while 58 per cent of ex-prisoners met other ex-prisoners in the first five months after release, only 12 per cent of the meetings were planned (Glaser, 1964, 390). In fact, he found (1964, 391) there was a continuation of the 'aloof' attitude that the prisoners in his study had maintained toward one another in prison. Many ex-inmate meetings seem to occur as a result of going to the same bars or cafés, where they feel welcomed, or at least not rejected. Of course, sometimes an ex-prisoner might choose his friends among other ex-prisoners. Such a 'choice' would probably depend on whether or not he still had a wife and family, whether or not his friends and relatives were ex-prisoners, and whether or not those he worked with have been to prison. These are, in a sense, considerations unrelated to events within the prison. Because the rift between prison life and normal society is so great, much of what happens inside can have no relevance to success after release. In most prisons, for instance, work conditions are totally dissimilar from those outside and the inmate does not have to face the normal problems of obtaining a job or coping with drink or drugs. If he has a family, his problems while in prison are not those of living with or supporting its members, but rather of trying to keep in touch with them.

It seems important to realize, however, that while the actual events of prison life may not be important, the very fact of having been to prison, as an experience where a man does not have to cope with job or family, where he is completely torn from 'normal' existence, may indeed have some bearing on success after release. Skolnick has developed a theory about the prisoner's attitude to parole, stressing the importance of appropriate attitudes and expectations toward release and toward the parole officer.[8] While this may explain the behaviour of some ex-prisoners, it would seem not to apply to the 'typical' prisoner who is usually overwhelmed by the problems of survival on release and who probably quickly loses sight of 'appropriate' expectations.[9]

The Transitional Status of Parole

Martinson, Kassebaum, and Ward (1964) have noted that there is very little theory attempting to explain post-release behaviour of parolees. Studt's (1967) discussion of successful re-entry of offenders into the community is, however, a notable exception. She classes parole as just one of the status changes that can occur during a lifetime, analogous to the time after discharge from a prisoner-of-war camp or a hospital. It should be pointed out, however, that all the studies referred to by Studt implied that the released individual wanted to achieve a new status and that, in existential terms, he had 'freedom of choice.' While a parolee may want to become a 'law-abiding' citizen in theory, he may find it difficult in practice. His family, accustomed to his absence, may not give any support, either emotional or practical; he may have trouble finding accommodation or a job, especially if, as is often the case, his work skills are limited and he now has the added disadvantage of a record.

What was not taken into account in these reference studies is that the parolee has been assigned a status that is negatively valued in society. Developing the work of others, such as Garfinkel (1956) or Sarbin (1967), who are interested in the relation between status and behaviour, Studt (1967) looked at parole with this in mind. She found that in California, despite lip service paid to the idea of 'treatment,' most parole agencies define parolees as potentially 'dangerous persons' until proved otherwise, and therefore regard their function as essentially one of control. Apart from requiring regular concrete proof that the parolee is employed and living where he is supposed to live, the parole officer takes little further 'personal' interest. As further indicators of the parolee's degraded status, we see that he must declare to prospective employers that he is on parole; he may not be able to get a driver's licence without special permission. In addition to these aggravations, other people (for example, the supervisor who regards the parolee as unable to make decisions) may act toward the parolee in such a way as to make his adjustment to normal society more difficult or painful.

Case-load Experiments

We have noted that early research on the correctional effectiveness of parole was mainly concerned with trying to predict reconviction. Latterly, studies have become more descriptive and experimental, dealing with the effect of variations in case-loads on violation rates. It seems advisable to examine the findings critically because other research suggests that parole, as a form of compulsory casework, is not an effective method of reducing recidivism.

The classic random-allocation experiment is supposed to be the soundest test of the effectiveness of parole supervision. In such an experiment, two or more types of supervision or treatment are provided, and an unselected series of parolees is allocated at random to one or another of the treatments. This procedure avoids the bias that could occur with a human decision-maker who might unknowingly select the more promising men for a particular treatment. Experiments of this kind have been carried out in California for nearly twenty years. The clear conclusion to be drawn from them is that more intensive parole supervision does not produce major reductions in reconvictions rates, though it may increase the number of technical violations (Robison and Smith, 1971). In one piece of research (Havel and Sulka, 1962) differences were observed that suggested smaller case-loads were more effective, especially in the case of the parolee who was neither a very good, not a particularly bad, reconviction risk. Unfortunately, further work (Havel, 1965) failed to confirm the earlier results, though it did suggest that the time allowed the officer to devote to supervision was important. In any event, it is difficult to see any logical reason why 'average' types should be especially amenable to individual casework. One might logically expect the high-risk group to be more responsive to increased attention, especially if it involved intensive 'police'-type supervision likely to deter them from further crime.[10]

Differential Treatment

As a result of the Grant and Grant (1959) study of US Naval delinquents the unpredictability of treatment effectiveness has been explained by the theory that any particular method is likely to affect some positively and others negatively. In line with this thinking, studies such as the classic example of the California Community Treatment Project of the California Youth Authority have been set up which attempt to classify and then match both treatment and offender for the highest probability of success. In the California study some results do suggest positive effects due to small case-loads, such as greater rapport, particularly in dealing with school, employment, or family, but in general the results are still uncertain. Unfortunately the investigators used technical violation rates as an index of success, although they were aware that differential decision-making was a factor in success and indeed was a treatment tool. These rates are particularly unsatisfactory because they themselves are affected by the intensity of the supervision and by the experimental nature of the programme, both of which may affect the supervisor's use of, or discretion in the use of, the power to report violations.[11] Comparisons using more objective criteria such as convictions for felony have so far given less encouraging results.[12] One of the findings of the California study, though not directly related to the effectiveness of supervision, was that in general parole did not result in an increase in the probability of arrest for felony or other more serious offences (although if re-arrest did occur, it was earlier, because of an earlier release). The Community Treatment Project also tried to assess the effects of different treatments on other areas of the individual's life, such as family adjustment or school performance. As yet no analysis of their findings has been published.

Hood and Sparks (1970) have reviewed critically a number of other studies purporting to show the differential effect of types of treatment upon different types of offender. Several of the studies failed to demonstrate any significant differential effects, but the California Pilot Intensive Counselling Project did find consistently better results when treatment was given to a particular 'amenable' group (Adams, 1961). A study by Hall and others (1966), which claimed to have found differential treatment effects with adult prisoners, furnishes a typical example of the problems encountered in this kind of research. The statistical evaluation that was used (a base expectancy method derived from configuration tables; Glaser, 1964, 292–301) is one that 'capitalizes on chance.' Without repeating the observations and obtaining similar results one cannot be sure that the findings were not spurious. Even though the research workers themselves pointed out the need for 'replication,' they still suggested that the differences they found probably resulted from the treatment programme. In spite of methodological difficulties, research into differential treatment effects continues in an attempt to advance from tenuous to more concrete findings.

There does, however, seem to be a catch in these programmes.

Even in the Community Treatment Project, where allocation to certain treatments is ostensibly based on suitability, it appears, in fact, that those individuals who are defined as high-risk (i.e., those who, in the absence of such programmes, would be sent to prison) are for the most part the ones who are given the intensive supervision (Robison et al., 1969, esp. 39–42). It would seem that the public, which has 'believed in' the effectiveness of prison for so long, can only tolerate this type of offender being released as long as some kind of 'protection' is provided. In this case it looks as though this 'protection' is being provided under the guise of 'differential treatment programme,' but it would be simpler to admit that releasing high-risk offenders is only justifiable (in terms of public opinion) when close tabs are kept on them.

Numbers and Significance

The statistical significance in any experiment is, to some degree, a function of the size of the sample. If a treatment's effect is small, a large sample will be required to show significance; conversely, if the sample is very small, only large effects will produce significance. However, it should be realized that a real but statistically insignificant effect from a small sample may be of greater economic importance than a small, statistically significant, result from a very large sample.[13]

In the report of Phase III of the Special Intensive Parole Unit: California (SIPU), there were 911 parolees supervised intensively in small case-loads compared with 2806 supervised in regular case-loads. The difference, in terms of percentage arrested, is shown in Table 1.1. This difference in distribution of parolees among the four outcome categories is statistically significant (Havel and Sulka, 1962), but the size of the effect is too small to be economically very useful. The small case-loads were 35 per officer, approximately half the regular case-loads, and the number of persons arrested was 5 per cent less for small case-loads than for regular case-loads. With a total of 3717 parolees, to achieve a 5 per cent decrease in arrests about 50 additional parole officers would be needed. In terms of cost-benefit, the cost of the additional officers might exceed the cost of the (185) arrests prevented. This schematic analysis is meant merely to illustrate the point that a statistically significant effect may or may not be important according to the values and costs involved. Using a much more sophisticated analysis employing a system model of criminal justice administration, the repercussions on other aspects of the system of halving the parole case-load could be seen more clearly, and rational changes could be made more easily.[14] However, in actual practice the current allocation of funds is so far from the optimum in relation to goals of social defence that the assumption of system analysis – working on marginals – would break down.

TABLE 1.1

Percentage of small case-load and regular case-load parolees arrested in a twelve-month follow-up

	Parole outcome				
	No arrest	Minor arrest	Major arrest	Return to prison	Total
Small case-load	42.0	20.6	13.0	24.4	100
Regular case-load	37.2	22.5	12.0	28.3	100

The important point to remember is that a small but significant treatment effect in an experimental study is only likely to appear if large numbers of individuals are involved. In the San Francisco Project, where only a small total of 307 parolees was involved, distributed between minimum (118 cases), ideal (119 cases), and intensive treatment (70), it is hardly surprising that the researchers were unable to find differences in outcome of statistical significance. Their findings provide evidence that the number of technical violations are greatly affected by the type of supervision, but show little else. Unless controls are applied measuring the discretion of the parole supervision in deciding what behaviour constitutes a violation, and the period at risk – the time from release to end of parole during which an arrest could occur – calculated, no firm conclusions can be drawn and the statistics may indicate more about the administrative decisions of the parole agents than about the behaviour of the parolees.[15]

Empirical Studies on the Decision to Revoke Parole

Takagi and Robison (1968; 1969) have shown that the decision to revoke is not a 'constant.' Takagi (1969) presented for judgment ten actual case histories from parole files. He found that the decision to revoke varied significantly not only between individual parole officers, but also between officers of different status, and between different parole agencies. The same relationship has been found concerning variability in sentencing by different magistrates (Hood, 1962; Hogarth, 1971). It would seem, then, that in the case of the decision to revoke parole the prisoner's rights are unprotected in that erratic variations are not unusual. Takagi also found that some of these variations resulted from different emphases; in one parole unit case needs were seen as important, whereas another stressed the maintenance of standards. (Takagi, 1969; Takagi and Robison, 1969). The significance of his results, from a small sample, indicate that these variations are quite considerable. His findings may cast further doubt on the conclusions from the large-scale case-load research of the SIPU, where the results were significant, but only with large numbers of parolees. No checks were made to find out what was the basis of the decision to revoke. In line with Takagi's findings, then, differential decision-making might account for the difference found between the smaller and larger case-load groups.

Technical violations can also be affected by administrative fiat. Takagi (1967) set out the history of one agency to which money was allocated by a state legislature to enable supervisors' case-loads to be reduced from 70 to 35. Early evaluation failed to show the expected reduction in violation rates, but the agency felt that it needed to justify the enormous amount of funds that had been allocated to it. The chief administrator therefore called a meeting of his colleagues, and deliberately set about achieving lower violation rates. The supervisors involved in small case-loads were required to hold a conference with their superiors to see what could be done to avoid returning parolees to prison. Each supervising unit was to compete against the others to see which could produce the lowest technical violation rates. Among considerations for future promotions of senior personnel would be how well leadership had been provided in reducing the technical violation rates.[16] A year later, the resulting research report was able to show reductions in recommitment to prison among the parolees supervised in small case-loads. However, the numbers of parolees supervised in conventional size case-loads who were recommitted to prison were also reduced.

When the parole supervisor becomes aware of a violation and recommends revocation, it is this recommendation that initiates official parole board reaction. This appears to be an important determinant of the final revocation decision as it is rare that the parole board does not accept his recommendation. Takagi found in the 1700 cases reported by parole officers only 13 instances where superiors disagreed with the original recommendation (Takagi, 1967, 163–4). Robison (n.d.) reports similar findings concerning the decision to discharge offenders from parole.[17] Of course it may be that the parole supervisor's views are heavily influenced by those of his superiors.[18]

As Ward (1967) has pointed out, negative findings in evaluative research may have long-term repercussions. For example, the publication during Phase III of the SIPU of the negative findings of the earlier phases could well have affected the study situation. Perhaps it encouraged the parole officers to work better, and could definitely have resulted in a more lenient policy toward marginal cases of violation.[19] While we cannot tell if these hypotheses apply to Phase III they are consistent with the findings. Even with the results of Phase IV, Havel still came to the same conclusion; the statement 'smaller case-loads do give better results' depends on the criteria of 'success.' Apparently they do help keep one free of arrest (during the parole period) but do not, ultimately, prevent return to prison.[20]

Influence of Revocation and Rule Enforcement

Another interesting omission in contemporary research is the lack of comparisons between new treatments and no treatment at all. Few studies, for example, in the research on case-load variations, compare men released under varying degrees of parole supervision with those released without parole,[21] and few compare offenders on probation with those conditionally discharged without supervision. Even in the San Francisco project, which seemed to show that minimal supervision was as effective as more intensive supervision, the minimum supervision group was still subject to the conditions of probation and parole, and therefore liable to revocation. 'Minimum' supervision, contrary to popularly held ideas, is still supervision. Little is known about the effect of living with the threat of revocation as opposed to release without conditions. It should be realized that in Canada, as elsewhere, a parolee who is reconvicted or who has his parole revoked is liable to serve some sizeable proportion of the remainder of his sentence. The potential severity of this penalty, and the way it is calculated, vary greatly between jurisdictions. Such variations are important, since this is a threat that seems likely to have some influence upon many of areas of a parolee's life. He may, for instance, make more effort to obtain and keep a job because he sees this as a way of maintaining his freedom. Similarly, it would be naive to think that a parolee reports regularly to his supervisor simply because he feels he benefits by the experience. In both instances the parolee conforms to the rules, but it may not be because he thinks the rules *per se* are good. Alternatively, the parolee may pretend to conform by making sure that the parole supervisor and the police receive only 'appropriate' information He may tell the supervisor about problems that he knows the supervisor thinks are important but that are unlikely to lead to the imposition of further restrictions. As most contacts with the supervisor take place in his office, and since the supervisor rarely spends more than an hour a month in face-to-face contact with the parolee, even in the supposedly intensive supervision of small case-loads, it is probably easy for the parolee to disguise what he is doing. Although some regulations (such as those of the work unit in California) require the supervisor to make some outside contacts, it still does not insure an 'accurate' picture.

The findings of studies carried out to see how parole supervisors spend their time, and how they redistribute their activities when case-loads are reduced[22] all point to the same general conclusion. Reduction in case-load by as much as half, for instance from 70 to 35 parolees per supervisor, does not bring about any great change in the way supervisors distribute their time between different activities, particularly in regard to the proportion of their time spend in face-to-face contact. The explanation for this seems to lie in the carry-over of work habits geared to larger case-loads. The result is that surveillance remains fairly minimal. As Robison (1969, 81) has pointed out, a supervisor with a 40-man case-load, who spends 25 per cent of his working time in face-to-face contact with parolees, would still average only one hour per month with each client, and from the studies cited above, even that could be an overestimate. Besides, the gulf between the hundreds of hours of day-to-day living, when the parolee is not under surveillance, and the one hour of direct contact, is much more than a matter of length of time. In a participant observation study of a sophisticated residential training school for delinquent boys, where treatment by individual interviews was in operation, Polsky (1962, 166) has noted that 'In a short walk from the clinic to the cottage the boy passes from one society to another.' The difference would be, in anything, greater for the parolee.

Parole agreements in the North American systems are permeated by a large number of specific prohibitions; total abstention from intoxicating liquor, association with undesirables, use of narcotics, gambling, possessing a gun, and incurring debts are some examples. Almost certainly these restrictions, with which it may be difficult to comply, do not encourage the parolee to be frank with his supervisor. It is also questionable to what extent these rather rigid rules, which were presumably instituted in the belief that they aid 'rehabilitation,' actually do lead to a change in lifestyle, or merely result in more sophisticated game-playing. Studies have shown that men who are employed are less likely to be involved in crime, but it is not clear whether it is the characteristics of the men who become unemployed or the actual state of unemployment that leads them to crime; so that while the requirement to work, to 'lead an industrious life' may press gang parolees into taking up jobs, we still do not know what effect, if any, this has on the likelihood of criminal behaviour.

There are considerable differences in the extent to which parole conditions are enforced by supervising officers. Different parolees probably have different ideas which may result in an unstable balance between game-playing and genuine change in habits. The English parole licence, with its general requirement of good behaviour but its absence of specific rules, has been praised in North America.[23] Under any system, however, the limits of the parole agreement are negotiated between parolee and supervisor, although these are subject to the general boundaries of the parole board's previous revocation decisions. A number of

American studies have shown that few of the technical violations that come to the notice of supervisors actually result in revocation.[24] The interaction between parolee and supervisor is an important element in understanding the potential influence of supervision on the parolee's life style, although this influence may be more through threat than case-work. Over-concentration of research upon the case-work relationship has led to neglect of other influences on success rates. In the San Francisco project offenders in a non-experimental section who completed their probation or parole successfully were asked their views on the contribution of supervision to their success. It appeared that, in general, the part played by the family and associates was more important than the activity of the supervisor. This seems obvious, and yet very little research as focused on other aspects of the parolees' environment, such as parole restrictions or coercion to take a job.

One of the few research projects on the effects of coercive case-work was concerned with 'Enforced Clinic Treatment of Parole Criminal Alcoholics' (Gallant et al., 1967). Since earlier work has shown the extent of alcoholism as a problem among offenders released from state penitentiaries, and since alcoholism is believed to be a factor in crime, the need for such an experiment is obvious.[25] The size of the sample was small (only 19 male alcoholics paroled) but statistically significant results emerged in relation to recidivism and other criteria. This suggests that this may be an important method of treatment which warrants fuller investigation with larger samples. In addition, these results suggest that if reduced case-load size is to have an effect in reducing recidivism, it must be accompanied by some effort to identify and deal with each parolee's specific problems.

Tentative Conclusions about the Effectiveness of Correctional Treatments

We have now examined some of the crucial issues. What is the trend of the findings that have emerged from the literature on the effectiveness of parole? Robison and Smith, Adams, and Hood and Sparks have also reviewed some general conclusions.[26] One of the most important shortcomings of most research so far has been the failure to consider any criteria of effectiveness other than those relating to re-arrest. It may be, as parole supervisors interested in helping 'clients' are quick to point out, that 'extraneous' factors affect arrest histories, and that therefore arrest does not really measure the success of rehabilitative work; it is probable that the effectiveness of a treatment programme can only be understood by considering other kinds of 'outcome' such as employment, family, or use of alcohol. So far as they go, the research findings point to two alternative hypotheses. Compulsory parole supervision in the community has no effect on an offender's likelihood of reconviction, or if it has an effect, it is too small to be of economic importance. If, in addition, one takes note of the work on variation in revocation decisions, the likelihood that existing treatment programmes have any substantial effect in reducing crime seems even less. Finally, if cost to society is considered, it appears that the extra money invested in these schemes yields an insignificant return.

The evidence so far suggests that the assistance provided by the parole supervisor is of minor importance in affecting the criminal behaviour of parolees. The question still remains, however, of to what extent the supervisor may help the parolee in other respects, such as finding and keeping a job, resolving marital disputes, lending money, finding accommodation, referring to alcoholism clinics or providing the friendly 'listening ear.' With regard to the threat of revocation, and the effect of imprisonment generally, too many questions remain unanswered. As far as threat of revocation is concerned, the parolee may be coerced into a greater effort to fulfil social requirements, or merely stimulated to fool his supervisor.

Despite the repetitive discussion of measures of success, reconviction and re-arrest must remain important criteria in assessing the effectiveness of sentences and penal treatments. The most important elements appear to be the selection policy of the parole boards, the offender's previous history, the offender's behaviour after release, and the reaction to it of the parole supervisor, police, and public. Finally, and possibly more important than the rest, this success is subject to a whole range of chance events and decisions that defy deterministic analysis.

We have attempted to be realistic in assessing the effectiveness of parole in changing behaviour. This is not necessarily to challenge its *raison d'être*, for while it may fail in one area, it has other valuable functions; avoidance of the construction cost of new prisons, the relief of overcrowding, humanitarian considerations, and the need to placate public opinion with the claim that justice is being done and protection being given, even though criminals are being set free.

These sceptical conclusions may lead the parole officer to feel that he is being used by the system without being able to accomplish anything constructive. He may challenge the conclusions because he can recall some cases in which he felt that he was instrumental in successful rehabilitation. It is not denied that a parole supervisor may play an important role in the lives of some parolees, although examples are rarer than the case-work literature would lead one to believe. Supervisors may make life more comfortable for the parolee, and may help him with his personal troubles, but this does not seem to have much bearing upon recidivism, except, perhaps, where the parolee's problem (e.g., alcoholism) is one that can lead to recidivism unless it is resolved. Until descriptive work has identified specific problems in the parolee's situation, independently and importantly related to outcome, such as drink, unemployment, type of associates, or family relationships, vast experimental projects will be unlikely to yield much result. If this were done, however, it might be possible to find a more positive role for the supervisor to play. On the other hand, it may be that our criminal justice, welfare, and social service dollars may be better spent in other ways.

The empirical data on which much of this monograph is based will be used to answer or at least clarify most of the questions raised in this chapter. What sort of man is released from a penitentiary in Ontario? What was the impact of that prison experience on him, his various life careers, and his family? What is it like to be released from a prison, and how important is that experience to the likelihood of later arrest? We will look at the intervening variables that might be affected by parole supervision and consider their importance relative to prison and parole variables. What is the relation to recidivism of the parole supervisor's discretion to suspend and revoke? Do the heavy periods of prison hanging over the parolee deter him from offences? As implied in this chapter, we must also touch on the process of selection for parole. As preliminaries to the main analysis, we will look at penitentiaries and parole, and their use in Canada in the next chapter, and then the research design in chapter 3. Both these chapters provide the minimal background to an understanding of our findings.

NOTES TO CHAPTER 1

1 For disparities in sentencing associated more with the sentencer than with the 'facts' of the case, see Hogarth (1971); Jobson (1971)

2 It is not suggested here that the Adult Authority of California decides whether or not to release on the basis of treatment considerations, but that the Department of Corrections (which carries out parole supervision) has been interested in treatment possibilities. A review of public pronouncements from proponents of parole contained in annual reports, or statements by chairmen of parole boards, emphasize the value of parole as a method of treatment. For a history of both parole and parole research, see Hawkins (1971, chaps. 1, 2, 6, 9, and 10)

3 See Adams (1967). His conclusions should be read with caution: cost-benefit advantages are not the same as treatment effects

4 Clemmer (1958). Only comparatively recently did sociologists extend their interest to other 'total institutions,' such as hospitals, schools, etc. See, for example, Goffman (1961)

5 Sykes (1958); Morris (1963); Mathieson (1965). See also Cloward, *et al.* (1960); Cressey (1958)

6 Deprivation of liberty, of course, is a punishment in itself. The significance of degradation in this discussion is first in whether it has any long-term effects, and, if so, in the proportion of prisoners affected by it. See also Wheeler (1961)

7 Takagi (1965); Himelson and Takagi (1963). See also Irwin and Cressey (1962); Irwin (1970)

8 Skolnick (1960) points out that he does not pretend to solve completely the

methodological problems which would be involved in carrying out relevant research. As such, Skolnick's is typical of theories not developed in close relationship with the data; he did, however, try to construct hypotheses which would be tested

9 See, for instance, the expectations of occupational advance held by the prisoners studied by Glaser (1964, 311–16). See also Strathy (1961) for some of the problems and results produced by testing some of the hypotheses put forward by Skolnick (1960) and James (1971)

10 See Zimring (1971); Zimring and Hawkins (1967). See also Willcock (1967)

11 The discussion in the section on the decision to revoke parole (below) emphasizes factors other than the behaviour of the parolee which can influence the revocation decision. See also Lerman, (1968)

12 While every conviction for felony may not provide a very satisfactory measure because there are many factors which contribute to unreliability, such as plea-bargaining or the charge which the police decide to bring, these should apply equally to both parolees under intensive supervision and controls under standard supervision

13 California provides numerous examples of programmes mounted after cost benefit calculations were carried out rather than statistical tests of significance.

14 This assumes that one can apply rational models to the administration of criminal justice. This idyllic situation does not even exist in California, though the 'Work Unit' and 'Probation Subsidy' projects are near equivalents. In this connection see McGee (1967)

15 The study is, perhaps, able to draw some conclusions about probation officer activity

16 Takagi (1967, chap. 5). The parole administrator also went round the offices emphasizing the importance of keeping men on the street

17 See also Robison (1969, 124–8); Robison (1971)

18 Takagi (1967, 167). For an interesting example of how the parole supervisor can back up his own point of view see Robison's Bay Area Research Unit paper, 'Two Years on Continuous Parole' (March 1967), which is part of his '2943 PC Decision Making Study' (n.d.). In this paper the use of 'turnabout sentences' is described. A turnabout sentence was defined as a compound sentence or a pair of linked sentences in which favourable and unfavourable evaluations of parolees' attitudes or behaviour are combined. Their significance rests in their order; thus a negative turnabout would be 'He has been steadily employed but he recently went on a drunken binge.' A positive turnabout, in contrast, would be 'He recently went on a drunken binge, but has been steadily employed.' Although turnabouts were used in their negative form in only 15 per cent of the cases, they supported a decision to discharge from parole in 79 per cent of those cases, and were against discharge in 12 per cent of those cases. Positive turnabouts were used in 29 per cent of the cases, in 62 per cent of which a discharge was recommended and in 88 per cent of which the recommendation was not to discharge. This type of definition of a variable illustrates a shift from emphasis on the 'characteristics' of parolees to an emphasis on their 'characterization' – terms used by Robison in his research. It is the importance of this shift in emphasis that is being discussed in the text.

19 These problems result from evaluation research, where 'double blind' methods are not used. In the SIPU studies the parole supervisors knew they were being studied and knew on which parolees they ought to have an impact

20 Havel (1965). See also (1961)

21 For an interesting exception, see the unpublished progress reports of the work by J. Ciale et al. carried out at the Department of Criminology, University of Montreal, on comparisons between parolees and men released at expiration of sentence. See also Robison and Smith (1971, 78–9)

22 See, for instance, Johnson (1961); MacGregor and Fowler (1965); Miles (1964)

23 See, for example, Arluke (1969)

24 See, for instance, Hunt (1964)

25 See, for instance, Guze *et al.* (1962)

26 Robison and Smith (1971); Adams (1967); Hood (1967); Sparks (1968). The substance of the latter two reports is contained in Hood and Sparks (1970, chaps. 6 and 7). See also n. 10

2

Parole and Unconditional Discharge from Federal Penitentiary Sentences in Canada

As we saw in the previous chapter, the literature has not made comparisons between men released from prison under parole supervision and those released unconditionally at expiration of sentence.[1] What is the impact on the man of the formal controls on the one hand, and, on the other, the threat of revocation for violation of the rules, or the threat (that always exists even in minimum supervision) of extra prison time additional to any new sentence incurred? This study has made a comparison on the basis of these differences.

Some earlier research has either implicitly or explicitly concerned itself with the ability of the parole board to select efficiently for parole. However, at the time of this study, nearly half of those released at expiration of sentence had never applied for parole. Therefore, in terms of post-release behaviour, it will be possible to contrast the impact of parole on those selected, not only with those refused parole, but also with those who never applied. This distinction between those who applied and those who did not will be shown to be particularly important to explain the illusory effectiveness of parole in Ontario, Canada.

In this study the principal subjects are men released from a penitentiary. But what is a penitentiary? How do men usually get sent there? Is it a common form of sentence? Once the men are in a penitentiary, who decides when they will be released? How frequently are men released on parole? How many prisoners apply for parole? This chapter outlines, *at the time of the study*, the workings of the Canadian Penitentiary System and describes the basic characteristics of National Parole from a penitentiary. It also looks at the use of penitentiaries and parole from 1959 through 1968, the year of the study, to 1971.

Federal Penitentiary Sentences

Under the British North America Act, the responsibility for criminal justice in Canada was divided between the provinces and the federal government. The (longest) sentence of the majority of persons in Canadian penitentiaries is given after conviction on indictment for a violation of the Criminal Code, which is a federal statute, although a few inmates were convicted of violations of other federal statutes. Under the Criminal Code a person convicted of an offence may be sentenced to a definite period in prison. If this sentence is two years or more it is served in a federal penitentiary, and if it is two years minus a day – a common sentence – or less, it is served in a provincial reformatory. Persons who escape from a provincial reformatory may be sentenced to a federal penitentiary for an aggregate period of less than two years. Approximately 6 per cent of all those sentenced for indictable offences were sent to penitentiaries in 1966 (*Ouimet Report*, 1969). Most of the subjects of this study were originally sentenced to two years or more. An important minority were re-sentenced escapers from provincial reformatories.

The only indefinite sentences being served in federal penitentiaries are for persons convicted as dangerous sex offenders, habitual criminals, or of committing murder.[2] Long-term prisoners made up a minute proportion of the release population and so were of minor quantitative concern in this study.[3] Qualitatively, however, the problems faced by these men on release might be great.

The Canadian sentencing system, which parallels the definite sentencing structure found in England, is markedly different from the indeterminate sentencing structure found in some other parts of North America, such as the states of California or Washington. A sentence handed down by a judge in Canada is a maximum or 'nominal' sentence which may be reduced by remission and further reduced by parole. A man sentenced to a definite sentence in a Canadian federal penitentiary is eligible for two types of remission.[4] Firstly, on admission he is granted 'statutory' remission equal to a quarter of his definite nominal sentence. Secondly, he is able to 'earn' remission at the rate of three days a month for good behaviour. If a prisoner receives all his earned remission, and does not lose statutory remission for any major offence within the institution, he would serve approximately two-thirds (0.681) of his nominal sentence, if he did not receive parole.

Penitentiaries

On any one day the federal penitentiaries in Ontario, which are typical of those across Canada, held approximately 2000 of the 7000 adult males sentenced to federal institutions. This study did not concern itself with provincial institutions, where on any one day 4500 men were held in Ontario out of 12,000 in Canada. The types of institutions from which the men were released are classified under three headings – maximum, medium, and minimum security. Those in the study are typical of such institutions. Approximately half of all federal penitentiary inmates were being held in maximum security in 1968–9, and one-third in medium security. By 1970–71, 37 per cent were in maximum and 50 per cent in medium (see Appendix B).

Holding between 700 and 800 inmates at the time of the study on any one day, the maximum security institution – Kingston Penitentiary – is typical of many prisons to be found in the western hemisphere. It was modelled on the Auburn system, and first received inmates in 1835 (Edmison, 1965, 285). In 1968, a typical day involved solitary eating in cells, working in groups in the workshop during the day, and few or no recreational activities in the evening. As the initial classification procedure was completed there, every person in the study passed through this institution. Some attempt was made to keep such new arrivals separate from the general population, but nearly two out of five of them had been to a penitentiary before. In any case, all would have passed through a local jail where segregation was not practically feasible, so that they all would have associated with other criminals before Kingston.

There were three medium security institutions. The first was Collins Bay, an older institution where unmanned guard towers are still visible on the corners of the perimeter wall. Although there was more freedom of movement and more work in groups than in Kingston, the architecture restricted much of the activity. This institution tried to emphasize vocational training for the younger prisoner, of whom there were 400–500 on any one day. The second medium security institution, Joyceville, holding an equivalent number of men, was one of the first to be built in a recent construction programme preceding the penitentiary service's ten-year building programme.[5] At the time of this study there was much freedom of movement and discussion among inmates and between inmates and staff. The major feature of this institution was the well-thought out and well-built workshops designed as miniature models of industrial situations which could provide some non-financial rewards to the men who went through them. The third institution, Warkworth, was opened during the course of the study and at that time had not settled into a distinct pattern of operation. A shortage of inmates and over-abundance of staff were its major characteristics. The work opportunities there were very limited during the course of the study.

The minimum security institutions included correctional camps and farms, characterized by small numbers of inmates supervised by small numbers of correctional staff. The principal work carried out in each was bush clearing or farming. The farms were attached to medium security institutions. The camps were relatively independent and were further from major cities than the other penitentiaries.

Parole from a Penitentiary

Briefly, National Parole in Canada is a means by which prison inmates who make successful applications are released early for periods approximately equal to that portion of their nominal sentences not already served.[6] After release parolees are supervised, must report to the police, and are required to live within certain restrictions and conditions broadly defined in their parole agreements (see Appendix A).

Under the Parole Regulations, providing he has served a minimum of nine months, the inmate of a federal penitentiary with a definite sentence was normally elegible for parole after serving four years, or one-third of his sentence, whichever is the lesser. Other than for inmates serving life sentences, the National Parole Board is in fact empowered, under special circumstances, to release an inmate at any stage during his sentence. However, this power is rarely used and then, with occasional exceptions (some of which have received considerable publicity) only to bring the release date forward by a month. In practice, the National Parole Board exercises its jurisdiction to release men between the one-third and two-thirds points of a definite 'nominal' sentence.[7]

Those serving indefinite sentences are normally eligible for parole after a certain portion of their sentence has been served. This portion was seven years for life sentences and ten years for commuted life sentences. However, those under preventive detention have their cases reviewed each year. Under the terms of the Parole Act every other person, which means the vast majority, held in a federal penitentiary must have his parole situation 'automatically reviewed' by the parole board every two years after his initial parole eligibility date, regardless of whether or not he makes a written application. In practice, this automatic review does not lead to the granting of parole, for which a written application by the inmate is a *sine qua non*. The application is requested approximately five months before either his parole eligibility date or some later date at which he would like to be paroled. On its receipt, the parole service collects various biographical details, opinions, and recommendations about the applicant on which the decision to grant parole may be based.

Material for the board concerning an applicant and his parole potential are first prepared in the institution in which he is held. Normally included are opinions of the inmate's workshop instructor and cell range officer and, most important, the classification officer's detailed report which organizes the other prison material. Opinions and recommendations for parole by any other member of the institutional staff may also be included. Together these form the 'Warden's Report.' The parole applicant is then interviewed by the regional representative or a member of the National Parole Service working under the regional representative. When this study began the regional representative was responsible only for preparing his own comments and collecting interview and other material concerning the applicant. He then sent the file to Ottawa, where it was summarized by a parole analyst for the board's decision.[8] The views of the sentencing judge, the police, and the community agencies also may be available or solicited. The parole Board has several options in relation to a particular parole application from a penitentiary that are of concern to us here. First, it can 'grant' parole, meaning that the man will be released on or about a certain date. Secondly, if less than two years remain until the applicant's scheduled release date, they might 'deny' parole, and thirdly, if more than two years remain, the question of parole might be 'deferred.'

Instead of denying parole to an applicant, the parole board can grant a minimum parole in principle. Minimum parole is a means whereby an inmate may be released from an institution one month earlier (up to six months) for every year of his sentence. Thus a man originally sentenced to three years can be released three months before his normal expected release date; he will then serve on parole (in the community) those three months plus his statutory remission. It is 'in principle,' as it is usually granted several months before the actual release date and is dependent on certain conditions, such as living arrangements or employment, being fulfilled. The final decision to grant minimum parole lies with the regional representative and the parole applicant, who sometimes turns it down.

The parolee's time served in the community may be divided into two portions; first, the time that he would have served in the institution until he was released; secondly, the statutory remission time. Because he is not able to earn remission while on parole, he serves a much longer time under parole supervision (often twice as long) than he had left to serve in the penitentiary. If parole is revoked without a conviction for a new offence, he will be returned to the penitentiary with a new sentence equivalent to the original nominal sentence less the time previously spent in the institution. Revocation, then, in these circumstances, results in a longer total time spent in the penitentiary.[9] (The additional time is approximately equal to one-quarter of the time originally spent in the penitentiary before parole.)

The Terms of Parole

Usually there are three people who share the responsibility of supervising the parolee in the community. The first clause of the parole agreement states that the parolee should ... 'remain until the expiry of his sentence under the authority of the National Parole Service regional representative.' The second person is the parole supervisor, who may in some cases be a member of the National Parole Service (and can thus combine the first two supervisory roles). However, in Ontario it was more usual for the parole supervisor to be an employee of either the Ontario Probation Service or a John Howard Society. The third person is the local police chief in the area to which the applicant is paroled, although in a metropolitan police force the *de facto* person might be an intelligence officer or a desk sergeant.

There are other standard requirements in the parole agreement: that the parolee should remain in the area to which he was paroled; endeavour to maintain steady employment; obtain advance approval before buying a motor vehicle, incurring debts, getting married, or carrying weapons; abide by the instructions of his supervisor or regional representative and generally keep the law. Special requirements such as abstinence from intoxicants are also frequently given. Later in this book we will see the difference between a parole agreement on paper and its enforcement and enforcability in practice.

Parole Termination

If it is felt that parole should be terminated for some reason the procedure is initiated by a recommendation to suspend from the regional representative. The parolee would then be arrested (in Ontario, this is usually done by the RCMP rather than the local police, although the latter probably know more about his criminal activities) and held in a local jail while a written statement on the reasons for suspension is prepared and sent to Ottawa. The parole board then has two options. In the first instance, it can decide whether to 'revoke' or 'continue.' Grounds for revocation are these: evidence of a further offence not punishable by two or more years of imprisonment; violation of any of the requirements (such as those cited previously) of the parole agreement. Parole may also have been terminated through forfeiture. If, for example, a parolee is convicted of an indictable offence, punishable by two or more years of imprisonment, his parole is automatically forfeited. This is not subject to the discretion of the parole board, although it may have been preceded by suspension. A parolee can be re-paroled after either forfeiture or revocation. If the board decides to continue parole after suspension, a decision is not usually taken for at least six weeks from the original suspension date. However, the parole board's figures show that approximately 90 per cent of suspensions are followed by revocation or forfeiture or both. (Until 1968 there were approximately as many revocations as forfeitures each year.)

Use of Penitentiary and Parole

In relation to the total number of persons convicted of indictable offences in Canada, prison sentences are used in about 40 per cent and penitentiary for about 6 per cent of all cases in each year. The relative use of the penitentiary by the courts increased from 1950 through 1962 followed by a gradual decline back to 6 per cent in 1968 (*Ouimet Report*, 1969, 480, Fig. F4). Approximately one-third of all those juveniles or adults held under court sentence in institutions are adults in penitentiaries. Of these, nearly 2000 were in Ontario. This population had remained constant from about 1965, but was expected to increase rapidly in 1971 (see Appendix B.)

Although prison populations in Canada had been rising steadily in the early sixties, most daily average populations remained steady during the period 1965–70. In contrast to this the use of probation, which had also been rising steadily from the early fifties, and the use of parole, which had declined marginally until 1963 but then increased, continued to rise but at an increased rate. The men in this study were being released during 1968, which was a mid-point in that increase. In 1963, 1968, and 1970, respectively 57, 71, and 83 per cent of the eligible penitentiary inmates applied for parole. In those same years, 26, 42, and 64 per cent of those penitentiary applications were granted. As a result, in the fiscal year 1968–9 there were 1400 men released on parole and 2100 men released at expiration of sentence (see Figure 2.1).

The parole board had been in existence from 1959–68 at the time of this study. Figure 2.II summarizes four important trends during its existence through to 1971. Further details may be found in Appendix C.

Relative to 1963, the number of paroles granted had doubled by 1968, both in absolute terms and with respect to the number of applications. For instance, there were 1331 paroles granted from federal institutions out of 3518 applications in 1967 compared with 663 out of 1789 in 1963. By 1971 the 1968 rate had doubled once again to 2785 out of 4559, but was apparently decreasing. There had been a general tendency for the proportion of those in federal institutions elegible and applying for parole to fluctuate with a slight time lag behind the proportion of paroles granted, so that a rise in the proportion granted appeared to trigger more applications and to result in dramatic increases in the actual number granted. In turn, increases in the number of paroles granted are apparently associated with a disproportionate increase in parole 'failures.' Forfeitures were multiplied seven times for a three-fold increase in parole granted and a four-fold increase in revocations. In 1963, 1968, and 1970 respectively, 120, 309, and 784 paroles were forfeited (the parolee might have been paroled in any year previously) and 120, 242, and 438 were revoked.

Figure 2:I
Number of penitentiary inmates released, Canada 1959-70
By type of release

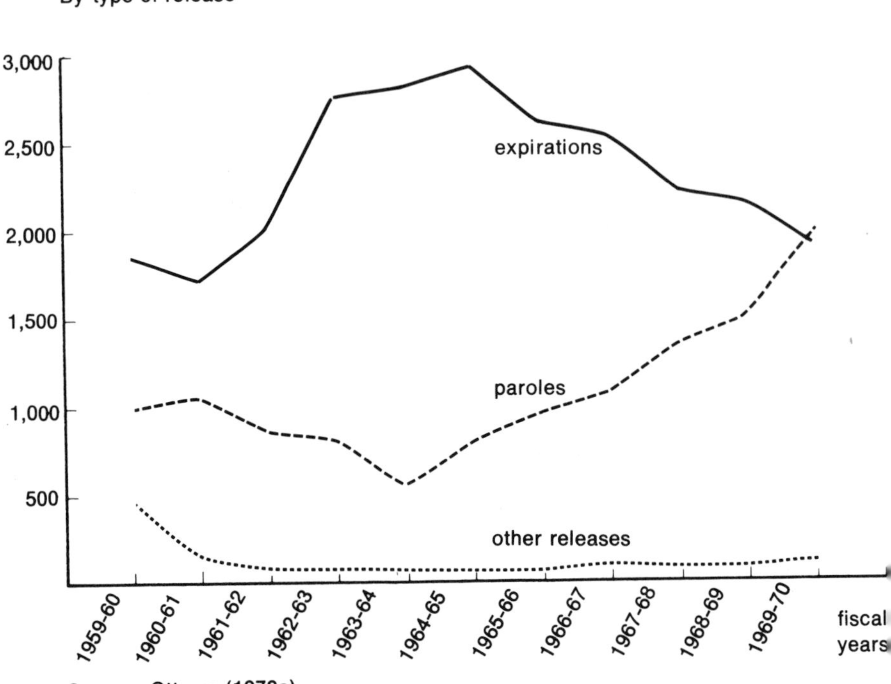

Source: Ottawa (1972a)

The remainder of this monograph will be devoted to our study in Ontario. We should bear in mind that National Parole is a release procedure dependent on application by the inmate, and, subsequently, approval by the board. It is at the discretion of the National Parole Board to grant, generally speaking, between one-third and two-thirds of the nominal sentence of an inmate. At the time of the study the proportion of those applying for and of those granted parole from federal penitentiaries in Canada was increasing dramatically. The number of forfeitures was also increasing on an annual basis, at an apparently disproportionate rate.

NOTES TO CHAPTER 2

1 Since the research for this monograph was completed a number of studies, mostly unpublished, have been made available comparing reconviction rates for parolees and dischargees. See Ciale (1969), K. Holt (1972), Langlois (1972), Landreville (1967, 1969), Solicitor General (1972)

2 *Criminal Code* RSC 1970, c. 34, Part XXI Preventive Detention (s. 687–695); *ibid.*, Part VI Homicide (s. 205–223)

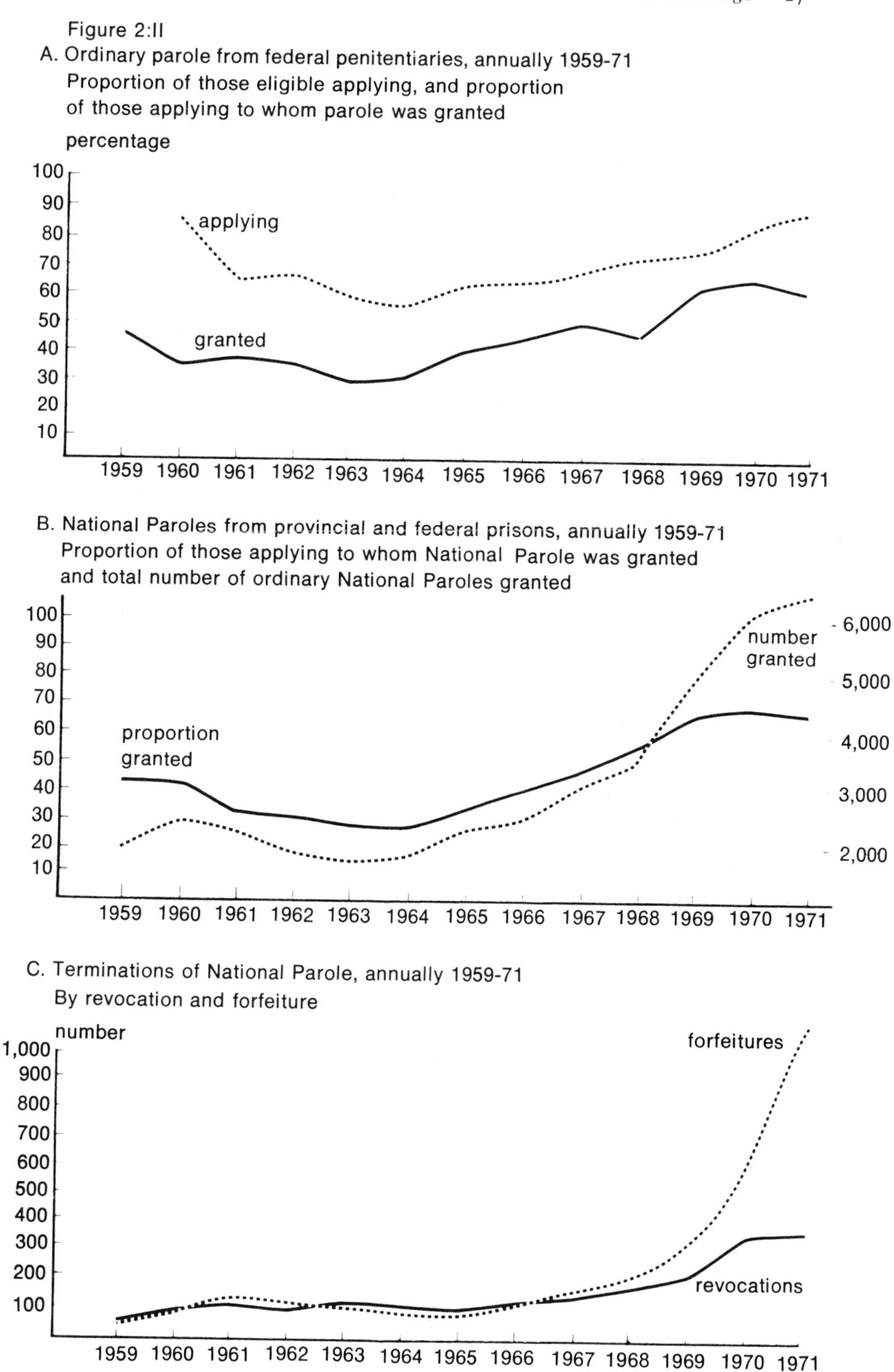
Figure 2:II
A. Ordinary parole from federal penitentiaries, annually 1959-71
Proportion of those eligible applying, and proportion of those applying to whom parole was granted
percentage
100
90
80
70
60
50
40
30
20
10
applying
granted
1959
1960
1961
1962
1963
1964
1965
1966
1967
1968
1969
1970
1971
B. National Paroles from provincial and federal prisons, annually 1959-71
Proportion of those applying to whom National Parole was granted and total number of ordinary National Paroles granted
100
90
80
70
60
50
40
30
20
10
proportion granted
number granted
6,000
5,000
4,000
3,000
2,000
1959
1960
1961
1962
1963
1964
1965
1966
1967
1968
1969
1970
1971
C. Terminations of National Parole, annually 1959-71
By revocation and forfeiture
number
1,000
900
800
700
600
500
400
300
200
100
forfeitures
revocations
1959
1960
1961
1962
1963
1964
1965
1966
1967
1968
1969
1970
1971

3 In 1968 there were eighteen inmates in the whole of Canada who had spent more than twenty years in institutions since their admission to a federal penitentiary; of these fourteen had been declared insane and were held in provincial mental hospitals. Department of the Solicitor-General, reply to written question in the House of Commons

4 *Penitentiary Act* SC 1960–61, c. 53, Statutory Remission (s. 22 and 23); *ibid.*, Earned Remission (s. 24)

5 At a time when the average daily population was falling, the new institutions completed and under construction were increasing

6 There is a number of decisions for which the National Parole Board is responsible; these include parole for deportation, parole with gradual, temporary parole, suspension of driving prohibitions and suspension of corporal punishment. This study is only concerned with ordinary and minimum parole.

7 See 'Parole Act Parole Regulations' (1960, 636, para. 2). The exceptions to the one-third of nominal sentences rule for very short, very long, and indefinite sentences are specified in this paragraph. These were slightly modified in June, 1969, and the powers of the Board were curtailed for certain types of life sentences. At the time of the study the regulations read as follows:
2(1) The portion of the term of imprisonment that an inmate shall ordinarily serve before parole may be granted is as follows: (*a*) where the sentence of imprisonment is not a sentence of imprisonment for life or a sentence of preventive detention, one-third of the term of imprisonment imposed or four years, whichever is the lesser, but in the case of a sentence of imprisonment of two years or more to a federal penal institution, at least one year; (*b*) where the sentence of imprisonment is for life but not a sentence of preventive detention or a sentence of life imprisonment to which a sentence of death has been commuted, seven years; and (*c*) where the sentence is one of life imprisonment to which a sentence of death has been commuted, ten years.
(2) Notwithstanding subsection (1), where, in the opinion of the Board special circumstances exist, the Board may grant parole to an inmate before he has served the portion of his sentence of imprisonment required under subsection (1) to have been served before a parole may be granted

8 A 'parole analyst' is a civil servant generally with legal training. Conflict between recommendations by the regional representative and the parole analyst led to reduction in the powers of the latter's position

9 This extra time is equal to one-quarter of the time spent (plus earned remission during that time) before parole was granted. In addition, the period when parole was suspended but not revoked would be dead time. This legislation was further clarified during the course of the study in *Regina* v *Morin* [1969 66 WWR 566]. However, it did not seem to be widely known to parole supervisors, penitentiary personnel, or even one member of the parole board. It was changed in 1969 so that earned remission was lost on revocation, but time to serve was calculated from the date of suspension rather than the date of revocation. Parole Act amended, SC 1969–70 c.31, s.2(1).

3

Obtaining Data

In chapter I we saw that previous research into the effectiveness of parole was inconclusive: little was known about what, if any, effect the prison experience had on a man after release, or about whether or not persons sent to prison have special characteristics which explain its apparent effects. The discretionary aspect of administrative factors may influence revocation and arrest, which would, in turn, affect their use as criteria of outcome.

In this chapter, we will return to the other emphasis of this study, the attempt to understand the ex-prisoner's social history, followed by a brief discussion of the use of prediction as a tool for what are, in effect, two separate samples, dischargees and parolees. (They are different because parolees undergo two modes of selection: by themselves and by the parole board.)

There are two polar approaches that could be used to understand the post-release career of the ex-prisoner. In the clinical perspective intensive investigation is made of a few individual cases, while in the statistical approach comparisons are made between variables known at the time of admission to the institution in an attempt to relate them to recidivism at a later date.

Clinical Approach

Aspects of a clinical approach were used to try to understand the man's experiences and feelings about the penitentiary and release into the community, as well as to learn the essential social history of a particular subject and develop an understanding of the relationships between experiences that occurred in his earlier years and his current behaviour.

An important aspect of the case history, as used (consciously or unconsciously) by clinicians, psychiatrists, and social workers, is the notion of 'career' or 'process' which provides a dynamic but unprovable explanation of individual behaviour. There are two components of 'career' – the idea that a person's behaviour is a product of his past experience as it is modified by problems and situations that now confront him, and an attempt on the part of the clinician to understand this 'career' from the actor's perspective (the case history cannot include every event, but inevitably selects certain behaviour that one or other sees as important).

No studies have tried to relate early to late post-release behaviour. The clinician or his counterpart, however, does this in effect on an individual basis when he describes the process whereby a case slowly deteriorates into failure or develops successfully. To test the extent to which the clinician's dynamic model of the development of post-release behaviour can be systematized, this study was designed to measure aspects of behaviour at various distinct time periods in an attempt to relate them to each other and to various outcome criteria.

In order to understand the subject's view of the world and consequently, perhaps, how he will act, the clinician tries to put himself in the place of the subject in an attempt to understand his feelings, perceptions, and experiences. The clinician will discuss his own understanding of the situation with the client so that he may get as accurate a picture as possible of his social world. The main disadvantage of the clinician's approach is that his conclusions or predictions about future behaviour are usually based on a sample of one or, at most, a sample biased by his own past and present case-loads. In order to generalize from a sample group to a total population, one needs to know the exact relationship between the two. As not much is known about how subjects get to the clinician, it is not possible to know how typical any case is.

In addition, the clinician will often concentrate on certain aspects (i.e., the psychiatrist may focus on the 'neurotic' or the 'pathological') of the individual's behaviour while neglecting others.

The Statistical Approach

In contrast, the statistical approach emphasizes the needs for objectivity in order to eliminate bias and systematically to test hypotheses against the real world. Whereas the clinician will infer that future behaviour can only be understood from a detailed knowledge of a case, the statistician believes that the ultimate test of the explanation of behaviour must lie in a measured test such as the prediction of a defined criterion.

Even so, our main interest in prediction techniques in this study is to control for the selection factors that differentiate our criterion groups: parolees and dischargees, or high-security and low-security prisoners. If we know that age and previous reconvictions predict arrest, we can combine these into an equation that predicts for the typical prisoner his probability of re-arrest, and we can then assess whether in general such prisoners released on parole were arrested more or less frequently than the equation predicted.

This simple approach requires a number of precautions, which are often overlooked, such as the testing of an equation on a new sample. This requires an apparent wastage of cases that are expensive and difficult to obtain, but which if omitted makes false claims to the accuracy of the equation. The methodological limitations on prediction equations have recently been discussed in Simon (1971); we will not discuss them further.

According to Simon, and our own findings concur, the statistical approach has reached a plateau in efficiency as far as the ways of combining variables into scores predicting recidivism is concerned. However, the types of variable collected may affect efficiency. Sawyer (1966) has shown that clinically collected data did not improve on psychometric scores. Moreover, Gottfredson and Ballard (1966) and Gough, Wenk, and Rozynko (1965) have shown that there are advantages to the inclusion of psychometric scores in addition to hard background data in equations to predict future recidivism. Still, the improvement in predictive efficiency is not large.

As Simon has pointed out, none of the other researchers has used information about the person's functioning in the community to predict later behaviour. Yet the parole officer emphasizes this. In this study, we will take a close look at the importance of these post-release variables.

The Data Collected

The subjects of this study were selected as representative of those men usually in prison for more than a year of any level of security, released at times throughout the calendar year. The 423 men finally included in the study were drawn from a representative sample of 291 parole applicants expected to be released, and 272 dischargees released from certain Ontario federal penitentiaries during 1968. The samples were based on those men whose stated destination was in a specified area of Southern Ontario. A man[1] was eligible to be included in the study if he were: (*a*) an inmate of any penitentiary[2] in Ontario except correctional camp L;[3] *and* (*b*) due to be released during the twelve-and-a-half months starting 15 December 1967;[4] *and* (*c*) due to be released with a first destination in Ontario which was either Toronto, Hamilton, Kingston, Windsor, Ottawa, or London;[5] *or* an area within 100 miles of Toronto; *and* (*d*) capable of understanding spoken English or French to the extent of taking part in personal interviews after release.[6]

These criteria exclude any inmate who was transferred to a hospital at the time of the intended interview but who might still be released from the institution.

A man was included in the *parole applicant sample* if he fulfilled the above criteria and if he was being actively considered by the parole board for release on parole and at that stage had had a community inquiry requested by the parole board.[7] He became a member of the *parole sample*, if he was actually released during the period covered in (*b*). He was included in the dischargee sample if he fulfilled the above criteria and was selected in a one-in-two quasi-random process which consisted of taking every second name on the release list of men who fulfilled the above criteria, stratified by institution. A few parole applicants, refused parole, later became members of the dischargee sample.

Data on the previous careers of the sample were taken from penitentiary files, and obtained in interviews after the ex-prisoner's first month in the community. The men were also asked to complete a group of psychological attitude tests before release.

Two female research interviewers were employed to carry out the interviewing for the study. At approximately one month from the man's expected date of release a group meeting was held in each institution. The groups ranged anywhere from six to thirty, although they were typically near ten. Parole applicants and dischargees were brought together separately.[8] In these meetings the interviewer explained in an informal manner the purposes and extent of the study and encouraged questions from those present. They were then given the opportunity to leave if they did not wish to co-operate. Those who remained were asked to sign a sheet releasing information from the penitentiary files to the project and stating that they had agreed to co-operate in the study. They were then asked to complete an attitude questionnaire consisting of five instruments.[9]

At the group interviews the tests were administered under research conditions, the major aim being to insure that the subjects perceived the interviewer as unconnected with the prison administration and with no 'power' over their future lives. The same female research interviewer who conducted the group interview contacted the subject again in the community.

TABLE 3.1

Co-operation by mode of release

	Co-operated	Attempted to be seen	Percentage co-operating of those listed to be seen	Finally released during 12-month period
Parole applicants/parolees	261	291	89.7	210
Dischargees	213	272	78.3	213
Ex-prisoners	474	563	84.2	423

NOTE: Proportion co-operating by mode of release $\chi^2 = 13.68$; $df = 1$; $p < 0.001$

Pre-release Co-operation

The co-operation was, for parole applicants, approximately 90 per cent, and for dischargees, a little under 80 per cent. The full details are given in Table 3.1. This difference may be explained by the fact that there was probably a greater incentive for the parole applicants to go to the interview, as they might think that it would give an impression of co-operation with the institutional authorities. However, some informal inquiries suggested that some individual refusals were from men who did not want to interrupt jobs that they considered important. Refusals at the interview itself came almost entirely from one group, where an institutional 'trouble-maker' persuaded a group of inmates to walk out. Refusals were allowed to withdraw freely, which was thought to contribute to confidence in the project as being really confidential and voluntary.

Every institution undertook to make attendance at the meeting outlining the study compulsory after which each man was free to volunteer or not. The main reasons for co-operating included curiosity, seeing other inmates who were friends, diversion from prison routine, interest in female interviewers.[10] In the maximum security penitentiary lack of co-operation, which was rare, was mainly due to the unavailability of some inmates who were held in segregation.[11] However, more dischargees held in other institutions were not given the opportunity to co-operate, either because they were not brought to the interview room or did not wish to be brought into the classification area. Those not brought for interview were mainly in the medium-security institutions, and ten of them occurred in the initial pilot sample which has been included in the study. The correctional officer assigned to collect the group may have had something to do with the proportion of those eligible who actually came to the meeting. In general, he would say, 'You are wanted in

Classification' without further explanation and without any extra effort to explain the reasons for, or the details of, the study. Another reason for the exclusion of otherwise eligible men was that they had been transferred to another institution which had already been visited, but in some cases it was possible to interview these persons on the next visit. The exclusion of 15 per cent of the eligible sample did not appear to affect its representativeness. A later analysis, which compared the co-operating sample with total releases either from Ontario or all Canadian penitentiaries on variables such as post-release arrests, reconvictions, age, previous convictions, and committal offence, confirmed this. At this stage in co-operation, Wilkins' suggestion (Mannheim and Wilkins, 1955, 56–7), that those whose files are not obtained have important differentiating characteristics, could not be extended to those not brought up for interview. The exception in our study must be those men held in segregation. While they were too few in number to affect the other comparisons, we should realize that there are important quantitative problems of transition from segregation cells to the free community. These, however, could not be investigated adequately in this study.

Quality of Data

Mannheim and Wilkins (1955, 56–7) point out that subjective judgments have been used a good deal in criminological research. In this study, it has been our policy to obtain 'hard' quantifiable data whenever possible. We wanted to know the precise age of a man, his actual earnings, the specific details of how he applied for jobs, and in exactly what ways the police, potential employers, or the public discriminated against him. Considerable 'soft' or subjective data have also been included, not only because these are the essence of the experience of being released, but also because these links are necessary to provide a reliable base for a theory of why the men behave as they do.

Subjective judgments are also important indicators of the person making the judgment. Some open-ended questions were presented to both the parole supervisor and the parolees and dischargees to see how subjective perceptions of problems related to hard data.

In recent prediction research in California, Wisconsin, and the United Kingdom (Simon, 1971), the data on which the research is based are restricted to what is included in the administrative file. This normally includes only the information required by the administrator or his professional staff. (The Glueck series of post-release interviews is an exception.[12]) One disadvantage is that this information is given to an 'official' person and may, therefore, be biased to please him or to ensure that he makes the desired decision. It is likely, for example, that there is an inmate folklore within prisons which describes how decisions are made about allocation of prisoners to specific posts within the institution. There is also a hierarchy of prestige of various posts, so that a prisoner may try to bias information he gives to officials concerned with job allocation in the direction of the post he wants.

An inmate, having already been held for a period of time in a local jail, was then transferred to the admitting penitentiary, which in 98 per cent of the cases studied was Kingston,[13] where he went through the admitting procedure. This involved bathing, measuring, and weighing. In addition, an official, in conjunction with the inmate, completed a Dominion Bureau of Statistics form. The officer had no reason to make any effort to verify the information given him and even if he wanted to, he would find it difficult as some 40 per cent of the inmates of the Ontario federal penitentiaries near Kingston come from Toronto, 150 miles away. This word of warning about the validity of the admitting information is particularly important, for it is the only information available on every person who co-operated in the study. It is also the information that usually forms the basis for prediction studies.

Data were also collected on the broad aspects of an inmate's institutional experience. It was hoped originally to collect detailed data on work adjustment, offences while in the institution, and peer group adjustment. However, the information in the files allowed only collection of details of the longest job held, the number of work changes while in the institution, details of offences against staff and inmates, and other offences. This was mostly complete. Further data were collected on release destinations and post-release assistance required from the John Howard Society. The official destination of the ex-prisoners was known in more than 95 per cent of the cases. However, this is not the same as actual destination, for it may be inferred from data collected in the one-month interview that more of the dischargees go to Toronto or spend a period of time in Toronto than would be indicated from the John Howard Society information.

We may note that in 1971, of the penitentiary population across Canada, 9 out of 10 were born in Canada (a higher percentage than the native-born in the total population); 8 out of 10 came from urban areas, had used alcohol moderately or to excess, and had been previously convicted; 7 out of 10 had not progressed beyond Grade 8 and were serving sentences of less than five years; 6 out of 10 were unemployed when arrested and were unmarried or legally separated; 4 out of 10 had served previous terms of imprisonment in penitentiaries.[14] Our 'typical' inmate released in Ontario is very similar. We will describe him on the basis of the category containing the largest frequency or the modal category on a number of other variables. Included after each variable is the actual percentage in the category.

The modal inmate was admitted to Kingston Penitentiary (98 per cent) in 1966 (41 per cent), for 'breaking, entering, and theft' as the most serious offence (20 per cent), for a sentence of 24 months (30 per cent). Within the grouping of crimes of violence, sex, property, drugs, his typical offence was property (67 per cent); at time of sentence he was aged 20–25 (33 per cent); he was born in Canada (92 per cent); single (53 per cent); Roman Catholic (36 per cent); he achieved a grade in school in the range 7 to 9 (62 per cent); had previous reformatory experience (26 per cent); had no tattoos (50 per cent), had no alias (83 per cent); had scars (94 per cent); had no disability (92 per cent); was medium built (56 per cent); did not take any formal training in the institution (75 per cent); if he did take training, he stayed in the course for 9 months or more (38 per cent), and did not graduate (52 per cent); said his destination was Toronto (43 per cent); if he was a dischargee he did not request help from the John Howard Society (66 per cent). The population is thus homogeneous (more than 90 per cent) on: admitting penitentiary – Kingston; country of origin – Canada; scars; no disability.

Post-release Data

The study originally aimed to collect information on a systematic basis in order to write a twelve-month 'biography' of each ex-prisoner, so that while we wanted to obtain information that was as nearly 'factual' as possible (to have an idea of his experiences and perceptions of events before they were either distorted or forgotten) it was necessary to limit research intrusion into his life. The descriptive data, then, were derived from three interviews following questionnaires designed to gather details of the ex-prisoner's experiences, problems, etc. during his first month, first six months, and first twelve months from release. Information about the social situation of a parolee was supplemented by a questionnaire completed by the parole supervisor at seven stages during the first twelve months; it asked for details of contacts between the parolee and his supervisor, and the supervisor's description of the parolee's problems, help given, and control used. Details of arrest(s) were obtained separately from police and Ontario jails.

Post-release Interviews

The questionnaires used by the interviewers were designed to collect data about the first month, the first six months, and the first twelve months from the ex-prisoner's date of release. The schedules were developed from pilot interviews[15] with two criterion groups of men released from the penitentiaries: men still free but attending a voluntary agency, and men re-incarcerated in a jail. The pilot interviews were based on the simple question, 'Tell me about being released from a penitentiary. I have never been in a penitentiary and I have never been released from a penitentiary and I am going to design a research study in this area and I want to find out about it.' Although there were initial suspicions, respondents in the pilot interviews were keen to discuss, at great length, their recent, and not so recent, penitentiary experiences and their perceptions of what happened to them on release and soon afterwards.

In designing each of the questionnaire schedules, attempts were made to limit the common problems of data reliability and interviewer bias by omitting questions which would require the interviewer to make judgements on the respondent's situation. The questions were, as far as possible, designed to elicit 'hard' data, such as the ex-prisoner's current employment, his income, his job changes over a certain period, the degree of skill required for the job, or particular problems that he had had with his employer or shop steward.

Some 'soft' or opinion questions, however, such as 'What sort of training should the penitentiary give you to equip you for work outside?' were included. The questions gave the ex-prisoner the chance to express himself, and gave him the feeling of being more involved in the study. The answers to these questions, while not used in the analysis of data, did provide a fuller understanding of problems in the work area.

The use of only hard data eliminates many problems of rating and interpretation, but the ex-prisoner may still distort the responses. To ask, for instance, 'How many job applications have you made?' assuming that both ex-prisoner and interviewer agree on a definition of an application, still allows the ex-prisoner to say he has made a dozen when in fact he knows that he has only made six. This type of distortion has been taken into account in the coding, where ranges have been used instead of exact numbers.

In order to obtain permission to collect data from the penitentiary files in the initial interview in the institution, each respondent was asked to sign a 'signature sheet.' This was a form which contained blank spaces for the various pieces of information required from the inmate's file. At the bottom of this sheet was a brief disclaimer giving authority to the Penitentiary Service to release the information to the research project. The purpose and importance of the signature were carefully explained to the respondents. While this is important in order to protect the human rights of the research subjects, it also made them fully aware that the research workers had access to material in their files. At this same time, the interviewer mentioned that co-operation in the study meant that we would be contacting their parole supervisors and the police to obtain further information on their pre-release and, more importantly, post-release histories. The commonly-held view among inmates, who do not seem to be very 'sophisticated' about research, was that access to this information and the psychological test inventories would tell the research team much more about the individual respondent then he knew himself. This put pressure on the respondent to avoid exaggeration and to be more truthful than he might otherwise have been. Another check on accuracy was built into the three follow-up interviews, each of which included a number of questions duplicating almost exactly those in earlier interview schedules.

Although it was planned to interview each ex-prisoner as close as possible to the due time of the questionnaire, the instruments were designed to cover the particular time period and could be administered later. For the one-month the majority of interviews were completed within three months of release, and for the twelve-month within fifteen months of release. The six-month was administered more variably, many being given in a shortened version in conjunction with the twelve-month.

The one-month interview was designed to get information in four main areas. We wanted to know details about the social history of the ex-prisoner before his incarceration, such as the nature of his offence, the actions of court and jail, and his views on why he had committed the particular crime. We wanted to see what if any effects the attempts to help him by psychiatrists, classification officers, or various agencies while in prison, had on his post-release behaviour. Perhaps the largest section was concerned with work in the institution and its relationship to work outside. The questionnaire also asked about the inmate's feelings about and perceptions of the release experience, the people to whom he turned for help and the type of help received, the jobs he held or tried to hold, family relationships, friends he saw, drink, and part-time activities. Some more general items thought to be salient to ex-inmates made up the final section. The questionnaire was effectively structured around the areas frequently mentioned by men in the tape-recorded pilot interviews as being related to ex-inmates' post-release behaviour. Several questions were asked of the parolee regarding his relationship with the parole supervisor, some of which were paralleled in the supervisor's questionnaire concerning the parolee.

In these interviews we were particularly concerned with describing as accurately as possible the ex-prisoner's level of functioning on the different dimensions, and how he achieved these levels. The other important emphasis was placed on getting an idea of the feelings and experiences of the ex-prisoner. For instance, the work on transition states described in chapter 5 below, although related to levels of functioning, is directly concerned with perceptions of a person being released from prison. A further group of opinion questions were included, whose immediate aim was to provide cross-validation material on the harder questions as well as to give the respondent the feeling that he was particularly important to the study.

The six-month and twelve-month questionnaires were basically similar, although some questions were explored further as a result of the 'non-scheduled' discussion held with the respondents and others in the field, including supervisors and ex-prisoners, about problems encountered at these later time periods. The area of concentration of the six-month and twelve-month interviews were more the area of family life, although areas already covered in the one-month interview, such as work adjustment and employment changes, were not overlooked.

The Interviews

One of the problems of the interview technique is to show that the responses are valid, and reliably obtained. This we were able to establish for the 'hard' facts, such as where an ex-prisoner was employed, or how much he earned. When one is trying to outline a 'career' or 'biography' from the actor's point of view, reliability and validity are less stable. In this case, the voluntary character of the interviews, the lack of 'power' of the interviewers over the lives of the men, as well as the interpersonal skills of the interviewers, seem to be essential elements for valid responses. As far as reliability is concerned, we felt that the variety of data sources tapped and the number of interviews held with each man provided subtantial checks. Initially there was little beyond hunch to help in the important choice of interviewers.[16] There seemed to be many advantages to choosing females and initially a younger and a more middle-aged person were employed. The latter had the additional advantage in that a non-authoritarian relationship between prisoners and their mothers is common.[17] One criticism of this choice of interviewers was that there would be language barriers, and that ex-inmates would feel restricted when describing their lives. Some empirical support for this argument is lent by the major differences in responses to the questions concerning homosexuality in prison from those given in studies using male interviewers.

The practice of many of the correctional agencies in the area of the study provided perfect differentiation between the correctional authorities and others. At that time no female was employed on the staffs of the penitentiaries as a correctional or diagnostic officer. One agency undertaking about 50 per cent of the supervision of parolees in the study employed no female case-workers in the province. The other agency undertaking a similar proportion of parole supervision rarely used its female workers, who were a small proportion of its staff working with adults, for the supervision of men. The parole service itself, which undertook the direct supervision of less than 5 per cent of the cases in the study, employed one female officer whose primary role was preparation of reports for Ottawa for the parole decision. Another agency with whom many of the respondents in the study had had contact was the police, and again, females were restricted in general terms to the juvenile division and female offenders. Although some of the respondents might have had contact with females in juvenile institutions, they were unlikely to come across them in positions of authority or administrative roles that related to adult offences. Thus the interviewers were clearly seen to have no relationship to correctional, parole, or police authority.

While this has advantages for perception of the interviewers by the respondents as separate from the administration, it posed many problems as far as obtaining co-operation from institutional administrators who were worried about the effect of female interviewers on morale and about unspecified awkward situations which might arise during the course of the pre-release interviews.

The successful completion of the initial pilot group interviews and the insistence by the interviewers that penitentiary personnel should not be present in the interviewing room not only had the effect of winning the confidence of most institution staff, but made clear to the respondents that the interviewers were not a 'branch of the parole board' or 'group spying for Ottawa.' These respondents returned to their duties with an impression of a female study team from the university, interested in understanding their problems, and who were, therefore, people with whom it might be enjoyable to co-operate.

The Representativeness of the Data

The interviewers arranged the post-release interview times and plans *at the convenience of the respondent*. This was done to maximize the possibilities for co-operation and the validity of the responses themselves. Many interviews, therefore, took place in the evenings or at weekends for those ex-prisoners who were employed. At the one-month stage, proportionately less interviews took place in the evenings than at six or twelve months by which time more of the ex-prisoners had obtained employment. Many of the initial interviews took place in the Centre of Criminology at the University of Toronto but by six and twelve months, as the ex-prisoners' lives became more caught up in their families and work, and as the novelty of visiting the university wore off, the interviews were held in the ex-prisoners' homes with the additional problem

TABLE 3.2

Numbers and percentages arrested within 24 months by mode of release and by whether the ex-prisoner was interviewed on one-, six-, and twelve-month schedules

	Parolee no. %	Dischargee no. %	Total no. %
Interviewed at 1 month	85/191 = 44.5	90/125 = 72.0	175/316 = 55.4
Not interviewed at 1 month	8/19 = 42.1	54/88 = 61.4	62/107 = 57.9
Co-operation rate* (%)	92.0	61.1	76.9
Interviewed at 6 months	51/136 = 37.5	43/68 = 63.2	94/204 = 46.1
Not interviewed at 6 months	42/74 = 56.7	101/145 = 69.6	143/219 = 65.3
Co-operation rate* (%)	70.1	37.9	54.5
Interviewed at 12 months	38/113 = 33.6	31/57 = 54.3	69/170 = 40.6
Not interviewed at 12 months	55/97 = 56.7	113/156 = 72.4	168/253 = 66.4
Co-operation rate* (%)	68.9	44.1	58.1
Total	93/210 = 44.3	144/213 = 67.6	237/423 = 56.0

*On the respective interview schedules by mode of release, co-operation rate is defined as that proportion of those *eligible* for interview who were interviewed concerning their experiences in the community. *Eligible* is defined as describing an ex-prisoner *not* either arrested or known to have moved out of the area during the eligibility time period for a previous questionnaire

of others, such as wives, being present. In a few instances the offices of after-care agencies were used for the interviews.

The main method of contacting parolees was through information returned to the research unit by parole supervisors. For the dischargee, initial contacts were made in a variety of ways, including sending lists of those co-operating in the study to after-care agencies to see if they had called there. The grapevine was a further source. However, a more important means was details of arrest obtained from the police which led to an interview in an institution with a re-arrested individual; his information often led us to another dischargee who was still free.

The primary reason for non-co-operation at all stages was the difficulty of contacting the ex-prisoner, who had often left the area or was moving from town to town. Only three dischargees and four parolees refused a post-release interview when contacted. In Table 3.2, even in the interview concerned with the first five weeks in the community, only 92 per cent of the eligible parolees and 61 per cent of the eligible dischargees were interviewed. By six and twelve months these proportions had fallen even lower. At six months, 70 per cent of the eligible parolees and 38 per cent of the eligible dischargees, and at 12 months 69 per cent and 44 per cent respectively, co-operated in the interviews. This reduced the total number of schedules returned to 203 at six months, and 171 at twelve months. By many standards these are impressive figures for voluntary co-operation by ex-prisoners. However, in terms of presenting a representative view of how the ex-prisoners experience the six- and twelve-month periods from their date of release, there are many limitations. For parolees, significantly fewer of those interviewed at six and twelve months had been arrested within twenty-four months than those not interviewed. For the one-month questionnaire, the principal bias in the sample was in the higher proportion of those dischargees interviewed who were arrested within twelve months. However, the bias for the dischargees was reversed by six and twelve months. Significantly fewer dischargees interviewed at twelve months had been arrested within twenty-four months. This would be expected from the proportion of dischargees arrested in the first twelve months.

Though there were no differences at one month, there were significantly fewer of the younger parolees interviewed at both six and twelve months. The interviewers were less successful in obtaining co-operation at the later stages from that younger group of ex-prisoners who, we will see, were typically released from Collins Bay, posed problems for their parole supervisors, were highly mobile, and were eventually rearrested. However, some such individuals were included.

A table of the numbers and proportions of those interviewed, by the number of previous arrests and by mode of release, was prepared. By previous arrest, there are no differences in proportions for the one-month questionnaire. Though there are no differences at six months for dischargees, there is a tendency for more dischargees with fewer previous arrests to be interviewed at twelve months. At six months there is a tendency for parolees with fewer arrests to have been interviewed. This parallel tendency for parolees is significant at twelve months. These latter significant differences appear to result from a relationship between eligibility for interview and number of previous arrests; thus those with few arrests are less likely to be arrested within the first twelve months, and so more likely to be available for interview.

It will be shown that age and the variable concerned with the seriousness of previous commitments to penal institutions (which correlated very highly with the number of previous arrests) could be used to produce a reliable prediction equation of arrest within twenty-four months. The analysis has shown that there were no major differences within parolees and dischargees on these two variables for each of the interview schedules. There were, however, larger differences in the numbers of each group arrested.

The extent of the missing data on the six- and twelve-month questionnaires resulted in a preliminary decision to consider 'zero order' responses alone of the ex-prisoners who co-operated in these interviews. As the background material for making some allowance for missing data is available, more sophisticated analysis on the material from the one-month questionnaire could be, and was, carried out.

NOTES TO CHAPTER 3

1 Female prisoners were excluded from the study as the numbers being released from the one federal penitentiary for women were too small to justify a study of this type. The basic social environment such as family or employment faced by a female on release from prison may have similarities to that of the male. However, there are differences that would introduce further complications. It is also unlikely that the interviewing methods adopted in this study, particularly the use of female interviewers, would have resulted in the same co-operation as was found with the men after release

2 The first decision taken was to consider only those persons released from institutions after spending at least one year continously in prison. In order to consider in some detail the effect of length of imprisonment, it was necessary to restrict the institutions considered to those taking men serving periods in prison of at least a year in the majority of cases. This decision necessitated the selection of federal penitentiaries and the exclusion of provincial reformatories

3 The differences in recidivism rates that are *prima facie* associated with release from the different levels of institution within the Canadian Federal Penitentiary System necessitated a sample which was representative of all grades of institution. However, there were two correctional camps with about 60 inmates each situated more than 100 miles from the research centre. One of these was excluded and a total sample taken from the other

4 An examination of recidivism rates in other studies showed that there are some minor variations in rates over time which appear to be related to the month in which the person is released. Many authors note that the number of arrests varies by month. Although the evidence is as conflicting and as weak as the other evidence in the field of recidivism, it is nevertheless important that a sample studied should cover the full calendar year

5 The destination of approximately 5 per cent of the men being released from the federal penitentiaries in Ontario is outside Ontario and of approximately 10 per cent within Ontario but outside Southern Ontario as defined in this study. It was decided, for the obvious reasons of cost, to exclude these men from the study. It is likely that there are some differences between the men so excluded and the men included. For instance, a number go to the Maritimes, where different models of supervision, local conditions such as scanty population and distance, as well as differences in availability of employment, may (or may not) make important differences in the problems which they meet. Further, there may also be differences in law enforcement practice in areas outside of Southern Ontario which cannot be accounted for in this study. All these considerations limit the general applicability of our findings

6 A Hungarian or Italian inmate who knows no English obviously presents different problems from many of the other ex-prisoners. However, he will also present similar problems to those men whose ability to communicate in English is not limited. Whether the results are applicable to this group or not, it was so small (less than 10) as not to justify a special research effort to include it. Any such special facilities would also have presented biases in the asking of questions for which no adequate controls would have been available

7 In 1962, 1963, and 1964, 83 per cent of those granted community enquires were finally granted parole, whereas 17 per cent of those not granted community enquiries were finally granted parole. The parole board estimated 90 per cent and less than 5 per

cent respectively for 1968. See analysis prepared for Macnaughton-Smith (1973)

8 The lists of men to be included in the interview were compiled from a list of all parole applicants on whom community enquires were being prepared during that month, and for the dischargees from lists of men due to be released in the next month prepared by each institution

9 This included the adult version of the Jesness Inventory, self-perception items, and three scales not analysed in this report – Sarbin Conduct Impairment, Mylonas Attitudes to Legal Institutions, and Crissman Moral Judgement Attitudes

10 The reasons for co-operating elaborated here and other comments on interviews are partly based on reports prepared by the interviewers themselves

11 The interviewers were allowed to see these men only at the discretion of the institution. The number eligible to be included in the study, but not brought up, was ten

12 Glueck and Glueck, (1930). Laune (1936) included simple sociometric data collected from other prisoners about the subject in the study. This information was then used to try to improve the prediction of the subject's success. Like many other studies it was unsuccessful in improving on the other 'hard' data that is available on men. See Ohlin and Lawrence (1952). Laune's data were based on only 150 subjects, of whom only 110 were available for study by Ohlin and Lawrence. It is possible that Laune assumed that the other prisoners rating the subjects would be doing so on relevant dimensions from their knowledge of the inmates' behaviour in the institution. However, the other prisoners may be too concerned with the subjects' reactions to the total institution, which may, *per se*, be irrelevant to behaviour in the community. It is unlikely that co-prisoners will give better information than professional workers, psychological instruments, or data on administrative files, or be very accurate in identifying the important dimensions which would relate to adjustment in the community. Thus, serious consideration was given in this study to including ratings by other inmates on the subjects in the work situation along dimensions which would be suggested by the researchers. Before the dimensions were adequately identified, it was decided that the inclusion of such data in this study would prolong it beyond any controllable length

13 Dischargees 99.5 per cent parolees 95.5 per cent

14 From *Canada's Correctional Services* (booklet, 1971)

15 Although the pilot interviews identified salient areas and led us towards the ex-prisoners' concepts of a theory of prison and parole, we were also influenced by work with similar orientations, particularly Lohman et al., (1966); Glaser (1964); Studt (1971). Some individual questions relating to employment were modified as a result of a rationale developed by Shearing (1968)

16 Hyman (1954, 366, Appendix on NORC Training and Field Procedures). In textbooks on social research design there is much philosophical discussion of criteria to be used in the selection of interviewers. Further, there has been a number of empirical studies comparing the efficiency and effectiveness of interviewers with respect to different ages, sex, socio-economic grouping, and training. The conclusions are equivocal. In dealing with populations that have had considerable experience of compulsory 'treatment' there are added problems in selection of interviewers. The work of Kroger, for instance, has illustrated how sophisticated attitude test scores can be influenced by a respondent's perception of the use which is to be made of the particular instrument. This has been discussed often with regard to opinion questions among sociologists. A classic example of this is Korn's (1965) review of Glaser (1964), where the simple tabulation of responses without due regard to the methods by which they were obtained was strongly criticised. The review also includes a classic statement of the reliability-validity problems by reversing, 'it never happened, but it's all true' to 'it all happened, but it's not true,' when discussing many of the opinion responses analysed by Glaser. The validity and reliability of individual questions is either considered when the analysis of that question is presented, or has resulted in the omission of analysis of the question. Glaser may or may not have produced a satisfactory answer in that particular case; however, the question of in what ways the respondents were to perceive the interviewers in

general still remains. Unfortunately, the research design can do no more than set the balance of probabilities in favour of a particular perception. To take an extreme case, a policeman is unlikely to be able to obtain any reliable information on unrecorded indictable crime because his role as a policeman which might entail unpleasant experience for the interviewee. Similarly, a classification officer in an institution whose role combines that of understanding the parole applicant and then making a recommendation with regard to level of security and later on his parole is likely to obtain biased information. The incentives and deterrents which might sanction untruthful answers amongst a socially deviant population are recognized as being important. Also, this particular socially deviant populations' experience with manipulative questioners in unfavourable situations is widespread. Policemen, lawyers, or social workers are each liable to try to manipulate the deviant to give the information, and possibly the answers, required for their purpose

17 This was later to be confirmed in this study in the addendum (Waller, 1971)

4

The Men Released From Prison

In the previous chapter we saw a break-down of the men's backgrounds based on data selected from penitentiary files. We now turn to a fuller discussion of those data, as they are all that are available on every one of the 423 subjects in the study. These data can provide some answers to questions such as these: Who is an ex-prisoner? How long was he in the penitentiary? What offences did he commit? Had he been in prison before? How old was he when released? How do parolees differ from dischargees? How do those arrested differ from those who are not?

It seems obvious, of course, that in any attempt to discover who 'the ex-prisoner' is, one must talk to him. The other focus, of this chapter will therefore be an analysis of the information that came out of interviews with these men.

Comparison Between Parolees and Dischargees and Between those Arrested and not After Release

The principal differences between parolees and dischargees on a number of variables are summarized in Table 4.1. The differences on the same variables between those still free and those arrested within twelve months are also tabulated. The outstanding conclusion must be that the differences between parolees and dischargees are more and larger than between those arrested and those not arrested.

The means for the parolees and dischargees were compared using

TABLE 4.1

Summary of comparison of means for biographical variables (Grouped on *t*-test by mode of release and arrest or not)

	Parolee† against dischargee	Men free against men arrested within 12 months
The parolee/man free was (or had) on average		
Fewer previous commitments to adult institutions/less likely to have been to a jail, reformatory or penitentiary	***	.
Admitted to the penitentiary later	*	.
Convicted of a more serious offence/not returned as parole violator	**	.
Longer aggregate sentence	***	**
Older at release	.	***
Employed on admission to the penitentiary	.	**
Married/had more dependents	*	.
Higher grade	**	.
Less use of drugs	*	.
In penitentiary		
More skilled job	*	.
Held the job less long	**	.
Less offences against staff	**	*
Less offences without a victim	**	.
Fewer months in training, if taken	**	.

. Not significant; * significant with probability 0.05; ** significant with probability 0.01; *** significant with probability 0.001. Range of *n*: For most, parolees 200–210; dischargees 200–213.
†Selection for parole involves application by the inmate and granting by parole board

the *t*-test.[1] Causes or other implications should be drawn only cautiously from the *t*-test. For instance, it should not be assumed that parolees are selected for parole because they have more children; it is more probable that they were selected because they were married or, much more likely, as a result of some combination of other variables not discussed.

The aggregate sentence of parolees is longer than that of dischargees. For the parolee the modal category was three years (30 per cent), but 20 per cent had sentences of two years and, importantly, more than 22 per cent had aggregate sentences of over five years. The modal dischargee had an aggregate sentence of three years (45 per cent), although 29 per cent had a sentence of two years, and less than 5 per cent had aggregate sentences of over five years. As the aggregate length of sentences increases the proportion of persons released on parole increases. Thus, 40 per cent of those with aggregate sentences of two years or less, 62 per cent of those with between four and five years, and 87 per cent of those with between seven and ten years were released on parole. For a release population, this implies that selection for parole favours those with longer aggregate sentence ranges, but results in shor-

TABLE 4.2

Most serious offence on admission to penitentiary by mode of release and age

	Murder	Sex	Wounding	Robbery	Breaking, entering	Escape	Theft	Fraud	Narcotics	Parole Violation	Other	
Dischargees		10.3%		13.1%				77.0%				100%
Over 25	5	7	6	15	29	4	28	20	1	4	3	
Under 25			4	13	21	31	11	6	2	1	2	
Total	5	7	10	28	50	35	39	26	3	5	5	213
Parolees		14.8%		17.1%				68.1%				100%
Over 25	11	9	3	23	36	4	11	21	3	1	5	
Under 25	3	2	3	13	25	22	11	1	2	—	1	
Total	14	11	6	36	61	26	22	22	5	1	6	210
Total	19	18	16	64	111	61	61	48	8	6	11	423
Parolees/parolees + dischargees	73.7	61.1	37.5	56.3	55.0	42.6	36.1	45.8	62.5	16.7	54.5	49.6

ter periods of time spent in the institution. In relation to longer sentences they will still serve long periods if parole is either revoked or forfeited. If this group had regular failure rates, it would tend to fill up the penitentiaries.

Since parole is a form of early release, we see that generally speaking the parolee, compared to the dischargee, serves less time in the institution, the mean admission year for dischargees being 1966 and for parolees 1967. This, however, hides a more complicated relationship. Parole is more likely to be given to persons admitted in 1967. Included in this group are those persons who had escaped from reformatories but whose original sentence had been less than two years, and a few whose earlier parole had been revoked. Persons serving three or four years in a penitentiary would be more likely to be released at expiration of sentence, though for sentences longer than four years parole was the more likely mode of release.

The parolee's offence was more serious than the dischargee's (see Table 4.2). The break-down by individual offence illustrates this more clearly. A higher proportion of those released on parole were originally convicted of murder, narcotic offences, sex offences, robbery, breaking and entering, or other offences; for crimes such as theft, wounding, escape, and fraud a greater proportion were was released at expiration of sentence.

In the criminological literature on adult offenders it is often shown

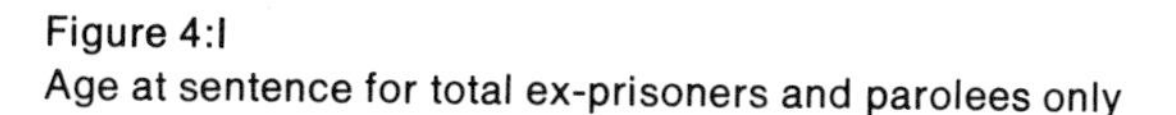

Figure 4:I
Age at sentence for total ex-prisoners and parolees only

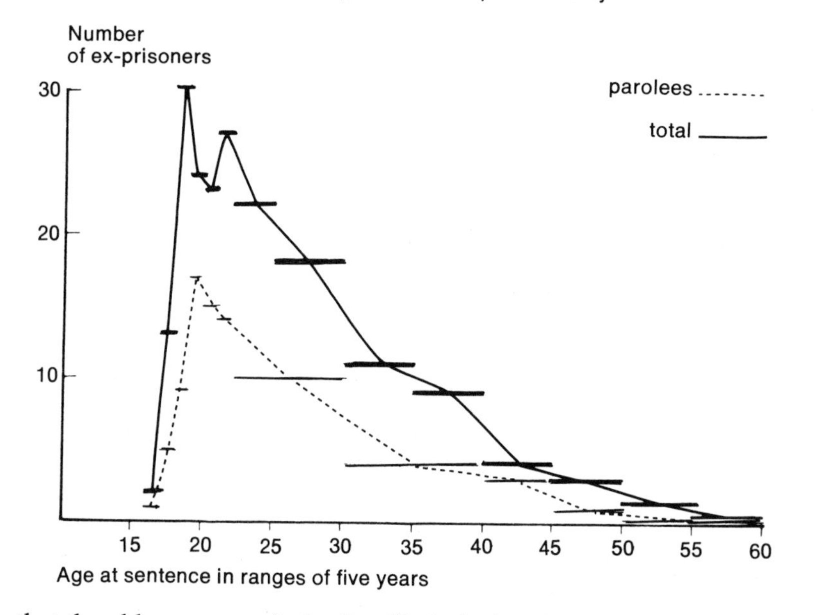

that the older a person is the less likely he is to be reconvicted (a finding which will be substantiated in this study). One might expect, therefore, that if the parole boards make selections on the basis of risk, there would be significant age differences between parolees and dischargees. This, however, was not the case for the men in this study. The histogram of age at sentence is laid out in Figure 4.1. The histogram of age at release is very similar. In over-all terms, there is little difference between the two populations, other than a marginal tendency for more of those aged 20 or younger to be unconditionally discharged at sentence and more of those aged 20–21 to be released on parole.

Despite the lack of difference in age, there was a tendency for more parolees to be married. Table 4.3 lays out marital status on admission to the institution by mode of release. In the release population, a person is more likely to be released on parole if he is married or separated at time of admission to the institutions, and more likely to be a dischargee if he's single or in some other category.

In terms of educational grade on admission to the institution the parolees' mean is higher than the dischargees'. The histogram laying out grade by mode of release is displayed in Figure 4.II. For grades below 6 more of those released were dischargees; for those in the range 6–9, they were approximately equal, but for grades over 9 more were released on parole.

There were significant differences in the means on a number of vari-

TABLE 4.3

Marital status by mode of release

	D	P	T	% parolees/total
Single	123	99	222	44.6
Married	54	78	132	59.1
Common-law union	13	11	24	45.8
Widow	3	2	5	40.0
Separated	9	15	24	62.5
Divorced	7	3	10	30.0
NS	4	2	6	33.3
Total	213	210	423	49.6

TABLE 4.4

Numbers and proportions of ex-prisoners who had previously been sentenced to jail, reformatory, and penitentiary, by mode of release

	Dischargees	Parolees	Total
Jail	108/213 = 56.7%	77/210 = 36.7%	185/423 = 43.7%
Reformatory	172/213 = 80.8%	145/210 = 69.0%	317/423 = 74.9%
Penitentiary	100/213 = 46.9%	70/210 = 33.3%	170/423 = 40.2%

ables concerned with previous records. In all cases parolees were less likely to have served time or to have served as much time. Table 4.4 lays out the proportions of the dischargees and parolees who had served time by jail, reformatory, and penitentiary. As many as 4 out of 5 dischargees and 7 out of 10 parolees had previously served time in a reformatory.

Figure 4:II
School grades achieved as recorded by admission office, by mode of release

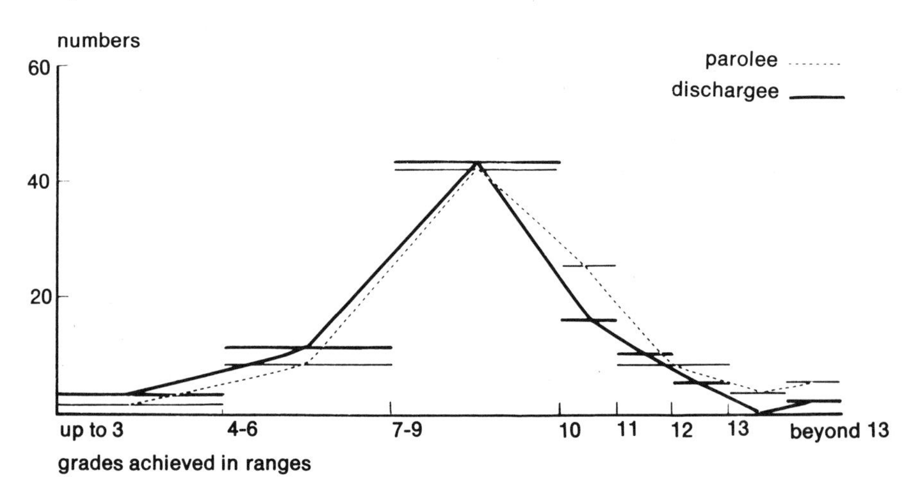

Mode of release, age and previous penal record are cross-tabulated in Table 4.5. These will be shown to be of considerable importance in later analysis. Penal record could be used as highly efficient predictor of whether or not a person was a parolee: 70 per cent of those with no previous commitments were released on parole. In contrast, of those who had jail, reformatory, and penitentiary commitments, who comprised 19 per cent of the total population, only 34 per cent were released on parole. Many are unaware of the extent of recidivism among the prison population. In this study only 13 per cent of the total had no previous commitment to an adult penal institution; 71 per cent of the dischargees and 40 per cent of the parolees with no previous adult commitment were under 25. It will be shown later that many of these younger ex-prisoners had had commitments to training school and that many of all ages had had previous arrests. In fact, there were only 14 of the ex-prisoners for whom it was a first arrest.

Psychometric Testing of Prisoners

There were a number of psychometric test scores collected for the ex-prisoners. The principal tests included the Minnesota Multiphasic Personality Inventory (MMPI), an adult version of the Jesness Inventory, and the California Psychological Inventory (CPI). Many theories of behaviour have been tested using such ways of measuring personality. We included them as data in this study for two reasons; first, as comparative data on prison population studies elsewhere; second, as data to be used in the development of prediction equations for various criteria of adjustment in the community. These tests were also included to enlarge the background information. The details of the situation under which the tests were administered, the general aims of the tests, and the specific findings are described elsewhere (Waller, 1971). Although we are not concerned directly with why persons do or do not apply for parole, or why those persons who do are selected or rejected, the current release population of parolees and dischargees from the same institutions, during the same time period, provides two neat criterion groups for pointing out, first of all, the characteristics that differentiate the parolees from the dischargees and, secondly, for inferring from these some details of the combined effect of the decision-making process of the parole board and that of the inmates. These characteristics should throw more light on the differences between the parolees and the dischargees which may be important for an understanding of their responses and behaviour after release.

The principal conclusions from the detailed analysis are, however, reviewed. While the norms of the penitentiary release population under study here are very different from the general population norms for these

TABLE 4.5

Previous recorded adult commitments by mode of release and by proportion under twenty-five

	No previous commitment	Previously committed to							
		Jail	Reformatory	Penitentiary	Jail and reformatory	Jail and penitentiary	Reformatory and penitentiary	Jail, reformatory, and penitentiary	
	1	2	3	4	5	6	7	8	N
Dischargees	17	9	50	5	36	10	33	53	213
% under 25	70.6	55.6	52.0	40.0	27.8	0.0	12.1	5.7	
Parolees	38	14	61	5	28	9	28	27	210
% under 25	39.5	14.3	60.7	0.0	32.1	22.2	0.0	3.7	
Total	55	23	111	10	64	19	61	80	423
Parolees/dischargees + parolees	69.1	60.9	55.0	50.0	43.8	47.4	45.9	33.8	49.6
% of total	13.0	5.4	26.2	2.4	15.1	4.5	14.4	13.9	

tests, they are similar on most scales to other prison populations.[2] Further, the means of parolees differ from those for dischargees in the same way that non-violators differ from violators in California and the other jurisdictions where the tests were used. However, with the possible exception of the Jesness Inventory, the differences between those re-arrested and those not are much smaller and less clear than the differences between parolees and dischargees.

Considerable regression analysis was carried out using individual test scores to predict re-conviction within twelve months. Although apparently statistically significant multiple correlation coefficients could be produced on a construction sample, these rarely validated on the test sample and so will not be discussed further. However, regression analysis predicting release on parole or discharge did result in validated equations, though these were less efficient than equations based on other data.

In later analysis personality was measured by the linear sum of selected scale scores within the CPI and Jesness Inventory. The scales selected, called combination scores, were those where the compared means of parolees and dischargees had significant statistical differences. The scores are the same as those which provide an estimate of the personality of the more or less successful, socially adjusted person.

The most important measures of self-concept which were administered before release were seven items used in a study in Ohio (Ali, 1966) that were found to differentiate technical (revocation) from criminal (forfeiture) violators. Three of these items were basically concerned with whether or not the respondent thought he would fail after release and whether or not the penitentiary had made him worse. The items were, in a sense, 'unsophisticated' in that they simply asked the respondent the direct question. The CPI, Jesness, and self-perception items were administered to the men when their statuses were either 'parole applicant' or 'future dischargee'; the MMPI, however, was completed on entry to the institution. These items clearly differentiated parolees from dischargees, a fact which makes it seem that being interviewed as a parole applicant may result in a 'halo effect'. However, within each of the sub-groups of parolees and dischargees, scores on these items were related to arrest.

Discussion

As a result of informal discussions with the parole board, it was expected that the criteria used for decisions on parole applications would be social. For this reason variables such as weight, race, and religion were not thought to differentiate parolees and dischargees; *t*-test bore this out.

The parole board, on the face of it at least, must strike a balance in its decisions between such considerations as retribution, consistency, rehabilitation, and, all important, protection for the public. It may be, of course, that these are only 'overt' aims to which the board refers in its annual reports, or alternatively aims which others attribute to it; possibly, day-to-day problems are more important elements of the decision-making process than these goals.

Undoubtedly, risk is a big factor. What is the probability that the paroled individual will commit further offences of a certain seriousness? The board knows that any sensational offence involving a parolee is likely to get a lot of attention, both from the media and from politicians. As a result, it seems likely that they grant parole on the basis of what the offender, as a 'rational man,' would do. The social and psychological environment, in addition to the background of the offender, probably are used to give an indication of what the risks are. Where these elements point to the likelihood of new (serious) offences, the inmate is unlikely to receive parole.

We can see, also that the offender's background, especially in relation to considerations of retribution and consistency, is very important.[3] From this point of view it is surprising that parolees did not differ from dischargees on variables such as employment status at time of arrest, involvement with drink, number of offences against other inmates, and intelligence; surprising, because it would be expected that these would influence the parole board, especially when the current folklore on the 'causes' of crime relates such differences to recidivism. Another undifferentiated variable was age; this has already been discussed.

At the time this analysis was carried out, little was known about the differences between applicants and non-applicants for parole. It will be shown later that with the exception of the self-perception items, there are few administrative pre-release variables differentiating the two groups.

All the variables considered until now were obtained from penitentiary files or from psychometric tests completed before release. We will now turn to information obtained from the man after he was released. Most of these data come from the interview concerned with his first five weeks in the community.

National and Family Origins

Of 317 persons (for whom the one-month questionnaire was completed) 286, or about 9 out of 10, said they were born in Canada.[4]

Of those born in Canada	Parolees*	Dischargees
Ontario	80	72
Maritimes	10	18
Quebec	7	7
Western provinces	2	3

*Approximate percentage

As far as upbringing is concerned, these are the figures:

Brought up in the place where they were born	64	60
For most of the time until age 15 by parents	75	75
Principally by state-aided methods	<10	<10

Quite a number of both groups had been in training schools or foster homes for short periods of time, three out of 10 having been to training school. It is surprising that the parole board does not discriminate against offenders with training school experience as they would be, generally speaking, worse parole risks. This may be explained by the fact that this information is not readily available on file, as it forms part of a separate 'juvenile' record.

Those who had been brought up with a father figure were asked to name his typical occupation: 55 per cent of the dischargees and 46 per cent of the parolees mentioned an occupation which could be categorized in the Dominion Bureau of Statistics (now known as Statistics Canada) scales as crafts, production processes, or related work; 11 per cent of dischargees' and 16 per cent of parolees' were involved in the transportation and communications area; 12 per cent and 16 per cent, respectively, were involved in service or recreation industries.

The ex-prisoner's socio-economic background was indexed by his father's occupation. Typically, the father was a higher-level blue-collar worker, while a few were involved in unskilled white-collar jobs. There was only a slight and non-significant tendency for parolees' fathers' jobs to have a higher prestige rating. However, the lower the father's job prestige scale rating the more likely it was that the ex-prisoner would be arrested within the first twelve months. The percentage differences, however, are not very large, and therefore they constitute weak evidence for the theory that the social class origins of ex-prisoners affect their chances of being reconvicted.

The ex-prisoners first left 'home' (the time criterion being at least six months) at a wide range of ages. Over half left at 16 or younger, some for the first time as a result of an arrest. Three out of four ex-prisoners left home between their 13th and 18th birthdays. In total terms, 43 per cent had left home at the age of 15 or earlier and nearly 90 per cent before the age of 20. There is a slight tendency for dischargees to have left earlier than parolees. For 27 per cent of the total population this was as a result of an arrest.

As might be expected, 50 per cent of those who were not living with both parents or who were not brought up by both parents had left home before the age of 15, compared to only 40 per cent of those who were living with both parents. This difference was mainly accounted for by persons brought up in foster homes and training schools or by their mothers alone.

What is the relationship between families and delinquency? Cormier (1965, esp. 101) has identified families that produce only one habitual delinquent – the black sheep – and families with a number of delinquent children, the parents being delinquent also – the multi-delinquent family. In his work on the multi-delinquent family he noted that it is a major source of criminality. In a study of 50 families, which produced 249 sons and 144 daughters, 149 of the sons were known delinquents, of whom 117 had served one or more penitentiary sentences. The criminality of the parents was often unknown to the children as it had taken place when the children were young. The father's crime was often less serious than the son's.

In this study we found that one in six ex-prisoners knew that their fathers had been charged with offences. Like the sons, most of the fathers' offences were against property, although some involved drunkenness. One in three members of the sample had brothers who had been charged. These were distributed in a similar fashion to the typical charges on which the ex-prisoners themselves had been convicted; assault, robbery, breaking and entering, theft, and fraud. A small number of less serious offences was also recorded. Only a small number of the sample had sisters who had been charged with offences. Two of these involved offences against the person; the remainder were prostitution, offences due to alcohol consumption, and vagrancy. Nearly one in two of the ex-prisoners thought that one of their family had been charged by the police at some time. There were comparatively few members of the sample who had both fathers and brothers who had been involved in offences, although there were many who had more than one brother involved. Since one might expect the parole board to discriminate between offenders with and without family members involved in crime, it is interesting to note (although the differences are not significant) that marginally more parolees than dischargees had brothers and sisters involved in offences. Although family involvement in crime was not related to conviction within the first twelve months for the dischargees, there was a tendency among parolees for those with neither brother(s) nor father convicted of a criminal offence to have a lower reconviction rate (20 per cent compared to 35 per cent).

Age at first arrest has frequently been shown to correlate with recidivism; the younger the first arrest the more likely an ex-prisoner is to be reconvicted on release. For both samples, involvment with the police started from an early age. More than 37 per cent of the total group had been arrested for the first time before the age of 15, nearly 80 per cent before the age of 20, and only 5 per cent of the parolees and 2 per cent of the dischargees over the age of 30. There was a slight tendency for the dischargee to have been arrested at an earlier age than the parolee.

Leaving home early was associated, though not necessarily coincident, with early arrest. As might be expected, 61 per cent of those persons leaving home at age 15 or younger were arrested at age 15 or younger, whereas only 16 per cent of those leaving home at 16 or over were arrested then. There is a consistent tendency for both parolees and dischargees, whose first arrest was before the age of 15, to be more likely to be arrested within twelve months from their date of release. Consistent with this is the finding that both parolees and dischargees who have had been in training school have higher probabilities of being reconvicted within twelve months from their date of release than those persons who had only been in reformatory or had been in neither reformatory nor training school.

For both parolees and dischargees interviewed there was a close relationship between penal record and age of leaving home; 50 per cent of those with a previous commitment to a reformatory or penitentiary left home at 15 or earlier in contrast to only 25 per cent of those with no previous penal record.[5]

Without any specific hypotheses, we investigated whether or not the original offence for which the ex-prisoner had been convicted was in any way related to these background characteristics, since Gibbons (1965) and others (Clinnard and Quinney, 1967) have suggested that there are differences in the biographical characteristics of persons convicted of certain types of offence. The main problem in carrying out this sort of analysis in the current study was the small number of persons convicted of offences other than robbery, breaking and entering, theft, and fraud. Biographical details, like age at first arrest, were found to be unrelated to original offence in this study.

There were marked tendencies for those convicted of offences against the person to have been brought up by both parents more often than by a combination of parents and institutions. There were also associations between age at leaving home and age at first arrest and whether or not the current offence was against the person. However, the direction of these relationships was different in the two groups. Fewer parolees who left home at age 15 or earlier had been convicted of an offence against the person, whereas more dischargees who had been convicted of offences against the person left home before age 15. Parallel findings were found for age at first arrest. More parolees who had been to neither reformatory nor training school were convicted of offences against the person, while for dischargees this was true of those who had been to one or the other. There is also a tendency for those who had been to reformatory to have less chance of having commited an offence against the person.

Although there was no difference for dischargees, for parolees 42 per cent of those brought up by both parents were single on admission to the penitentiary compared to 72 per cent of those brought up in some other way. A slightly greater proportion of those who left home before the age of 15 than those who left home when older, were single. There was a parallel tendency for the age at which a person was first arrested. Of the ex-prisoners who had been in training school or reformatory, 49 per cent of the parolees and 65 per cent of the dischargees were single. In contrast, 35 per cent of the parolees and 29 per cent of the dischargees who had not been in training school or reformatory were single. Those with previous time in an institution were more likely to be single at admission to penitentiary. Also, a relatively small proportion of dischargees with no previous prison commitments were single.

Of the dischargees 57 per cent had committed no offences against staff compared to 73 per cent of the parolees; 81 per cent of both groups who had committed no offences against staff had been brought up by their parents compared to 70 per cent who had. For parolees, there was no relationship between age at first leaving home or age of arrest and offences against staff, although there was a slight tendency for discharges with offences against staff to have been arrested earlier than those who did not. Those parolees and dischargees who had no commitment to training school or reformatory were more likely to have had no offences against staff during their current penitentiary sentence.

Lack of Relation to Arrest

The above are all variables that other authors have demonstrated empirically as having a relation to re-conviction. As such, one would expect that the parole board takes them into account in making its decisions. This is why it is so interesting that there are comparatively few differences between parolees and dischargees. However, in terms of our expectations of who would be a penitentiary inmate we found evidence to confirm and reject some of these earlier hypotheses.

These variables were included in the one-month questionnaire with the expectation that they would be useful in the development of a base expectancy equation or to provide some background information on the ex-prisoners in order to understand details of their post-release careers. It has been shown that there are many relationships, though not statistically significant ones, between these background variables and being reconvicted within twelve months from date of release. The more important of these variables are employment at the time of the offence, number of previous convictions, and offence, all of which, in our findings, were related to reconviction.

Pre-admission Work Experience

The post-release work histories of the men or their interest in training courses in the institution can be better understood after we have reviewed the ex-prisoner's work history before admission to the institution.

In Glaser's (1964) study of the post-release failure rate he found that the US Federal prison releases were differentiated on the basis of certain attributes of prisoners' previous work histories such as longest time on one job, and type of job on which longest employed. The arrests, however, are related to other characteristics of the ex-prisoner and his situation which would be expected to affect his chances of being rearrested on release. The basic distribution of attributes for this population in Ontario is similar to that found by Glaser.

The ex-prisoner was asked what was the longest job he had ever held before arrest. Table 4.6 shows the distribution of the responses for the parolees and dischargees. Although a considerable numer of ex-prisoners had worked at only one job continuously for short periods of time, there were many – nearly one-third of those responding to the one-month questionnaire – who had held jobs for more than two years.

Of the total ex-prisoners who took part in the one-month interview, 28 per cent claimed skills that were coded at the skilled level and 29 per cent at the semi-skilled;[6] a further 5 per cent claimed professional or managerial skills and 9 per cent claimed clerical skills. All the 'skilled' positions were in the craftsmen and production processes area, typically such occupations as welding and plumbing. The 'semi-skilled' skills were distributed over service and recreation, transportation, and craftsmen and production processes. The typical skills in these first two areas were cook and truck driver respectively.[7]

Related to occupation skill is the latest regular wage of the exprisoner before his arrest. The distribution of these wages is shown in Table 4.7 ranging from over $150 per week to under $50, with the mode lying in the range from $71.00 to $90.00. To put this in perspective, in 1967 the average weekly wage in Ontario was $106.00 (DBS, 1969). On

TABLE 4.6

Longest jobs ever held by ex-prisoners before arrest

	Dischargee		Parolee		Total	
		Cumulative (%)		Cumulative (%)		Cumulative (%)
Never worked	2	1.76	—		2	0.66
Off and on	2	3.52	3	1.60	5	2.32
1–3 months	14	15.90	25	14.96	39	15.32
4–6 months	13	27.40	15	22.98	28	24.65
7–9 months	10	36.24	12	29.39	22	31.98
10–12 months	13	47.74	21	40.61	34	43.31
13–15 months	2	49.50	4	42.74	6	45.31
16–18 months	8	56.57	16	51.29	24	53.31
19–21 months	1	57.45	1	51.82	2	53.97
22–24 months	14	69.83	21	63.04	35	65.63
3 years	14	82.21	18	72.66	32	76.29
4 years	5	86.63	13	79.61	18	82.29
5 years	3	89.28	8	83.88	11	85.95
6 years	2	91.04	5	86.55	7	88.28
7 years	2	92.80	6	89.75	8	90.94
8–12 years	5	97.22	10	95.09	15	95.94
13–17 years	2	98.98	1	95.62	3	96.94
18–22 years	0		3	97.22	3	97.94
23–28 years	0		4	99.35	4	99.27
Longer than 28 years	1	99.86	1	99.88	2	99.93
Total	113		187		300	
No response available	12		5		17	
Not interviewed	88		18		106	

all three indicators of job functioning before admission the ex-prisoner held a lower-order job than the average male, a finding now well documented in criminology.

These findings are not startling in comparison to the previous criminological literature. Our particular coding method would tend to put more people in higher-grade jobs than other systems as any doubt was always resolved in favour of a higher skill category. If the semi-skilled and unskilled labouring groups and the unskilled clerical categories are combined, 75 per cent of the dischargees arrived at the institution with few or no job skills.

Treatment by the Jail and Courts

At the one-month stage a number of brief questions were put to the ex-prisoner concerning such matters as whether or not he received bail, pleaded guilty, was investigated by a probation officer for a pre-sentence report, or whether he thought he deserved imprisonment. His experience of the local jail was also discussed.

One in three ex-prisoners received bail (with the parolees having a

TABLE 4.7

Latest regular wages of ex-prisoners before arrest

	Dischargees		Parolees		Total	
Weekly wage ($)		Cumulative (%)		Cumulative (%)		Cumulative (%)
30–50	24	21.2	23	12.6	47	15.9
51–70	26	44.2	40	34.5	66	38.2
71–90	20	61.9	53	63.5	73	62.9
91–110	16	76.1	22	75.5	38	75.7
111–130	12	86.7	15	83.7	27	84.8
131–150	5	91.1	16	92.4	21	91.9
151 or more	8	98.2	13	99.5	21	99.0
Earned illegally	2	100.0	1	100.0	3	100.0
Total	113		183		296	
No responses	12		9		21	
Not interviewed	88		18		106	

slight edge over dischargees). In 53 per cent of the cases bail was provided for both groups by the family or wife, by a friend in nearly 18 per cent of the cases; and by a bonding company, the ex-prisoner himself, or employer in the remainder. Of those who had not obtained bail, 39 per cent of the dischargees and 45 per cent of the parolees said that this was because of lack of money; 42 per cent of the dischargees, compared to 32 per cent of the parolees, said it was not worth trying to raise the money. One-third of the total sample spent two months or more in the local jail and one-third less than three weeks. For both groups the shorter the time spent in the local jail the less likely it was to be counted as a portion of their sentence.

Nearly half the sample said they had suffered physical effects from being confined in a local jail, such as weight loss, sleeplessness, losing hair or hair turning grey, feeling 'burnt up,' amnesia, depression, ulcers, and heart trouble, though loss of sleep and tenseness were most frequently mentioned: 37 per cent of the dischargees and 45 per cent of the parolees mentioned some adverse effect from their stay in a local jail; the longer the stay, the more likely they were to be mentioned.

Nearly 70 per cent of both groups pleaded guilty to the offences with which they were finally charged in court (there was a slight tendency for more of the parolees to plead guilty). It has been suggested that the chances of getting parole are better if a person pleads guilty to the charge and even better when he does not dispute the finding of the court by appealing or asking for a re-trial. Three out of five ex-prisoners said that they deserved imprisonment while one in four said they did not. A small group of whom there were proportionally more parolees, mentioned that they deserved it but not for so long.

Accounting for the Offence

The prisoner was asked in the one-month interview why he had committed the offence for which he was sentenced to the penitentiary. The answers given could be viewed in three ways: as rationalizations worked out from talking to probation officers, providing explanations to a sentencing court, talking to other inmates, correctional officers or classification staff in the institution; as reasons related to why the ex-prisoner thought he got caught; as reasons that were, in fact, important in understanding why he committed the act, the so-called 'genuine' reasons. Sykes and Matza (1957) have mentioned five different techniques for the neutralization of guilt or shame that they found in prisoners' responses: the denial of responsibility, the denial of injury, the denial of the victim, the condemnation of the condemners, and the appeal to higher loyalties.

In this study, however, although there were one or two who 'condemned their condemners' (if this is broadly interpreted to include those who said they were framed) and a small group whose responses could be classified as 'denial of responsibility' ('I did not know how to control myself') or an 'appeal to higher loyalites' (when he was the cuckolded lover in a triangle), for the most part the principal reasons given for committing the crime could not be interpreted as techniques for the neutralization of guilt.

Of the main reasons given by both groups 14 per cent mentioned financial gain, and 13 per cent said that they were out of work. Although neither said it was a matter of necessity, 35 per cent mentioned that some factor related to employment or money left them in a difficult situation such as an urgent need for money or being out of work). 30 per cent gave some reason related to emotion; they did not know how to control themselves because of drink, emotion, or jealousy usually the result of triangle love affairs, excitement, marriage difficulties, pressures too big for them. The other reasons included, 'being depressed,' 'the people he went around with were immature' or 'he was framed.' The category of being framed included statements such as, 'I was not really the villain' in the affair. There was also a group who did not know or would not say why they had committed the crime.

When the ex-prisoners were asked if they thought that the situations which led to the offences for which they had been committed still existed, 15 per cent said that one or more of the reasons was still there. The responses by the dischargees are less reliable, however, as many of them were already back in jail when they were asked whether or not the situation existed; even so 39 per cent of them thought that it did, with a marked tendency for it to exist more often in the group who gave as reasons things 'beyond control.'

These 'situation still exists' responses (one month after release) were compared to arrest within twelve months. These are the percentages of each group re-arrested:

Still exists	46 parolees	69 dischargees
Does not exist	24	55

These responses suggest that if the original situation in which the offence occurred no longer exists at resease, the ex-prisoner is less likely to be re-incarcerated. They suggest just how important the influence is of such factors as unemployment, the 'dissolution of the super-ego' in alcohol, the opportunity for financial gain by illegitimate means, the importance of the sorts of person with whom the ex-prisoners associate, and the related need for excitement. All these items were mentioned by at least 5 per cent of the parolees and many said these factors still existed after their release.

The Prisoner's Role

It has been inferred from sociologists' work on inmate roles within the institution that these roles have some relationship to behaviour outside (see chapter 1, n. 7). The study discussed earlier by Himelson and Takagi has shown the limitations of these theories for California.

In the hope that we might have found some relationship between the type of friends a prisoner had and his post-release behaviour, we asked the men to classify their prison friends and associates on the basis of ten alternative categories which were based on a California questionnaire (chapter 3, n. 15). 25 per cent described then as casual, 12 per cent as friends from previous incarcerations, 12 per cent as having similar interests. However, since 18 per cent gave an uncodeable response, and 7 per cent denied having any friends (the remaining responses were spread over combinations of the various groups) we felt that no valid inferences could be made.

Similar problems were encountered concerning a description of the role the ex-prisoner felt he played in the institution. The sample divided almost equally between the classic 'Square John' role and that of the 'loner' (one of whose attributes is 'doing his own time'). Only eight ex-prisoners saw themselves playing the role of the 'wheel' and only ten mentioned playing the 'rebel.' This suggests that these role categories are not very useful in Canadian prisons.

An open-ended question was also asked as to whether the ex-inmates had ever had any influence in the prison. 67 per cent claimed they did not, 12 per cent claimed some influence with inmates alone, 8 per cent with the staff or guards (with a slight tendency for more dischargees to feel this way), and 8 per cent with both.

This chapter has taken us toward our main interests in the study. We now know something about the backgrounds of the men who were released and their experience of the penitentiary. This will grow as we continue to try to understand their experience after release.

NOTES TO CHAPTER 4

1 Used in its purest form, the null hypothesis states that there is no difference between parolees and dischargees on the variable. The research hypothesis would be that there is a difference. The hypothesis that a particular variable would be a variable in which the two groups differed significantly was not put forward. It was generally hypothesized that there would be a large number of variables on which the two groups would differ signficantly and a number on which there would be no differences. Multiple *t*-tests have been carried out so that in using the 5 per cent level of significance 6 out of 120 variables would have been significant by chance. Further, differences between individual variables may be due to associations with other variables. For instance, more children are likely to be related to being married, so that if there is a signficant difference on number of children there is also likely to be a significant difference on whether married or not

2 Clark (1948); Clark (1953); Panton (1959); (1962); Gough, Wenk, and Rozynko (1965); Marx (1969); Davies (1967); Mott (1969)

3 The reader is referred to Hawkins (1971) for a fuller discussion of parole board decision-making. This author clearly recognizes that a model of parole decision-making policy cannot be based on simply minimizing the risk of a future offence, although a model of parole board decision-making which would explain much of its behaviour might be concerned with the minimization of risk

4 2.5 per cent of both groups were born in the United Kingdom. Less than 1 per cent was born in the US; 2.4 per cent of the dischargees compared to 1 per cent of the parolees were born in Hungary, and 6 per cent of the parolees compared to less than 1 per cent of the dischargees were born in other European countries which included Portugal, Poland, Greece, Czechoslovakia, Italy, Yugoslavia, and Germany

5 χ^2 cc = 7.34; df = 1; P < 0.01, two-tailed test

6 It is important to note that the description of skills used by the ex-prisoners and the probing carried out by the interviewers were in no way equivalent to the certification that might be carried out by a provincial government agency to register a particular person as having a particular type of skill. Also, there are many different interpretations of what is termed a semi-skilled occupation. The emphasis of the question was to bring out any asset that might possibly be termed a work skill that might assist in obtaining a job. Whereas a person can walk immediately into a casual labour job, he has to have had some experience, however limited, in driving before he will be entrusted with a truck or a taxi

7 A small number of the sample was involved at later time periods with obtaining licences to operate taxis and cartage businesses. However, when considering 'semi-skilled' skills the vast majority would have used them only as employees

8 See, for instance, USA (1967b, 3)

5

The Experience of Penitentiary and Release

We now turn to our investigation of the prisoner's experience after release. What, if any, preparation was the prison experience for life outside? What does he do and how does he feel the first day? How does the man feel he is treated by other people such as his neighbours and the police? Do all employers turn him down if he admits to a record? How typical is the unemployed ex-prisoner who lives alone in a rooming house in an urban area? When does he get a job – what sort is it? How quickly does he get into debt? What was the impact of prison on his family and how did he adjust after release? Who are his friends? Does he drink?

The next three chapters will look at the responses of the ex-prisoners to these sorts of questions. They were put at the five-week, six-month, and twelve-month stages in the interviews conducted by the research interviewers. Some of the material from the parole supervisor reports has also been included if it gave a fuller picture of the parolee's situation. In chapter 8 we will turn to a detailed analysis of the parole supervisor's information.

Gleaning in the Pen

Irwin (1970, 72) has coined the term 'gleaning' for the process whereby the prisoner makes the fullest possible use of his time in the penitentiary to acquire education that may be useful at a later date. If, for example, school or vocational training is available at the institution, he will enrol in order to acquire skills or experience related to some kind of legitimate work after release. In our sample 38 per cent of dischargees and 58 per cent of the parolees took classes. This does not necessarily mean that the prisoner intends to 'go straight' when he gets out. In fact, it has been suggested that prisons are the universities of crime (*Time*, 1971). 'Gleaning' then can be of the sort where the prisoner learns more sophisticated criminal techniques. As we have seen, most men sent to the penitentiaries have previously been to at least one prison. The phenomenon of the innocent learning from the criminally sophisticated is much more likely to occur in local jails. Even so, approximately half the men said that there was something new to be learned about crime in the penitentiaries. (In contrast, when asked whether it was possible to not learn about crime there, 91 per cent of the dischargees and 76 per cent of the parolees, replied in the negative.) The principal areas mentioned where knowledge could be 'gleaned' were safe breaking, bank robbery, circumventing burglar alarms, picking locks, nullifying electronic gadgets, passing cheques, stealing cars, and techniques of violence.

Effect of Stay in Penitentiary

The ex-prisoner was asked if he felt he had lost something more than time while he was inside. The proportions of both groups answering 'no' and 'yes' were basically the same – slightly more parolees felt that they had lost more of what they had worked towards while more dischargees felt greater bitterness. A minority, 19 out of 317, felt that they had gained something from their stay in the penitentiary.

When ex-prisoners were asked specifically if they thought they were the same men as when they went in, 43 per cent said that they were more mature, more grown-up, or something to that effect; 33 per cent were less specific and said they thought they were different, but did not say in what way. On the other hand, 25 per cent felt that they were the 'same guy' and that they had been 'in and out for years.' Surprising, perhaps, but only 7 per cent felt they were more bitter or mean.

The second part of the same question asked, 'In what way do you think your stay in the penitentiary affected you?' 20 per cent said that they saw it as a time to think about life, to look at things realistically and not run away. 14 per cent said it did not have any effect at all; 12 per cent mentioned they felt it made them more aggressive or belligerent. Approximately 5 per cent made one of the following responses: 'the penitentiary slows down your mental processes; it makes you know people more and changes your outlook on prisoners; makes you think what a waste of time the penitentiary itself is; it drives you crazy and makes you depressed; it leaves you scared and you hate it.'

The purpose of the penitentiary, as conceived by the Quakers in the 18th and 19th centuries, was to place a man in solitary confinement where, while serving his time, he would search his soul in order to be cleansed.[1] Undoubtedly, one hundred years later the institutions are more humane in terms of hours out of cells, recreation, guards' attitudes to physical violence, and particularly the medium- and minimum-security architecture. However, in 1968 many of the men still saw their penitentiary experience as a lonely, boring, painful, but challenging experience, that might bring about changes in oneself.

The ex-prisoner was asked what he thought rehabilitation was. Very few had a concrete definition. Although 4 per cent did not know what it was, most (45 per cent) thought that it related to changes within the individual or his personality and saw it as something which was up to the man himself. 12 per cent saw it as going back to society and living within the rules; 10 per cent as being able to explain oneself to other people, accept advice, and follow it; 4 per cent as preparing for the street, and 3 per cent as getting a job. The remainder mentioned individual situations. Since most ex-prisoners see rehabilitation as something that comes from within the individual it is not surprising to find that the penitentiary is generally ineffective. We also asked the ex-prisoner how effective he thought the rehabilitation programmes were, and if they were not, why:

Useless	57 parolees	76 dischargees[2]
Effective	19	13
Effective for some	24	12

In accounting for the failure of the programmes, 50 per cent of dischargees and 30 per cent of the parolees said that the administration was incompetent. In line with ex-prisoners' views on self-rehabilitation, 24 per cent of the dischargees and 28 per cent of the parolees blamed the prisoners themselves, mentioning their lack of interest, uncertainty, and lack of education or intelligence; 10 per cent of the dischargees and 18 per cent of the parolees did not give an opinion. The remaining responses were from a small group who mentioned public apathy about release problems, lack of facilities for helping them outside, and combinations of the administration and the types of prisoners in the institutions.

Concerns Before Release

We asked the ex-prisoner to tell us his principal concerns or worries before he was released.[3] As these recollections were likely influenced by experiences after release, we interpreted the responses in terms of the question 'Of the realistic worries or concerns you had before release,

TABLE 5.1

Ex-prisoners' worries before release in parolee rank order

Rank order						
Parolee	Dischargee		Parolee		Dischargee	
1	1	None	37	19.9%	29	24.3%
2	2	Finding employment	36	19.4%	22	18.5%
3	4	Family	22	11.8%	12	10.1%
4	5	Meals	19	10.2%	11	9.2%
5	6	Going back to prison	12	6.5%	7	5.9%
5	8	Common-law wife	12	6.5%	5	4.2%
7	9	Place to stay	11	5.9%	4	3.4%
8	3	Managing financially	9	4.8%	15	12.6%
9	6	Self identity	7	3.8%	7	5.9%
9	10	Acceptance	7	3.8%	2	1.7%
11	10	Keeping employment	6	3.2%	2	1.7%
12	14	Money-lending, bonds, etc.	4	2.1%	0	—
13	12	Friends	3	1.6%	2	1.7%
14	13	Age	1	0.5%	1	0.8%
Total			186	100%	119	100%
No responses available			6		6	
Not interviewed			18		88	

which were the most important?' Employment (as shown in Table 5.1) was felt to be important; 30 per cent mentioned this as a first concern and 33 per cent as a second. Family was mentioned as the first concern by 64 per cent and as the second by 10 per cent. Managing financially was mentioned by 24 per cent as their first concern, and by 20 per cent as their second. After these came worries about returning to prison, relationships with a common-law wife, and then a place to stay. Employment, of course, applied to everybody, whereas family, particularly in the case of a wife, applied differentially.

The ex-prisoners were also asked to whom they turned for help with their worries. Perhaps as a result of the type of concerns set out, 62 per cent with problems turned to nobody. In order of importance, however, the main categories of persons approached were other prisoners, the parole supervisor, a representative from the John Howard Society and the classification officer. As dischargees did not have parole supervisors they turned to the John Howard Society as an alternative. In general, those persons approached were felt to provide little assistance, but when they did, it was in the form of reassurance and being someone with whom to discuss things. In individual cases, however, help was received in obtaining a job, finding a place to stay, or getting into a union. 16 per cent of the parolees, compared to 12 per cent of the dischargees, replied that they had sought and received some help in obtaining jobs before

TABLE 5.2

Totals receiving any help at all

Rank order						
Dischargees	Parolees		Dischargees		Parolees	
		POSITIVE HELP				
3	1	Classification officer	11	16.2%	27	23.3%
1	2	John Howard Society	19	28.0%	26	22.4%
4	3	Work supervisor	6	8.8%	22	19.0%
2	4	Manpower	16	23.5%	12	10.3%
6	5	Padre	2	2.9%	9	7.8%
5	6	Guard on range	3	4.4%	4	3.4%
			57	83.8%	100	86.2%
		NEGATIVE HELP*	11	16.2%	16	13.8%
Total			68	100%	116	100%
Percentage of total interviewed			54.4%		60.4%	

* Classification officer = 6; guard = 2; JHS = 4; future parole supervisor = 3; Manpower = 6; Harold King Farm = 3; teacher = 1; doctor = 2; total = 27.

release. Interestingly, this small difference was due to parolees more frequently mentioning assistance from other prisoners. We might infer from this that there was greater pressure on the parolee to try to obtain a job in order to assure the parole board that he would have employment on release. The ex-prisoner was asked if any official in the prison *tried* to help him set up a release plan. 54 per cent of the dischargees and 60 per cent of the parolees replied in the affirmative. The interpretation of 'plan' was loose and came to mean any form of pre-release assistance.

Table 5.2 shows the main sources of help for both groups. A rank ordering of the official approached by the parolee shows that the classification officer was the person from whom he most often asked assistance. In order of frequency of mention, the others were the John Howard Society visiting representative, the work supervisor, and Manpower. In contrast, dischargees most often went to a representative of the John Howard Society, with Manpower a close second; the classification officer and work supervisor followed only at a later stage. The two outside agencies, the John Howard Society and Manpower, tended to be much more important for the dischargee than the work supervisor and the classification officer.

It is the classification officer who is involved in the preparation of the various papers for the parolee's application to the parole board, which means, consequently, that he has some interest in the parolee's post-release plans. The John Howard Society also has a policy of interviewing before release those they will later supervise in order to get various details about them and their pre-release plans for the community supervisor. In contrast, the classification officer is not, in his official capacity, required to help the dischargee; besides if they have a choice, many dischargees refuse to co-operate with the institutional authorities. The John Howard Society tries to see those due to be discharged, although it is not as efficiently organized as for parole; this is complicated by the fact that any relationship between a dischargee and an outside agency is voluntary. Manpower help is usually limited to giving the prisoner the address of the Manpower office in the area to which he will be released.

The Family and the Prisoner

Morris (1965) carried out a study in England of the effects of imprisonment on the prisoners' families. She had the advantage of talking to the wives themselves about how they experienced their husbands' imprisonment. It was not possible for us to do this type of survey; however, a question was put to the ex-prisoner concerning whether or not his wife changed residence after he was convicted. Of those who said they were married, 39 per cent of parolees said their wives did not change residence, compared to 23 per cent of the dischargees. Table 5.3 shows the nature of the wives' moves, and again there are interesting differences between the wives of dischargees and parolees. The parolee typically has a faithful wife who is able to use her own resources during the period of imprisonment. If this is not the case, she will most likely move in with her mother or move somewhere else by herself. On the other hand, the wife of the dischargee is more likely to move in with another man. Marital stability is a factor related to recidivism in many of the theories that might influence parole board selection; because of this the parole board

TABLE 5.3

Wives' changes of residence after conviction of ex-prisoners
(based on question asked in one-month questionnaire)

	Dischargee	Parolee	Total
No move	7	30	37
Moved, but living by herself	5	21	26
Moved in with another man	9	7	16
Moved in with other*	10	19	29
Total	31	77	108

* Mother, mother-in-law, sister
$\chi^2 = 9.28$; $df = 3$; $p < 0.05$

tends to select people with good family support. There is also some evidence (Davies, 1969) to suggest for probationers that offenders with supportive families are in fact less likely to be reconvicted.

Obviously visiting and correspondence regulations could be very important to the maintenance of ties between the ex-prisoner and family and friends outside. A great majority (81 per cent), however, felt that they did not interfere with their ability to plan for release; 52 per cent had no suggestions for improvements other than selection of guards. Although some thought day or weekend leave more comfortable, it was felt that private visiting arrangements would be an improvement.

We asked those ex-prisoners who said they were married whether or not their wives visited them; if so, did they make any arrangements for release at that time?

Not visited	26 parolees	47 dischargees[2]
Visited, but got no opportunity to plan for release	26	29
Visited, and made arrangements for release	26	15

The final question put to the ex-prisoner concerning his wife was where he thought she got the money to make the visit. The purpose of this was not to tie down exactly where the money came from but instead to give an indication of the extent of the wife's dependency. None of the dischargees thought their wives had borrowed from friends or family but rather that the money had come from either their own earnings or from welfare. 46 per cent of the wives visiting parolees (N = 50) had done so out of their own earnings, 24 per cent out of welfare or mother's allowance, while 22 per cent had borrowed from relatives or friends.

Outfitting the Man for Release

Glaser (1964), in dealing with financial resources at release has shown that there is considerable variation among the various prison systems in the US in the extent to which they issue free civilian or working clothing and provide transportation from prison, and in the amount of cash available to the prisoner.

In this study 59 per cent of the ex-prisoners had $100 or less on release,[4] 26 per cent had between $100 and $200, 9 per cent had between $200 and $300, and 5 per cent had in excess of $300. The money came from earnings from work in prison, hobby crafts sold,[5] and money sent in from outside.[6] 32 per cent of the ex-prisoners had had money put in their trust fund from outside sources. Of these, 30 per cent received money from their own investments, 20 per cent from their parents or family, 6 per cent from their wives, 8 per cent from friends, and 15 per cent received income tax rebates. Another 15 per cent received money from other sources.

At the time of this study, men released from Canadian federal penitentiaries were given a travel warrant by bus or train to their stated destination (42 per cent of the sample were going to Toronto). Every prisoner released was issued with a 'prison suit.' The ex-prisoners were asked how long they wore it.

Beyond the first day, out of necessity	9 parolees	13 dischargees[2]
Got out of it as fast as possible on the first day	23	33
Wore it at home only on first day or still wear it at home from time to time	68	54
Gave it away	53	35

Although as a general rule no work clothes are given to ex-prisoners, 21 persons in the sample said they had been given some. However, for the majority the problem was to recover the work clothes that they had used before their incarceration or to obtain clothes by some other means. 46 per cent had not obtained work clothes at the time of their one-month interview. However, 19 per cent had used their old clothes, 28 per cent had bought new ones, and the rest had got something from the John Howard Society, the St Vincent de Paul Society, or their mothers.

Transition from Prison to Community

The sort of adaptation that the ex-prisoner makes during his first few days on the street may be crucial in relation to his later adjustment. Some of the problems of leaving a total institution and re-entering the 'free world' have already been discussed. In the institution the prisoner's life is almost totally regimented, his identity being little more than a number. On release, he again becomes a free man; this means he continually makes his own decisions. Although he may anticipate doing all kinds of things on release, the transition to the free world is likely to be characterized by both exhilaration and uncomfortable anxiety. A major purpose of this study was to look at the various components of the transition experience. This section deals with the ex-prisoner's feelings on the first day out and during the first week.

Accommodation and Welcome

Typically the ex-prisoner is left to travel to his destination alone by bus. This indicates both the inaccessibility of the penitentiaries to prisoners' friends and family and also the general dearth of close ties with other persons who might come to pick him up.

More dischargees (62 per cent) than parolees (40 per cent) either receive no welcome or avoided whoever was there to meet them at the bus or train terminal. For the remainder who were met by someone, typically the parolee more than the dischargee was welcomed by his wife or common-law wife or by someone from his extended family.[7]

Ex-prisoners usually found accommodation through personal relationships. Newspapers, the John Howard Society, and 'accommodation being provided with jobs' account for less than 16 per cent of accommodation found by dischargees and less than 13 per cent found by parolees.

More than one in three of both groups obtained accommodation through their own resources; this classification included returning to a wife or common-law union. There is a slight tendency for more dischargees to find something through parents and for more parolees to do so through friends of their own age. This latter is of particular interest as it was found that, of the total jobs, more dischargees than parolees found them through friends of their own age. Also, proportionately twice as many dischargees as parolees obtained accommodation through the newspapers.

As the parolee is more likely to be met by members of his family, it was expected and found that more parolees spent their first nights at home with parents, or other members of their families, while a small number of dischargees spent their first nights with friends although there were proportionately more than parolees.

At 'home' with parents, wife, or girl friend	53 parolees	39 dischargees[2]
In a room or hotel, with or without a girl	19	32
With siblings or other relatives	13	13
With friends	4	10

Thus, even though the parolee finds out about accommodation through friends he is less likely to actually stay with them.

Only 6 per cent of parolees lived in a half-way house or farm during their first week. The numbers living in such situations declined to less than 1 per cent after the first 3 months. This is a normal finding, as the typical length of stay of an inmate in a half-way house or farm appears to be only six weeks. The type of residence of the dischargees interviewed at the one-month stage followed a basically similar distribution to the parolees, though more were living in rooms and only 2 per cent were living in a half-way house or farm. (We checked for dischargees with the half-way houses.) There were, however, one or two dischargees who went to half-way houses or farms at later periods after their release. These findings reflect the lack of any such hostels in the core of the major metropolitan area. The short stay may be due to the voluntary nature of the hostels.

There is a steady turnover of residences among parolees; this is more pronounced early where 7 per cent of both parolees and dischargees changed residence in the first week while less than 3 per cent per week changed in the nine to twelve month period. With minor fluctuations over the twelve months, 72 per cent of the parolees lived in urban areas, 20 per cent in suburban areas, and 8 per cent in rural areas. The types of community in which the dischargees were living at the one-month, six-month, and twelve-month interviews were basically similar to those of the parolees.

Interestingly, 24 per cent of the parolees and only 10 per cent of the dischargees went to a town which was not familiar to them. This difference is statistically significant. It reflects the deliberate policy of the parole board to parole some prisoners away from the community where the original offence occurred. Of those who were going back to familiar towns, some mentioned feelings of being lost, friends having moved and things generally seeming different; most remarked on new buildings but otherwise found that little had changed.

The First Day Out

The ex-prisoners were asked to identify what was the most important thing they did on their first day out. One in three mentioned being with family or relatives, 16 per cent enjoying freedom, and 15 per cent indulgence after the deprivations. A small number of parolees mentioned seeing their parole officer and staying away from drink.

The ex-prisoner was also asked to comment on how he felt about the whole release experience. 46 per cent said they felt relieved and dazed. However, depression, fear or anxiety were mentioned by 31 per cent as their main feelings. These feelings – which may certainly last beyond the first day – probably result from the ex-prisoner's transitional status and are, therefore, crucial to understanding the man as he is being released from prison. The items suggested are presented in Table 5.4. On the average, 62 per cent of the dischargees and 61 per cent of the parolees said they had not experienced individual transition symptoms.

TABLE 5.4

Percentage of ex-prisoners experiencing transition symptoms by mode of release

	Dischargees (%)	Parolees (%)	Parolees greater than dischargees (%)	Dischargees greater than parolees (%)
Trouble talking to people	38.3	43.7	5.4	—
Anxiety	53.0	62.3	9.3	—
Loneliness	45.2	40.5	—	4.7
Hard time remembering	24.4	23.5	—	0.9
Hard time getting used to things	41.7	44.8	3.1	—
Disappointment from things you were going to enjoy such as drink, sex, food	21.7	23.5	1.8	—
Sleeplessness	33.1	38.8	5.7	—
Depression	31.3	31.2	—	0.1
Feeling of looking like an ex-con	34.7	39.4	4.7	—

More parolees experienced anxiety, sleeplessness, and trouble talking to people, felt they looked like an ex-prisoner, had a hard time getting used to things, and experienced disappointment concerning things they had planned to enjoy. More dischargees had a tendency to experience such symptoms as loneliness, hard time remembering, and depression. The finding on loneliness is consistent with the tendency for the dischargees to have fewer friends or family to whom to turn.

The finding that the parolee experiences more anxiety is consistent with the psychometric data collected before release; the parolee tends to be more neurotic and less psychopathic in the sense that he is more able to experience guilt and worry. The experiencing of guilt and of finding problems within themselves will be found more often for parolees than dischargees. In informal discussion with the parole board, there seemed to be a preference to grant parole to those who admitted their guilt – as they believed such prisoners had come to face reality. However, it may also be that this is a characteristic closely associated with other variables that are themselves important to parole. The concern about looking like an ex-con is possibly due to more of the parolees wanting to make serious efforts to go straight or to self-consciousness associated with neuroticism.

Although most ex-prisoners had experienced only one or two of these transition symptoms at five weeks, there were a few who mentioned all the symptoms suggested by the literature. As would be expected, the proportion of items mentioned per ex-prisoner at the one-month stage had dropped by a fifth at six months and by approximately

TABLE 5.5

Hypothesized transition symptoms experienced by ex-prisoners, by mode of release and interview at six and twelve months, in rank order for parolees at six months

	6 months				12 months				Total	
	Dischargees		Parolees		Dischargees		Parolees		6 months	12 months
Depression	13	19.1%	26	19.1%	6	10.5%	21	18.6%	19.1%	15.8%
Anxiety	10	14.7%	29	21.4%	9	15.8%	19	16.8%	19.2%	16.4%
Trouble talking to people	4	5.9%	18	13.2%	4	7.0%	7	6.2%	10.8%	6.4%
Loneliness	9	13.2%	16	11.8%	2	3.5%	8	7.1%	12.3%	5.8%
Trouble making decisions	6	8.8%	14	10.3%	—		—		9.9%	—
Feeling of looking like an ex-con	4	5.9%	8	5.9%	2	3.5%	3	2.7%	5.9%	2.9%
Hard time getting used to things	4	5.9%	8	5.9%	—		4	3.5%	5.9%	2.3%
Sleeplessness	4	5.9%	7	5.1%	—		6	5.3%	5.4%	3.5%
Hard time remembering	—		4	2.9%	2	3.5%	3	2.7%	2.0%	2.9%
Total	54		121		25		71		175	96
Total interviewed	68		136		57		113		204	170

another third by twelve months. The rank orders at the six- and twelve-month stages were generally similar to those at the one-month stage. The full list of items experienced by the ex-prisoner has been laid out in Table 5.5. Though there has been a diminution in the frequency of the transition symptoms mentioned, they have not totally disappeared. Depression and anxiety were important for both parolees and dischargees at these later time periods. More than 1 in 10 of the ex-prisoners at the six-month stage had experienced depression, anxiety, trouble talking to people, and loneliness. The items such as 'hard time getting used to things,' which are more directly associated with the transition status, had virtually disappeared. It is possible that loneliness and trouble-making decisions would have been of more importance had larger samples been used, as the proportion of dischargees experiencing loneliness dropped disproportionately, implying that more had been arrested or had, perhaps, got back with friends from before. Later analysis will suggest that both of these hypotheses may have some validity. Thus those who have no family to turn to and those who turn to (what have been described by the interviewer and the parole supervisor as) undesirable associates were more likely to have been arrested earlier and were, therefore, less likely to be interviewed at a later stage.

In the face of difficulties such as obtaining a roof over his head, feeding himself, or paying for simple pleasures, the man released from prison may long for the 'comfortable' and 'secure' situation that existed before he was released. We asked, therefore, if he had felt at any time since his release that he was better off in prison. 13 per cent of dischargees and 17 per cent of parolees replied in the affirmative. As the numbers are small, the differences in the distribution would have to be large for reliable trends to be noticed. However, of these, there was a tendency for parolees to mention difficulty in getting a job (six parolees, one dischargee), or trouble with girl friend (seven parolees, no dischargees), and there were four parolees who mentioned pressure from their parole supervisors. The remaining responses were evenly distributed between the problems of finding three meals a day without a job, being bored in the free community as a result of familiarity with the 'joint way of life,' and a less specific category which included preference, when angry or depressed for being in the institution. Even so, between four and ten (or between 2 per cent and 5 per cent of the parolee sample) felt that they would have been better off in prison because of hounding by their parole officers. Again there is a general trend for the parolee to be more involved in personal relationships than the dischargee, although in the case of girl friends the relationship may not necessarily be positive; as a result, the parolee may try to escape pressures by going to prison. These findings – the difficulty of managing in the free community – might also be expected just as a result of release from a total institution.

In the face of these common difficulties it was expected that the ex-prisoner would have much to say to another ex-prisoner if he met him on the street. Two out of three met fellow ex-prisoners within their first five weeks from release. Of the total (who met other inmates) one in three had discussed how things had been going since release, including 7 per cent who mentioned discussing particular problems, such as obtaining a job or managing financially. One in five of the total said that they limited their interchange to a brief smile of 'hi, good-bye.' Few spent any time with ex-prisoners. Generally it seems that there is some loose sort of friendship between ex-prisoners centring around common problems.

In an attempt to see whether 'inmate culture' was something that still influenced the ex-prisoner's behaviour, we asked him whether or not he thought there were prisoners still in the institution who wondered how he was doing. If there were such persons we then asked whether their opinion was important to that ex-prisoner.

Were not sure, or said there were no such people	19 parolees	42 dischargees[2]
Yes, but their opinion was not very important to them now they had been released	45	30

The Effects of Having a Record

One of the perennial problems which the ex-prisoner is supposed to face is that of 'labelling.' A number of questions dealt indirectly with the disadvantages that the ex-prisoner felt he faced because of his criminal record. Labelling is a phenomenon both of the labeller taking action against the labellee, and of the labellee feeling discrimination as a result of a real or imaginary label. One question concerned whether or not the ex-prisoner thought he was treated differently by the people who knew he had a record than by those who were ignorant of it. To ensure that the important areas in which a record might affect his life were covered a series of specific probes were given. (Family and employment were treated separately.) The interviewer read to him in turn 'neighbours, welfare, manpower, adult re-training, police, hospitals.' The ex-prisoner could also mention other agencies, though in practice few did. In each case the ex-prisoner was asked to describe the way in which he thought he had been treated differently.

At five weeks, 18 per cent of both groups felt that there was some difference in the way that they had been treated by neighbours. Of these, 50 per cent of the dischargees and 71 per cent of the parolees felt uneasy in their contacts with neighbours; 14 per cent of the dischargees and 9 per cent of the parolees felt they got *more* help as a result of their record; 17 per cent of dischargees compared to 13 per cent of parolees mentioned a feeling of being treated differently by the police, although three ex-prisoners felt they got more help from the police as a result of their records.[8] At six months parolees felt they were most often discriminated against by neighbours, with Manpower ranking second, and police third. At six months dischargees ranked police first, followed by neighbours, welfare, and then Manpower. These adverse effects of labelling, however, were felt by only a minority.

Employment

A brief reading of the literature and a look at the actions of pressure groups who wanted to obtain changes in legislation pertaining to records would lead one to believe that the effects of labelling are only negative. In view of this, an unexpected finding was the number of ex-prisoners who mentioned positive help as a result of their criminal records. At both six and twelve months Manpower was mentioned as providing extra help to ex-prisoners because of this. Although there is a house rule for Manpower counsellors that they should inform an employer if his potential employee has a record, it appears that they use considerable discretion in interpreting this rule. Although it was not verified against the data, there was some reason to suppose that the negative feelings against Manpower were in fact against particular offices that interpreted this rule rigidly, whereas the positive feelings occurred in Manpower offices where discretion was used.

One of the few studies to investigate empirically this problem of 'record' was that of Schwartz and Skolnick (1962). A series of false job applications was made by the researchers to a series of firms. It was shown that if a man had been convicted of offences other than assault he was more likely to be hired than if he had never been convicted. Further, employers were more likely to hire a person acquitted of assault with a letter from a judge confirming acquittal, than a person acquitted without a letter or, finally, a person convicted. All these probabilities were lower than for a person with no court appearance.[9]

How important a factor is stigmatization as an explanation for difficulties in obtaining jobs? While stigmatization may play a role in the non-hiring of offenders, a much more important issue may be the lack of skills amongst the majority of prisoners, their inability to present references describing their ability to work, or their previous work history, which is usually irregular.[10]

The ex-prisoner was asked if any of the applications had requested information about his record. Where this information was requested, 47 per cent of the dischargees and 33 per cent of the parolees gave it on a form they completed as an applicant.

Of both the parolees and dischargees 58 per cent had either not completed any application or had not had to give any information concerning their records. They were then faced by the problem of explaining missing years in their employment history. For this group two out of three of the ex-prisoners claimed false jobs. Some of them said they had worked for their fathers or were self-employed, thus avoiding the possibility of tracking down the job. Others invented jobs in places a considerable distance from where they were trying to get a job or claimed periods in hospital. We also found that the men did not have a well worked out story to tell; they said whatever came to mind, thus making their chances of being found out and the likelihood of being accused of lying or withholding information much greater.

In the case of 54 dischargees and 91 parolees whose prospective employers were told of their records, we asked what their reactions were.

Turned down immediately	29 parolees	52 dischargees[2]
Not turned down immediately, but no further information requested	39	33
Not turned down immediately and further information about record requested	23	15

Part of the difference in the reception given to these men by their employers may be due to the type of jobs for which they were applying. The responses may also relate to the readiness of the dischargee to give unwarranted emphasis to his record as the reason for not getting jobs.

Secondly, as in earlier findings, the dischargee may simply be the less employable worker. However, Manpower may also account for part of this difference. As the parolee is referred to Manpower by his parole supervisor, he is known to be an offender, whereas the dischargee will often go to Manpower without admitting his record or without a referral. In the case of parolees, Manpower may select employers for whom the record is not important, or when making a referral, they may mention that he has a record before the parolee goes to see about the job. On the other hand, the dischargee is more often referred blind to employers and so will make some applications which could have been avoided had the referring agency known of his record.

The thorny question as to whether an ex-prisoner should declare his record when applying for jobs is well known. The brief analysis of the question above would lead one to expect that parolees worry less about declaring it than dischargees. In fact, a specific question was put to the ex-prisoner concerning what he was worried about most when applying for jobs. The question was intended to differentiate between worries due to lack of skill and experience as opposed to the record.

	parolees	dischargees[2]
Did not worry: they planned to lie or tell the truth	27	31
Did worry: because of the record	40	31
record and lack of working skills or experience	16	19
not obtaining or being able to live up to requirements of a job	14	14
lack of skill or work history singly	8	3

A final topic that has received considerable attention recently in Canada is the question of bonding ex-prisoners. There has been a move, supported by such pressure groups as the John Howard Society, to get the government to undertake bonding for ex-prisoners. The ex-prisoners were asked if they had ever been refused jobs because of bonding since their times of release; only 28 per cent said they had.[11] So that we see that is is, then, an issue for only a small number. The jobs for which they were applying were higher grade jobs, so it may be that they are more vocal in making their needs felt. However, refusal of a job because of bonding is still a very great disadvantage for this group. Considering the number of ex-prisoners who were engaged in the transportation area before admission to penitentiary and the number who were turned down for bonding in this area, we see that one fulfilling job opportunity has been limited.

Parolees were asked if their parole status made any difference in being considered for jobs. Only 31 felt that it made some difference; 22 of these felt that it was important because their employer was aware that they would stay at that job for some time though many added that they thought this was a minor consideration. Seven did not know what difference it made; one said his parole officer had spoken directly to his employer and another that there was more aggravation from his parole officer about getting a job. In general terms, the parolees at the six-month stage did not feel that their status made any difference when considered for the job: 64 per cent said definitely that it did not matter and a further 12 per cent said their employers did not know. Only 10 per cent were able to think of instances where parole had made any difference. Some of these included times when they were turned down for jobs and other times when the parole officer had helped them to get something.

Identifying the Ex-Con

As a result of the pilot interviews where it was suggested that an ex-prisoner is easily distinguished from those who have not been to prison, we included a question in which we asked the men in our sample if they could recognize others who had been inside. Only 9 per cent of the parolees and none of the dischargees said they could not. 25 per cent said that slang would be an indicator while 21 per cent cited attitudes. Some mentioned a combination of these two in addition to the manner of dress. (Three parolees said that he would look lost.)

The other side of this coin was whether or not men worried about the types of word they used. If slang does identify a person with a record, do the ex-prisoners make deliberate attempts to avoid using it? One in three of both groups said that they did, mostly in conversations with strangers, although also when applying for jobs, talking to friends or meeting girls, and at work generally.

Relations with Police

The feelings of many ex-prisoners that they are discriminated against by the police are not easily interpreted. They may be aware of other individuals who were involved in activities similar to their own who were not arrested by the police for whatever reason. However, it may be that those other people were more efficient criminals, did not leave fingerprints, were not drunk, were not involved in violence, or were simply not known to the police; in light of this it is impossible to know to what extent these feelings were justified without a thorough study of the use of police discretion in the arresting of persons involved in breaking and entering, theft and fraud, and, more generally, a study of general police decisions about allocation of resources. This would be particularly important for a comparison between the typical offences for which persons are sent to the penitentiary and offences involving usually larger amounts of money such as tax or stock exchange frauds.

A separate question was concerned with whether the ex-prisoner felt he would be suspected if an offence occurred in his own area and whether he would feel threatened by this suspicion. Of those not in jail at the the time of the interview, 56 per cent of the dischargees and 68 per cent of the parolees felt that they would neither be suspected nor feel threatened. As might be expected, there was a tendency for more of the dischargees, 33 per cent, than the parolees, 22 per cent, to feel that they would be suspected of an offence occurring in their area. However, none of these differences were statistically significant. At twelve months, one in two of the ex-prisoners had spoken to the police since their release. 20 per cent of the dischargees, compared to 10 per cent of the parolees felt that the police had been actively trailing them; of those not arrested at that time, 30 per cent of the dischargees compared to 20 per cent of the parolees said the police had threatened to arrest them.

One way to avoid arrest and prosecution or conviction is to act as an informer. Less than 5 per cent of the sample admitted giving information to the police. At twelve months the ex-prisoners were also asked if they had ever got a patch and how they would go about getting one. A patch is one of the many terms used by ex-prisoners to refer to the process by which a person tries to avoid arrest or prosecution and to bargain for a lower sentence: 33 per cent of the dischargees and 15 per cent of the parolees said they had at some time in their lives got a patch. Another one-third of the dischargees and half of the parolees said that they did not really know how to go about getting one. For those who had an idea, many mentioned, singly or in combination, police, crown lawyer, magistrate, and defence lawyer. It is not possible to say to what extent this reflects a 'real' understanding of the situation. Unlike governmental or other officials, who like to emphasize open and fair justice and who in some cases might lose their jobs, ex-prisoners have little reason to deny or fabricate. It seems obvious that bargaining occurs at all levels of both police and courts with some frequency.

NOTES TO CHAPTER 5

1 Interestingly, penitentiary has no clear etymological roots. One would presume that it refers to a place where one atones or amends for wrongdoing by experiencing remorse. However, *de facto* it has referred to the more severe and long-term prisons in both Europe and America from the 17th century onwards. Traditionally then, it has been a place where one sleeps in solitary confinement but during the day either (Pennsylvania separate system) works in one's cell, or (Auburn silent system) works in silence with others. The Auburn system was more productive and so defrayed more of the costs of imprisonment and spread widely in North America. Kingston Penitentiary follows the Auburn system. By 1860, thirty years after these two systems had reached their peaks, the silent rule had given away to more liberal association. See Tappan (1960, chap. 20, esp. 601–11)

2 Many of the tables in this chapter are designed to present principal findings in summary form. The percentages do not total 100, because categories with only small percentages were omitted from the text. The percentages refer to those interviewed (it is important to remember that there was s slight bias with regard to the original population of dischargees; those interviewed were more likely to be re-arrested)

3 The study was not concerned with pre-release dreams or aspirations. Irwin (1970, 86–106) has pointed out for prisoners being released from California prisons that in order to obtain parole, effectively the only mode of release, they are forced to shift from speculative future concerns to immediate and more mundane details. He points out that there is considerable variation, however, between types of prisoners and the extent to which they do any constructive planning

4 However much truth there is in the theory that people steal because they do not have

any money, the amount of cash available to an ex-prisoner on release and how he spends his money is obviously of considerable importance. In Glaser's (1964) study the median amount of total payments from all the various sources at release was between $55 and $57. Also, 75 per cent of Glaser's sample received less than $100 as the total funds due to them at release. It is not possible to show the exact distributions from the way in which his data were presented

5 Through the various hobbies that are available to inmates in the institutions, it is possible to earn extra money on top of the normal prison earnings. Petit point, oil painting, copper work, jewellery making, and leather craft are some of the hobbies available. The material is on display at the gates of the institutions and visitors or correctional officers may buy it. From time to time stores are set up at local community fêtes and the material is sold. The earnings from this are given to the inmate on release. Three of the ex-prisoners had earned more than $300 through this; 11 had earned $100 to $300; and 29 had earned less than $100. For a minority of the ex-prisoners who have kept their hobby crafts until release the prison hobbies are also of importance, for they realize cash after they are released from sales to their friends or acquaintances

6 An important element in the control of prisoners within the institution is a grading system, and related to the grading system is a system of daily payments. Money is earned in this system of grades as follows:

Grade 1	35¢ per day	20¢ spending money
Grade 2	45¢ per day	30¢ spending money
Grade 3	55¢ per day	35¢ spending money
Grade 4	65¢ per day	40¢ spending money

Other money sent to the prisoner while he is an inmate in the institution, or realized from sale of hobby crafts, is put in a trust fund

7 21 per cent of the total parolees, compared to 8 per cent of the dischargees, were met by their wives or common-law wives; 10 per cent of the parolees compared to 8 per cent of the dischargees were met by siblings; 16 per cent of the parolees compared to 13 per cent of the dischargees were met by parents, grandparents or their children. In contrast, 3 per cent of the parolees and 7 per cent of the dischargees were met by their friends. Only 5 per cent of the parolees were met by their parole officers

8 27 per cent of the dischargees compared to 9 per cent of the parolees felt there was initial shock at first but that afterwards their transactions were normal. 5 per cent of both groups felt that some wanted to get him into trouble deliberately. Of the 21 who mentioned any difference in welfare benefits, 9 per cent said that more help had been given. 8 per cent mentioned a feeling of uneasiness, and four men mentioned a general apathy on the part of the staff. 50 ex-prisoners noticed differences at Manpower, 11 per cent of these mentioning a general feeling of uneasiness, 15 per cent lackadaisical attitudes, and 20 per cent that they received more help. There was a slight tendency for more parolees to mention more help. Three dischargees felt uneasy about adult re-training while five parolees felt they received more help in this area

9 This sub-study had a number of methodological virtues but also some vices – the sample was confined to one geographical area and one type of job

10 Glaser (1964) pointed to the effect of the lack of work skills: 'The ex-prisoner's primary barrier to employment is not his criminal record so frequently as it is his lack of extensive skilled work experience'

11 Nine of these were white'collar jobs at the unskilled clerical level in the service and recreation, sales or clerical areas; six were in the transportation areas for drivers of various sorts; four were for semi-skilled or fully-skilled jobs in the craftsman production processes area, and one was for a mangerial job in sales. The ex-prisoners were also asked in which jobs up to now they had been bonded. 13 claimed to have been bonded. Of these, three had been bonded in the unskilled jobs in the service and recreation industry, one in an unskilled sales job, one in an unskilled clerical job, three in semi-skilled transportation jobs, and four in semi-skilled or unskilled pro-

duction processes jobs. This may be contrasted with 37 of the ex-prisoners who had been bonded before being sent to the Kingston penitentiaries. 11 of these had had jobs of managerial, supervisory, or foreman responsibility, 10 were concerned with transportation driving jobs, 10 were concerned with service and recreation skilled jobs, four had had clerical or sales jobs, and two others had had unskilled work in production processes

6

Obtaining a Job

In many informal discussions held with ex-prisoners while we were designing the research project, they emphasized that 'if you want to know whether an ex-prisoner is involved in crime, find out if he has a job.' Analysis of the relationships between pre-release data and recidivism within the first twelve months confirms the apparent relationship between unemployment and recidivism (at statistically significant levels). Table 6.1 shows, for the total sample, and for the respective sub-populations of dischargees and parolees, the proportions who were employed or unemployed at the time of their original offences and their arrest rates within twelve months: 42 per cent of the total sample were employed and 58 per cent were unemployed at the time of their original offences. Within twelve months of release the arrest rate for the employed men was only 29 per cent compared to 43 per cent for those unemployed. This pattern also holds true for the two sub-populations. There is also a slight tendency for more prisoners who were employed at the time of their offences to be granted parole.

Penitentiary Training

Because it is believed that the released prisoner has difficulty finding work as a result of his lack of job skills, vocational training is emphasized in the penitentiary programme in the hope that he can then qualify for skilled or semi-skilled work in the community. According to institutional

TABLE 6.1

Arrest rates by employment status at time of original offence, with breakdowns by mode of release and proportion arrested within twelve months

According to penitentiary files	Dischargees			Parolees			Total		
	N	Percentage of total	Percentage of N arrested	N	Percentage of total	Percentage of N arrested	N	Percentage of total	Percentage of N arrested
Employed at time of original offence	82	38.9	39.0	93	46.0	20.4	175	42.4	29.1
Unemployed at time of original offence	129	61.1	51.2	109	54.0	33.0	238	57.6	42.9
Total	211*	100	46.4	202†	100	27.2	413	100	37.0

The employment status of 2 dischargees* and 8 parolees† was not recorded

Original offence refers to the most serious offence for which they were committed to the penitentiary from where they were released in 1968

TABLE 6.2

Institution training and work experience similar to job held within five weeks from release

	Taken	Used	Used as % of taken (beware small N)
Carpentry	24	1	4.2
Welding	15	6	40.0
Barbering	12	5	41.7
Stationary engineer	10	5	50.0
Dining services	6	2	33.3
Motor mechanics	5	1	20.0
Plumbing	12	5	41.7
Machine shop	14	1	7.1
Mason	10	3	30.0
Painting	8	1	12.5
Printing	3	1	33.3
Vocational electric	8	0	—
Other	30	1	3.3
Total	156	32	20.5

files, only 23 per cent of the sample took any form of training in the institution (32 per cent of the parolees and 13 per cent of the dischargees). Those persons 'suitable' for trade training, on the basis of age and motivation, are more likely to be granted parole and therefore tend to be released during their training; consequently those released at expiration of sentence, who had taken training, had a slightly higher tendency – 53 per cent compared to 45 per cent – to have completed it.

Table 6.2 shows the number of ex-prisoners who had used their training in one or more jobs in the community during their first five weeks out. Only 10 per cent claimed to have held a job directly related to their work inside. Out of the 156 ex-prisoners who stated that they took some training, 21 per cent said they used it in some way at this time. This should in no way imply that a person who took some training, in welding for example, actually worked as a qualified welder outside or that he acquired some new skill. It merely means that the ex-prisoner felt that his training in the institution was related directly to a job he had held since his release.

By twelve months, we estimated that these proportions had doubled. 20 per cent of the total still free had used institutional training in some way. These proportions appear to be similar to those of the Gluecks (1968, 92–3), who found that 19.1 per cent of their delinquents had used the training taken within five years of release. However, for the US Federal Bureau of Prisons, Glaser (1964, 251) found that 29.7 per cent of 114 men who took part in an interview at the end of the first four months after release claimed that one or more of the jobs that they had held since release for more than one week were related to their prison work experience. Because of the small numbers involved, caution should be observed in interpreting the meaning of 'use' of training. However, more than 40 per cent of those with experience in stationary engineering, plumbing, barbering, and welding used it in some form outside.

Of course, its use depends on two things: the work opportunities outside, and the validity of the training acquired. The stationary engineers nearly all worked in positions of responsibility for the heating systems in the institution. They got these positions mainly as a result of having had similar experience before they were sent to the institution or during a previous sentence. The combination of previous and continued experience in the institution probably contributes to their opportunities to continue outside. Barbering, on the other hand, was one of the few skills that could be acquired in all three of the main institutions in this study; it is also a job in which, from the ex-prisoner's point of view, there seem to be realistic opportunities of being one's own boss.

The ex-prisoners were also asked what sort of training the penitentiary should give to equip them for work outside. 24 per cent mentioned that they thought the current training was aimed in the right direction, but should be brought up to date so that it was relevant to the work available outside; 11 per cent mentioned making available training for what the inmate wants to do; 8 per cent wanted educational up-grading; 9 per cent favoured leaving the initiative up to the inmates themselves; 5 per cent suggested work release in order to enable the prisoner to support his family; 5 per cent wanted more concentration on helping the ex-prisoner to live after release.[1]

A further negative reflection on institutional training is the fact that many of the ex-prisoners were involved in adult re-training programmes after release. At six months, 10 per cent of both groups were taking adult re-training courses. A further 25 per cent were considering it (although there was wide variation in the seriousness of their intent). Nearly one in two of those taking courses were involved in welding or sheet metal courses. Of particular interest is that over half of the adult re-training courses taken by ex-prisoners were less than twelve months in duration which means that they could have been adequately carried out while the man was an inmate. Some of these may simply have been stop-gaps, though they appeared to be closely related to an occupational goal. The citizen pays taxes to support the man in the institution during which time, in the majority of cases, the inmate is involved in occupations or in training irrelevant to his post-release career, though a minority may be advancing their educational qualifications, which are often a pre-

TABLE 6.3

Methods tried to obtain jobs within five weeks, by mode of release

	Dischargees				Parolees				Total	
	no.		%		no.		%			
1 *Impersonal methods*										
Individual employers	12		5.4		32		8.5		44	
Newspapers	26		11.7		58		15.4		84	
Employment agencies	2	40	0.9	18.0	5	95	1.3	25.2	7	135
2 *Own Resources*	38	38	17.1	17.1	64	64	17.0	17.0	102	102
3 *Manpower*	52	52	23.4	23.4	89	89	23.6	23.6	141	141
4 *Social agencies*										
JHS	22		9.9		28		7.4		50	
Welfare	9		4.1		3		0.8		12	
Parole officer	3*	34	1.4	15.4	14	45	3.7	11.9	17	79
5 *Friends*										
Own age	34		15.3		34		9.0		68	
Parents' age	2		0.9		5		1.3		7	
Priest	3	39	1.4	17.6	4	43	1.1	11.4	7	82
6 *Family*†										
Parents	9		4.1		16		4.3		25	
Brother, sister	6		2.7		17		4.5		23	
Other relatives	4	19	1.8	8.6	8	41	2.1	10.9	12	60
Total		222				377				599

* An OPS or NPS worker

† Wife was coded as own resources

$\chi^2 = 7.58$; $df = 4$; $p < 0.10$

requisite for training courses. On release many then take re-training programmes, which also cover living expenses (the money again coming from taxes), which last about the same time as many prison sentences. It may not be feasible to try to provide this kind of re-training in the prison when only a few prisoners are interested; these statistics, however, do question the wisdom of providing for the most part irrelevant 'vocational' training of the type now given in institutions. They point to the advantages of building such institutions near population centres where courses would be available. Gradual release or day parole – the National Parole equivalent of work furlough – was used very little in Ontario penitentiaries, in spite of the fact that it is an excellent opportunity for an inmate to follow meaningful and 'in demand' training courses while serving his sentence. Indeed, this was a suggestion put forward by many of the ex-prisoners; they seemed to be well aware of the limitations in the training courses and work opportunities in the institution. Since the time of the study such temporary leave measures have been used more extensively in Kingston.

Job-finding Methods

The ex-prisoner was asked how he went about getting a job, and how successful he was. An attempt was made to differentiate between methods that had been totally unsuccessful, those that looked as if they might have led to a job, and those through which he actually obtained a job. The ex-prisoner tried, on the average, two methods to get a job. This, however, does not represent the true number of job applications, so we also asked how many genuine applications he had made. The parolees, as expected, made more applications than the dischargees, probably because they were on parole and the parole supervisor might have emphasized finding employment as part of the parole agreement. Alternatively, the type of person selected for parole is more likely to make more applications.

Somewhat more dischargees (14 per cent, compared to 8 per cent for parolees) had turned down one or two job offers since release. A typical reason was that the pay was too low or the type of job not good enough. Wife, parents, friends, and supervisor were either not told that he had turned the job down or were generally supportive of his action. We will see later that dischargees are less likely to be employed, but when employed earn more than parolees; this implies that parolees make more effort to find jobs and turn down fewer, while the dischargees make less effort and turn down more.

Table 6.3 presents the classification of the various methods used by ex-prisoners to try to obtain jobs in the first five weeks (which may be

TABLE 6.4

Proportion of jobs obtained through various sources within five weeks, by mode of release

	Dischargees				Parolees					
	no.		%		no.		%		Total	
1 *Impersonal methods*										
Individual employers	7		19.8		26		18.4		33	
Newspapers	7		9.2		14		9.9		21	
Employment agencies	2	16	2.6	21.0	0	40	0	28.3	2	56
2 *Own resources*	15	15	19.8	19.8	27	27	19.2	19.2	42	42
3 *Manpower*	14	14	18.4	18.4	32	32	22.7	22.7	46	46
4 *Social agencies*										
John Howard Society	4		5.3		0		0		4	
Welfare	3		3.9		1		0.7		4	
Parole officer	0	7	0	9.2	7	8	5.0	5.7	7	15
5 *Friends*										
Own age	16		21.1		10		7.1		26	
Parents' age	0		0		1		0.7		1	
Priest	1	17	1.3	22.4	2	13	1.4	9.2	3	30
6 *Family*										
Parents	5		6.6		9		6.4		14	
Brother or sister	2		2.6		9		6.4		11	
Other relatives	0	7	0	9.2	3	21	2.1	14.9	3	28
Total		76				141			217	

contrasted with Table 6.4 for jobs actually obtained). Manpower was used by nearly one in four.

Within five weeks, 32 out of the 139 parolees who actually obtained jobs got them through Manpower. For the dischargees, the most important method of finding jobs was through friends of their own ages, and then through their own resources. In contrast, for parolees 'own resources' and 'individual employers' were the most important. Table 6.5 shows that there is very little difference for the two groups in their job sources at either six or twelve months. For both more than a third found their jobs through their own resources, and approximately one in five found them through Manpower, although these two tended to be used less at twelve than at six months. The direction of the changes over the later six months between the proportions obtaining jobs through friends of their own age varied by mode of release; the dischargees increased from 15 per cent to 20 per cent whereas the parolees decreased from 14 per cent to only 9 per cent. This reinforces the previous pattern noted for the dischargee to make more use of informal methods later, but for Manpower and direct methods to be more important for first jobs. If the 32 parolees obtaining jobs through Manpower within five weeks are represented as a proportion of the total number of parolees who tried

TABLE 6.5

Proportion of jobs obtained through various sources at six months and twelve months, by mode of release

	Dischargees (%)				Parolees (%)			
	6 months		12 months		6 months		12 months	
1 *Impersonal methods*								
Individual employers	8.8		0		4.5		4.9	
Newspapers	5.5		11.0		5.8		6.3	
Employment agencies	1.1	15.4	0	11.0	1.8	12.1	1.9	13.1
2 *Own resources*	36.3	36.3	33.0	33.0	42.6	42.6	37.9	37.9
3 *Manpower*	24.2	24.2	11.9	11.9	19.7	19.7	18.0	18.0
4 *Social agencies*								
John Howard Society	2.2		1.8		0.9		1.0	
Harold King Farm	2.2		0		0.4		0.5	
Welfare	0		0		0		0.5	
Parole officer	0	4.4	0	1.8	0.4	1.7	0.5	2.5
5 *Friends*								
Own age	15.4		20.2		13.9		8.7	
Parents' age	1.1		0		0.9		1.0	
Priest	1.1	17.6	10.1	30.3	0.4	15.2	3.9	13.6
6 *Family*								
Parents	1.1		2.8		4.0		2.4	
Brother or sister	1.1		1.8		2.7		1.5	
Other relatives	0	2.2	0.9	5.5	1.8	8.5	1.5	5.4
Not specified				6.4				9.0
Total		100.1		99.9		99.8		99.7
N		91		109		223		206

to get jobs through Manpower, 35 per cent obtained a job. In contrast, 27 per cent of those persons discharged found jobs through Manpower. The successful percentage of the total who tried a certain method is termed the *job-finding ratio*. There are considerable variations in the job-finding ratio between both the various methods tried and between parolees and dischargees.

These findings were compared with a population of parolees considered by Boulanger (1969, 37) in Montreal, Quebec, and US Federal ex-prisoners discussed by Glaser (1964, 349). The major differences in the distribution of methods of obtaining jobs are due to the proportions of persons finding jobs through public employment agencies. In Glaser's study, only 5 per cent of the sample found their first jobs through such an agency, compared to 18 per cent of dischargees and 23 per cent of parolees who found jobs through Manpower in this study. This may, in part, result from the requirement of the welfare agency in Toronto that a person be registered with Manpower before he can be considered for welfare. At least it reflects a totally different status of Manpower as far as men released from prison are concerned different from that of public employment agencies in the US. At the time of this study most Manpower offices had special placement officers to deal with ex-prisoners; this, too, may be another reason why ex-prisoners go there. However, during the study these special placement officers were being phased out and some offices did not have them.

Types of Employment

There is a sharp rise during the first three months in the number of parolees fully employed to 75 per cent of the population which remains fairly constant for the next nine months. There is a similar dramatic fall in the number of persons never employed or unemployed for more than five weeks during a particular time period, with approximately 8 or 9 per cent of the population forming a 'hard core' of unemployed parolees. There was a slowly declining proportion of parolees unemployed for less than five weeks. In contrast, 44 per cent of the dischargees interviewed concerning their first five weeks had not been employed during the first month, while 37 per cent had been unemployed for less than five weeks and only 15 per cent had gone straight to a job. At no stage in the first twelve months did the proportion employed of those dischargees interviewed ever go above 29 per cent. It is particularly interesting to note that, even in the implausible circumstance that all those dischargees who were not interviewed concerning their first six months and who were still in the community at six months, were counted as employed, the proportion of dischargees employed would still not reach that for parolees. One might expect the employment variable to differentiate parolees who would be arrested from those who would not. There was, however, only a slight tendency for those arrested within twenty-four months to be employed less. There were few differences in unemployment proportions between parolees not arrested and those arrested, although there were dramatic differences between the parolees and the dischargees.

A special job-coding schedule was developed to enable the parole supervisor to describe the important characteristics of the employment careers of the parolees. A duplicate version of this schedule was used to describe the employment careers of the dischargees in the one-, six-, and twelve-month questionnaires.

The job-coding schedule was developed on the assumption that the most important characteristics of employment are reflected in the length of time a person is at a job, the type and skill of work he does, whether or not the employment is full time, and his wages. Of course we are still left without knowing whether a person who goes from short job to short job, and is in effect, continuously employed, is at a higher or lower level of functioning than a person who holds the same job for the complete

Figure 6:I

Percentage of men who had held a cumulative number of jobs at twelve months from release, by mode of release

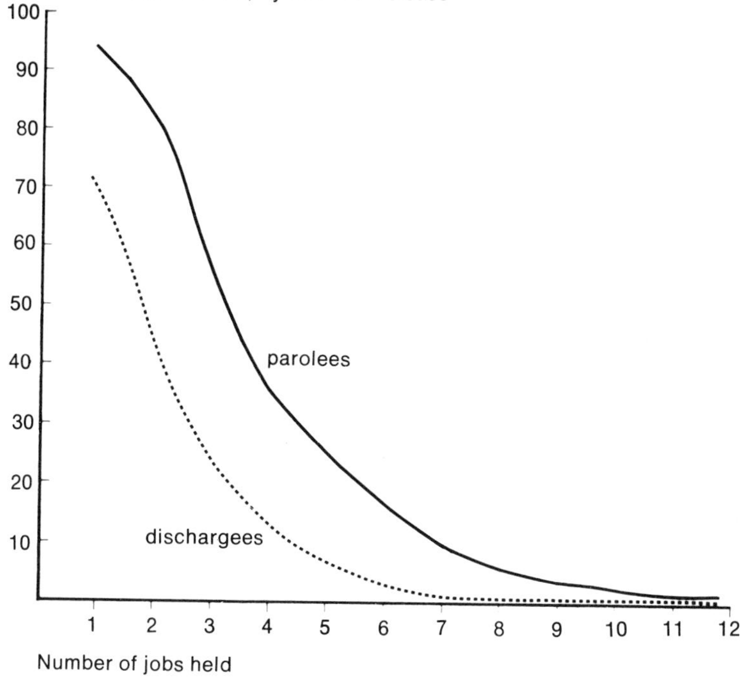

100
90
80
70
60
50
40
30
20
10

parolees
dischargees

1 2 3 4 5 6 7 8 9 10 11 12

Number of jobs held

period. These indices were not attempts to provide a single indicator of prestige, either. Despite these limitations, these dimensions function as crude indicators describing the general level of functioning of the ex-prisoners and particularly the parolees; as crude indicators they will later be related to criteria such as re-arrest.

Parolees held more jobs than dischargees, but for shorter periods of time. As illustrated in figure 6.I, by twelve months more than 50 per cent of the parolees had held three or more jobs, though only 24 per cent of the dischargees interviewed had done so. Nearly 10 per cent of the parolees had held seven or more jobs. 35 per cent of the parolees held their first jobs for less than a week, and 22 per cent held them for between one and three months. In contrast, less than 8 per cent of the dischargees held a first job for between one and three months. With the exception of the first job for the parolees, the modal time period for holding a job was between one and three months. As illustrated in Figure 6.II, 88 per cent of the jobs held by parolees were held for less than three months. In comparison, 68 per cent of the jobs held by dischargees were held for less than three months. The difference in the shape of these curves is

Figure 6:II
Cumulative proportion of jobs held for length of job, by mode of release

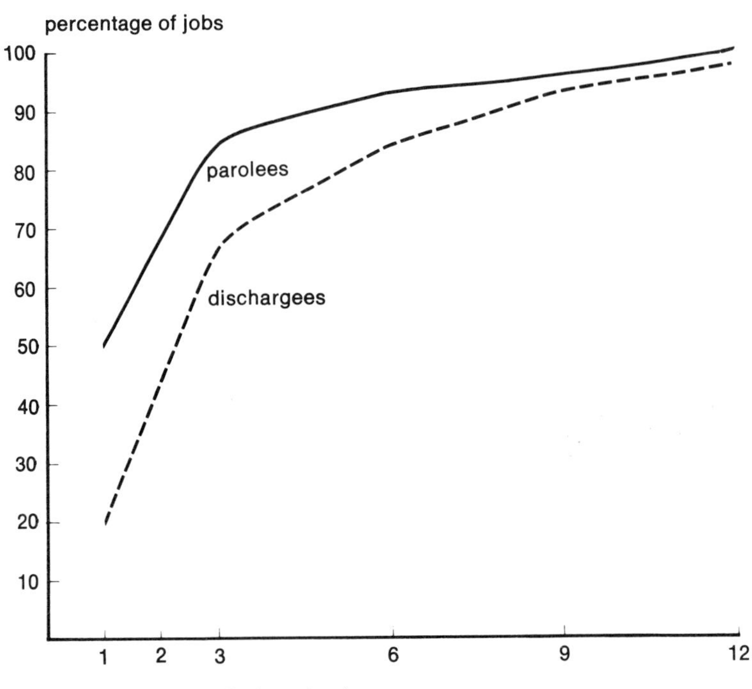

primarily the result of the proportions of first jobs held for short periods of time which was discussed above.

The parolee when employed tended to earn less than the dischargee. The wages earned by the ex-prisoner were coded in ranges of \$20.00 to \$30.00 starting, to over \$150.00 a week. A minority of the jobs were 'part-time,' or 'adult re-training,' where the wage coded was the payment made while the ex-prisoner was attending the particular course.

The modal wage for all the jobs – first, second, third, fourth, fifth, etc. – for both parolees and dischargees lay in the range of \$70.00 to \$90.00 a week (see Figure 6.III).

A mean wage was calculated by ignoring those parolees whose wage was not known and taking the mid-point of the range for each category. For the first job held by the parolees the mean wage was \$64.00, for the second \$74.00, third \$79.00, fourth \$74.00, fifth \$76.00, and sixth \$79.00. For the dischargees the mean wage was more variable starting at \$80.00, rising to \$86.00, and falling by the third job to \$72.00.

Figure 6:III
Cumulative percentage of ex-prisoners earnings, wages in ranges specified for total jobs, by mode of release
(including a histogram of wages)

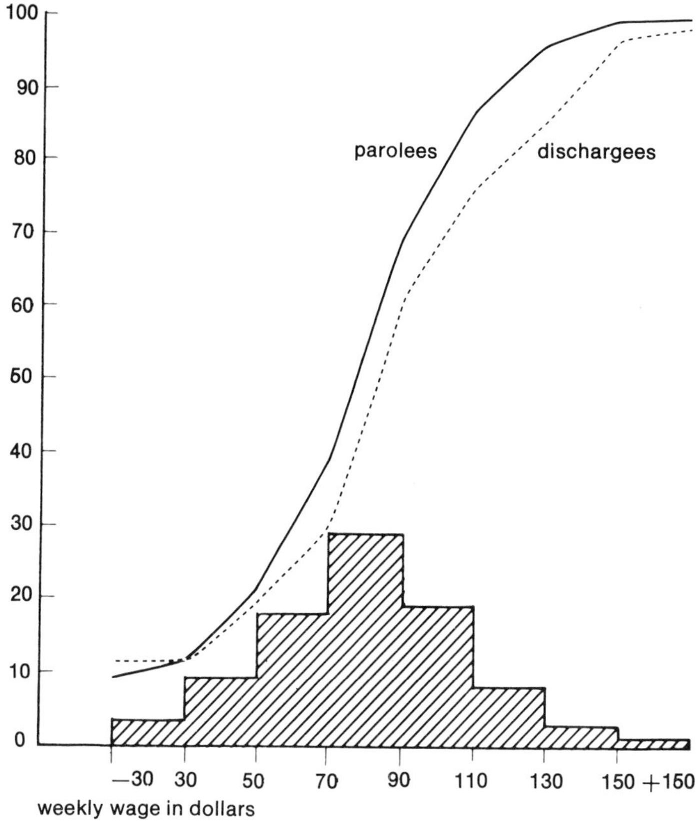

100 90 80 70 60 50 40 30 20 10 0

parolees dischargees

—30 30 50 70 90 110 130 150 +150
weekly wage in dollars

The mean for the parolees, $74.00 a week, was significantly different from that of dischargees which was $82.00 a week.

This wage differential suggests, along with the previous conclusions, that higher proportions of parolees are employed but for shorter lengths of time and that dischargees are less inclined than parolees to accept lower-paying jobs. This would appear to be a result of the supervisor's emphasis on employment; the parolee feels compelled to take a job and so takes those with lower wages. The dischargee will be more exacting, and prefers to stay unemployed rather than take a low-paying job. This tendency is particularly noticeable for the first job, where the parolee was prepared to accept a job for a short period with a mean wage of $64.00 a week, whereas the dischargee would only accept a job that the parolee would accept for his second job. The wage for the dischargee's job was nearly $80.00, a mean wage that was only nearly reached by the parolee at the third job.

In terms of the prestige scale, 26 per cent of the longest jobs involved unskilled light work, 18 per cent unskilled heavy work, 22 per cent semi-skilled blue-collar work. Only 6 per cent of ex-prisoners were described as holding white-collar jobs, and 6 per cent had their own businesses or supervisory roles. Of the highest wage jobs, 25 per cent were described as unskilled light work, 19 per cent unskilled heavy work, 26 per cent as semi-skilled blue-collar work, and 15 per cent as skilled blue-collar work. for the most part, the distribution of jobs in terms of the prestige scale between the length of time and wages is identical.

In terms of the prestige scale, 35 per cent of the dischargees were involved in semi-skilled occupations and 29 per cent in skilled blue-collar occupations although, as for the parolees, 25 per cent had unskilled labouring jobs. There was then, a tendency for the prestige scale ratings of the dischargees' jobs to be higher than those of parolees. This difference would seem to be consistent with the higher wages and differences in areas in which the dischargees and parolees worked. However, it is also possible that this is the result of a difference in emphasis in the coding.

Of the longest jobs held by parolees, 6 per cent were adult re-training and 5 per cent of the parolees earned their highest wages in adult re-training programmes. In contrast, there was only one dischargee who was involved in adult re-training for a long period of time and two dischargees who described it as their highest-paying jobs (there were only two dischargees involved in adult re-training who took part in the interview). For the parolees, 9 per cent of the longest jobs and 6 per cent of the highest earning jobs were part-time. In contrast, 13 per cent of the dischargees' jobs in both categories were part-time. Another major difference lies in the proportion of casual labour jobs: 8 per cent of the dischargees' jobs were recorded as casual, compared to 3 per cent of the longest parolee jobs and 5 per cent of the highest wage-earning jobs for the parolees. It is possible that this was another result of the parole agreement. Many supervisors do not like parolees to be involved in casual labour and try to encourage them to take steady employment.

Job Likes and Dislikes

Even in response to questioning, few ex-prisoners expressed any work satisfaction. At five weeks, 32 per cent of the total could find nothing they liked about their jobs, while 8 per cent stated that the main thing they liked was the money. In contrast, 21 per cent said that they enjoyed their work but did not know why; 19 per cent who liked the setting and freedom were often those who were doing jobs without immediate supervision, such as driving a truck; 4 per cent mentioned the people they worked with and 5 per cent the challenge and the opportunities for learning that the job offered. At six months, 58 per cent of the parolees and 31 per cent of the dischargees interviewed said that they had liked some aspect of their job giving similar reasons, although individual responses showed that the ex-prisoner had difficulty in identifying what 'aspect' it was that he liked.

At both six and twelve months about half of the ex-prisoners identified aspects of their jobs that they disliked, such as insufficient pay, discontinuous employment, dislike of their work colleagues, or working conditions, the difficulty of getting to the job, and not doing the type of work for which they felt suited. Only 6 per cent of the dischargees and 8 per cent of the parolees mentioned friction with their bosses as a reason for their dislike.

Those who found a job were asked if they ever looked for another. 26 per cent of the dischargees and 27 per cent of the parolees said 'yes.' They were asked to specify what means they used, but generally their replies were inconclusive. Some of the reasons given for changing jobs were the temporary nature of the current job, long hours and low pay, and better opportunities elsewhere. Only three individuals said that their records had anything to do with it.

During the first three months, approximately 6 per cent of the parolees changed their jobs at least once each month. In the periods of three months covered by the six-, nine-, and twelve-months questionnaires, the proportion changing jobs declined from 12 per cent to 5 per cent. 11 per cent of the dischargees interviewed had changed jobs one or more times within the first month and higher proportions had done so at the six- and twelve-month time periods. Although there were differences between the parolees and the dischargees on the job changes variable, there were no differences between those arrested within the parolee population and within the total population.

It is sometimes suggested that employers take advantage of men with records by giving them jobs that they would not give to others. It may be that such employers know that ex-prisoners would have difficulty finding a second job because of their records. We therefore asked whether any ex-prisoners felt that they had been taken advantage of in this way. Eight dischargees and twenty-five parolees felt they had, thirteen of the parolees saying that it affected their wages in some way and six saying that it had affected the particular job they were doing.

However, four of the parolees and two of the dischargees felt that their employers had looked after them more because of the records. These particular two dischargees were employed by persons who they said had records also. At twelve months, only 12 per cent of the parolees and 6 per cent of the dischargees interviewed thought that awareness of record had made any difference to the types of job, wages, or other aspects of employment. Two of the parolees felt that they were employed because they had records, attempts on their employers' parts to help them. Three dischargees and three parolees thought they had been fired because their employers had found out about their records after they had become employed.

Glaser (1964, 311–16) has pointed out that a slow rate of progress in the face of high employment expectations creates frustration. He found that many ex-prisoners have unrealistic expectations for the future. In this study we asked the ex-prisoner what he expected to be doing in one year, how he expected to achieve this, what he expected to be doing eventually, and how long he thought it would take. This question was not specifically related to job expectations although its situation in the questionnaire was such that it was generally interpreted to refer to work. Of the ex-prisoners, 16 per cent could not specify what they expected to be doing in a year's time. This reflects the general uncertainty and lack of confidence for the future that typifies some ex-prisoners. 21 per cent mentioned that they would like to be working at some particular type of job, and 24 per cent spoke of the ones at which they were currently working. Surprisingly, given Glaser's findings, only 5 per cent of the ex-prisoners wanted to own their own businesses. However, some planned to achieve upward occupational mobility through the educational system: 10 per cent mentioned going to either school or university or acquiring a job which had career opportunities following from it. It is hard to say to what extent these were realistic responses. Many ex-prisoners in fact drop out of re-training programmes, and some have difficulty keeping a steady job, although the attainment of such goal is possible for people with similar qualifications. In this case, however, these were not merely fanciful ideas, for many of the men had thought of a specific type of re-training and a certain job, or of saving money.

Later in the first twelve months more than three out of four ex-prisoners interviewed wanted to settle down in the right job. For the sixteen dischargees and seventy-three parolees who were employed at the time of the six-month interview, a third of the dischargees and two out of five parolees were planning to stay in their current jobs either for five years or more or indefinitely. Two out of five of the dischargees and one out of five of the parolees said they did not know, but that they were waiting for something better; 14 per cent of the parolees thought they would stay as long as their employer was ignorant of their record. One in four of the dischargees and one in ten of the parolees mentioned periods of less than a year.

Irwin (1970, 134) has pointed out that many prisoners feel heightened aspirations and a need to compensate for the fact that some of their lives have been taken away from them by their institutional sentences. It has been noted above that the post-release aspirations of our group were much more realistic than those of Irwin's sample. Nevertheless, the ex-prisoner was asked if he felt others had got ahead of him in the work world while he had been inside and, if so, he was asked to specify in what way: 31 per cent replied that they did not feel that this was the case; 25 per cent, however, mentioned getting a wife and family; 8 per cent, possessions, usually specifying own home, car, etc. In contrast to this, only 20 per cent of them mentioned a job. The parolee was more likely to mention job and less likely to mention family, perhaps because he was more ambitious and often already had a wife and family.

Handling Money

Because of the large number who mentioned some aspect of money or employment as a reason for their involvement in crime, we were concerned with both these variables after release, not only in relation to reinvolvement in criminal activities, but also in more general terms. First, how much money does the ex-prisoner have and where does it come from? Secondly, how does he budget this money? Earlier we saw that three out of five men were released from the penitentiary with less than $100.00.

Although one-sixth of the prisoners had all the money with which they had been released left at the end of their first day, 34 per cent said the money lasted them less than a week, and a further 24 per cent until the end of their second week. What did the ex-prisoner do with his money? Was it so little that it could only last a week or two? What did the money pay for?

Rent or hotel rooms	30 parolees	30 dischargees[2]
Food or groceries	52	38
Clothes or personal effects (cigarettes, confectionery, medicines, etc.)	77	65
Transportation	27	27
Women, drink, drugs, 'entertainment'	37	51

Although the numbers are small in the remaining categories, more parolees than dischargees spent money on their children, presents for their family, or work tools. As might be expected from the previous analysis of the differences between the two groups, the parolee spends money on food and his wife, whereas the dischargee spends more on entertainment and presents for friends, probably those he stays with.

The ex-prisoner was asked how long it was before he got his first pay cheque, and what he did for cash until that time: 16 per cent had received their first pay cheque within the first week; 20 per cent in the next two weeks; 15 per cent in the fourth week; 8 per cent in the fifth week. 63 per cent of the ex-prisoners had, then, received their first pay cheques within the first five weeks from their dates of release. There were a number of men for whom the question was not relevant; those, for example, who lived at the Harold King Farm did not have to meet any expenses while they were there. Of the others 23 per cent said they had enough; 13 per cent relied on members of their family other than their wives; 8 per cent relied on money that their wives had saved; 5 per cent on mother's allowance or other forms of welfare; 4 per cent on the John Howard Society. The remainder mentioned combinations of welfare and other sources.

To get some idea of the ways in which the income of the ex-prisoners was spent we asked them to estimate the percentage of a weekly pay cheque that went on food, clothes, transport, furniture, fun, and savings. From the attempts to code the responses to this second part of the question both at one month and at twelve months it was quite clear that the ex-prisoner did not have exact figures available.

51 per cent of the dischargees and 36 per cent of the parolees mentioned that they bought food; 7 per cent of the dischargees and 6 per cent of the parolees mentioned that their wives or mothers paid for food. 10 per cent of the dischargees and 2 per cent of the parolees had included food in the rent. This might be expected as more dischargees than parolees live in rooming houses. 25 per cent of the ex-prisoners replied positively that they did not save at all; 6 per cent saved less than $10; 5 per cent between $11 and $20; 5 per cent between $21 and $30; 6 per cent saved more. 11 per cent mentioned saving, but it was not possible to put this into ranges. The coder was also asked to comment on the pattern described by the ex-prisoner. 11 per cent of the dischargees, compared to 2 per cent of the parolees, were coded as spending their money on 'non-essentials.' For 6 per cent of both groups, the common-law wife or mother was looking after their money. 24 per cent of the dischargees and 18 per cent of the parolees were living with parents, friends, or in half-way houses so that they were not responsible for food, rent, etc. 18 per cent of the dischargees were not working, compared to 4 per cent of the parolees. 20 per cent of the dischargees and 7 per cent of the

parolees were in situations of both working and living with some person who was primarily responsible for budgeting.

During the pilot interview discussions it was pointed out that having a telephone may not be a good thing for the ex-prisoner as he could run up bills for long distance calls which he could not pay. Generally speaking, he found it difficult to obtain credit from companies other than the telephone company. A sizeable number, had, or had access to, a telephone: 39 per cent of the dischargees and 62 per cent of the parolees had a telephone; 46 per cent of the dischargees and 53 per cent of the parolees made long distance phone calls. We asked them to specify the place to which they had made the calls, but in the majority of cases this was not done. However, more than one-quarter of each group who had made phone calls did specify that they were within Ontario.

At one and twelve months we asked the ex-prisoners about borrowing money. Of those who had, there was a tendency for the dischargee to have borrowed larger amounts than the parolee. This might be expected, not only because of the different spending patterns of the two groups, but also because the dischargee is more likely to be unemployed at this stage.

– Had not borrowed	57 parolees	43 dischargees[2]
– Had borrowed: from family	54	42
from friends their own age	16	27
from John Howard Society	20	24

In cases where they borrowed from the bank, it was often done in the names of their wives in order to avoid trouble with the parole agency. This applied particularly to the ownership of cars.

The proportion of debts of which the parole supervisor was aware remained approximately constant at 55 per cent throughout the twelve months. Of the parolees known to have debts of some sort or other, there was a gradual increase from 17 per cent in the first week to 45 per cent at the twelve-month stage; the same was true for those arrested. Although the supervisor was not always aware of the debt situation, particularly in the earlier stages, those arrested later tended to have more debts as time went on. Where the parolee was in debt, it was typically in the range of \$100–\$500. Usually these debts were incurred for such items as furniture, clothing, or cars.

The ex-prisoners were also asked if they had any real estate, and if so, to specify the approximate value of what they owned. Less than 5 per cent of the ex-prisoners said that they owned more than \$10,000 although another 20 per cent said that they owned between \$1000 and \$10,000. Although the question was not put to the ex-prisoners, it would seem that some of the victims in their offences could have brought civil suits against them for damages.

At the twelve-month stage the ex-prisoner was asked if he had any property registered in his own name. Approximately one in five had. In two-thirds of the cases the property was a car, in others it included houses, trucks, and land; 7 per cent of the ex-prisoners had registered property (cars and real estate) in their wives' names.

NOTES TO CHAPTER 6

1 A large range of other suggestions was put forward but with little overlap: 2 per cent, for example, mentioned training in jobs that do not require much education and that the men like, particularly the operation of heavy equipment and truck driving. Finally, there were suggestions about work with pay, creating an interest in a job, and making the hours worked in the institution count towards a trade

2 Percentages do not add to 100 because categories with only small percentages were omitted from the text. The percentages refer to those interviewed.

7

Family, Friends, and Detachment

Throughout the analysis, we have differentiated between public agencies (such as Manpower), supervision agencies, friends, and the families of procreation or origin. It has been shown that there are considerable differences in tendency between parolees and dischargees in their contacts with these groups. Criminological literature is full of support for the folklore that a person's associates markedly affect possible involvement in crime. The theory of 'differential association' is the most sophisticated of these theories and states briefly that a person's attitudes and motivations are affected by those of the people with whom he associates: that is, those persons who associate with others holding 'criminal values' are more likely to involve themselves in crime (Sutherland and Cressey, 1964; 1970). Secondly, those people without friends lack the reasons to try to achieve their goals through legitimate means, and are more likely to find extra-legal ways of achieving short-term ends.[1] It would appear that friends play the same role in the ex-prisoner's post-release career as did the family in the Gluecks' study (1962); support from parents (in the case of a younger person) or husband or wife is important for preventing re-arrest and conviction.

Does prison break up the family and reinforce criminal associations after release? What happens to the marriage after release? Does the wife go on with the ex-prisoner, perhaps on a different footing, or does she leave him? Less than 5 per cent of all males of all ages in Ontario were divorced in 1961. In comparison, there were 10 out of 423 men (with mean age of twenty-eight) who were divorced on admission; another 89 (32 per cent) of those interviewed after release who stated that they were married said their marriage had broken up. 55 per cent of these 89 said the marriage broke up more than two years before the offence which sent them to Kingston; 9 per cent said the break-up occurred while they were inside; 7 per cent, when they got home; 10 per cent, soon after their arrest. Therefore 19 per cent of this 89 felt that arrest and the time inside coincided with the break-up of their marriages. Unfortunately we did not find out whether they saw the arrest as the straw that broke the camel's back or as a major calamity that broke up an otherwise on-going marriage.

Only half of the parolees returned to live with their wives on release. By the end of twelve months, however, a nearly similar proportion of parolees had set up common-law unions or new marriages. Of those parolees who would be arrested within twenty-four months, a consistently higher proportion were single than for the total population of parolees. Similarly, the proportion of those married and living with their wives was approximately 10 per cent less.

It has been suggested by a number of authors who stress the importance of transition problems that there are major let-downs when the ex-prisoner arrives in the community. Skolnick (1960), in his developmental theory of parole, suggests that prisoners' anticipations of relationships that they will have with their parole supervisors in the community are important, given certain other conditions, to the adjustment they make in the community. This hypothesis might be transposed to their relationships with their wives. To try to investigate this area further the ex-prisoner was asked if his marriage was going as he expected it would before he was released. Of the 72 persons to whom this question applied, 46 per cent said that it had gone as they expected, and that they were happy or that it had gone well. 18 per cent said it had been strange or difficult at first but had gone better since then and 11 per cent mentioned that they had come out to find their wives living with somebody else. Some of these were parolees who on release had found, to their surprise, that their wives were living in the US, planning divorce or thinking of separating. Of the remainder, 14 per cent mentioned items such as 'his wife had the baby of another man though he was prepared to accept it' or 'problems due to the fact that he did not have a job'; 6 per cent, such things as 'he didn't expect to be back with his wife but they are together now,' or he was planning to get married to his common-law wife. Two out of three who went back to a wife felt that their families had changed since they were arrested, a few mentioning that the children had grown up. The remainder remarked on changes that they felt had taken place in their wives; 15 per cent said that their wives spoke up for themselves much more than before as a result of learning to manage on their own.

In the six-month questionnaire the ex-prisoner was asked to think back to his expectations of married life before being released and compare these with his experience. Often the comments from the ex-prisoners were not explicit, although the majority thought marriage had gone as they expected, and approximately one in four said it had gone better. Only one in three of the parolees who were married were able to recall ways in which the marriage had worsened, some reasons given being as 'lack of contact,' 'loss of thread,' 'more problems,' and 'inability to communicate.'

In an attempt to identify the strong points of his marital relationship, the ex-prisoner was asked what made marriage worthwhile for him. One-third of the parolees said companionship and love for each other, and one-third mentioned family life – wife and children. A wide range of other responses were mainly concerned with the feelings of being wanted and needed by another person.

An attempt was made to try to understand the nature of the major problem areas between the ex-prisoner and his wife. One out of three of both groups felt that there were none. Those there were mainly concerned money, jealousy, or various problems related to the ex-prisoner's employment situation.[2] Although they began after release, most of these major problems from then on were not seen as occurring at any particular point in time. In one in five of the marriages they resulted in disputes that led either to the wife walking out or to violence between the husband and wife.

In the twelve-month questionnaire, the ex-prisoner was asked, 'you must have been thinking about married life before coming out. Has it gone as expected?' The interviewer also asked what things were going well. These questions were applicable to 40 per cent of the parolees and 28 per cent of the dischargees, of whom three dischargees and two parolees had just married. Having the companionship of another person who cared for them was again one of the main things that made marriage worthwhile, although some mentioned amusement and interest in their children. A small group cited the convenience of sexual relations, particularly within a common law union. There was also some concern as to how long the marriage would last.

Children

At twelve months, 30 per cent of the parolees and 40 per cent of the dischargees with children had not seen them more than once a month since release. Approximately one in five were not able to see their children. This may influence post-release behaviour. Firstly, the child may be a link with the straight community helping the ex-prisoner to avoid situations that might lead to his arrest. Likewise, a child may be the thread that keeps a faltering marriage together.

Of the whole group, 18 per cent of the dischargees and 37 per cent of the parolees were seeing one or more children.[3]

What were the children told about their father's whereabouts during his incarceration? 52 per cent of the children (this included many whom the prisoner would not see on a regular basis after release) were told the truth; 22 per cent that their father was ill or had gone overseas with the army. In 10 per cent of the cases, the older children were told the truth and the younger ones that their father was in hospital. In 14 per cent of the cases, the ex-prisoner did not know what his children knew; 2 per cent said the other kids on the street had told them the truth.

The mother had supported the children during the prison term in a number of different ways. More of the dischargees' wives had had to resort to welfare or children's aid. However, 30 per cent of each group had supported their children through work. It is often suggested that a prison sentence does more than punish the offender; it can create hardships for the wife and children who may have to go on welfare and it removes the 'father figure' from the family. Where the man returns to the family long-term debilitating effects resulting from his removal appear to occur in only a minority of cases.

Family of Origin

It appears that the ex-prisoner may have been before conviction and is rejected by normal society with regard to employment and friends. 22 per cent of the parolees and 39 per cent of the dischargees were living alone. However, 40 per cent of the parolees and 38 per cent of the dischargees were living with parents or relatives. (Those parolees living with parents or relatives during their first five weeks from release were more likely to be arrested within twelve months.) How important were the men's relationships with their families?

At one month, nearly two out of three of the ex-prisoners described their relationships with their mothers as close or very close. One in four of the parolees described it as average, and one in four of the dischargees as difficult or said that they had not heard from them for a long time. 29 per cent of the parolees described their relationships with their fathers as average and 40 per cent of the dischargees and 24 per cent of the parolees as difficult, very difficult, or said they had not heard from him for some time.

At twelve months, though one in four of the ex-prisoners were not seeing their mothers, nearly one in three were seeing them at least twice a week; there were more dischargees than parolees doing so. About one in five could not see them because they were living abroad, not in Ontario, or were dead. In contrast, 14 per cent of the dischargees and 21 per cent of the parolees were seeing their fathers at least twice a week. Approximately 1 in five of both groups saw elder brothers; 14 per cent of the parolees and 9 per cent of the dischargees, younger brothers. One in five were seeing elder sisters and one in ten, younger sisters. A few saw other relatives, but not regularly. It appears, then, that the relationship with the mother is indeed strong, insofar as frequency of contact can measure this.

Close Friends

It seems reasonable to suppose that the person(s) an ex-prisoner describes as a very close or 'best' friend might have some influence on post-release behaviour. One in five denied having any friends at all and many said there was no one they would describe as a 'best' friend. In the cases where there was a close friend, 40 per cent identified an ordinary 'square' citizen, a neighbour, or a couple.[4] 12 per cent of the dischargees and 5 per cent of the parolees mentioned persons known to have criminal records; 6 per cent men with whom they worked; 8 per cent of the parolees compared to 4 per cent of the dischargees mentioned girlfriends who could not be defined as common-law wives. The remaining responses included a sponsor from Alcoholics Anonymous, boss, foreman or a colleague at work, and, in 14 per cent of the cases, father-in-law. 3 per cent of the parolees named their parole supervisors as best friends; while this was an indicator of a real and important benefit to the parolee, it also reflected his extreme loneliness. All these parole supervisors were individuals who took the job out of the office and were prepared to make personal sacrifices to help the parolees.

32 per cent of the dischargees and 38 per cent of the parolees at six months, and 50 per cent of the dischargees and 59 per cent of the parolees at twelve months, were not able to identify best friends. It is not clear if this progression is due to factors associated with the passage of time; does the ex-prisoner realize that those whom he defined as his best friends were in fact just trying to be helpful after release and that the relationships were not enduring? Or alternatively, is this of an artificial nature due to the differences in the proportions of the ex-prisoners who co-operated at six months and twelve months? The rest (approximately 45 per cent) mentioned a man they worked with (10 per cent); a father-in-law, brother-in-law (7 per cent); a girlfriend (8 per cent); another inmate (22 per cent).

Many of these friends were already known to the ex-prisoner before he was admitted to Kingston Penitentiary. However, of those friendships made since then, one in two of the dischargees and one in three of the parolees had met their friends in the penitentiary during sentence. One in four of the dischargees and two out of five of the parolees had met their friends at their places of employment. By twelve months, fewer of the ex-prisoners still free had met their best friends in the penitentiary, while more of the ex-prisoners had, for example, met them on the job and at home.

Prisoners use the term Square John frequently. This usually describes a person who goes out to work, has a family, and does not steal. 42 per cent of the ex-prisoners said that they did not know nor had they tried to meet Square Johns. Within five weeks 12 per cent said they knew only Square Johns; 10 per cent mentioned the men with whom they worked. 4 per cent said they had tried to find friends but did not elaborate how or whom, and 3 per cent said that they had tried but could find no one. 38 per cent of the dischargees and 60 per cent of the parolees at six months, and 58 per cent of the dischargees and 65 per cent of the parolees at twelve months described their best friends as Square Johns.

Handling Undesirable Associates

Quite a number of dischargees who were living in large urban areas, such as Toronto, could be found relatively easily through certain hotels that are well-known to ex-prisoners (and presumably to the police). One of the more important reasons why ex-prisoners go to these hotels is that they are places where a person with a record (particularly from a penitentiary) who has pulled off worthwhile 'scores' has some prestige. Secondly, many feel very lonely on release and they are almost certain to find someone they know, or at least someone for company for an evening. As the dischargee has a longer history of frequent imprisonment, he is less likely to be in a position to choose alternatives to these sorts of hotels for finding friends or acquaintances.

Ex-prisoners emphasized that people who really want to go straight make special efforts to avoid their old associates. We asked if they tried to avoid any of their pre-arrest friends after release. 47 per cent of the parolees and 34 per cent of the dischargees said that they were deliberately trying to avoid all of their friends from before. Only 16 per cent of these parolees said that, in terms of the Parole Agreement, their parole would be revoked if they were seen with such persons. At six months ex-prisoners were asked the same question. There was a slight but non-significant tendency for more parolees (48 per cent) than dischargees (37 per cent) to be making more effort to avoid these people. The responses to this question suggest that the threat in the parole conditions only stopped about 16 per cent from being 'seen' with 'undesirable' associates.

At the one-month stage, 44 per cent of the dischargees told the interviewer that they had both desirable and undesirable associates, whereas only 20 per cent could say they had desirable associates only. From three months, nearly 50 per cent of those who would be arrested within the first twenty-four months, compared to 25 per cent of the total, were described by their parole supervisors as associating with desirable *and* undesirable associates. For the arrested sub-group the proportion increased from 15 per cent to 47 per cent within the first three months, showing that the parolee can pick up such associations very quickly after release.

At the one-month stage a fair proportion of ex-prisoners had met other ex-prisoners, but for the most part the encounters had been brief. At the six-month stage every dischargee interviewed had met someone he knew from the penitentiary. In contrast, there were 15 per cent of the parolees who said that they had still not met other ex-inmates. The parolees were rather more likely to limit the conversation to 'hi-good-bye,' or, 'how have things been going,' rather than to discuss a particular problem such as finding a job.

Meeting People

For both parolees (30 per cent) and dischargees (20 per cent) there was a steady proportion with no girlfriends. During the first three months there was a gradual increase in the proportion of parolees described as having steady or occasional girlfriends. For the dischargees, the proportion of those describing themselves as dating occasionally declined from 40 per cent at the one-month stage to only 20 per cent at the twelve-month stage. There was also a gradual increase from 18 per cent to 25 per cent who said they had steady girlfriends.

Generally speaking, it took nearly three months before parole supervisors knew about parolees' girlfriends or other associates. This is probably only natural as the parolee takes time after release to seek out his old friends or find new ones. 10 per cent of the parolees were described as having no associates.

It was expected that the ex-prisoner might have problems in getting to know people. However, four out of five of the ex-prisoners claimed that they had no difficulty. Significantly fewer (35 per cent) parolees than (54 per cent) dischargees said that they felt lonely. These figures remained constant throughout the twelve months. These proportions, however, are not surprising in view of what we found out earlier about the parolee's family and living situation. Did they have any trouble making friends because they were 'ex-cons'? 82 per cent of the ex-prisoners replied 'No.' 5 per cent said that the penitentiary had hurt them so much or that they had spent so much time inside that they now found it difficult to make friends; 2 per cent said that they were not sure, and 1 per cent mentioned being turned down by people who did not want to associate with them. By twelve months less than 10 per cent of the ex-prisoners said that they had had any trouble making friends, but if they did, they said it was because of the unfriendly natures of some people. Many of those who had had no difficulty said that they avoided meeting new people and that their friends had known for some time that they had records.

Spare Time

In view of the fact that a need for excitement was cited as one of the reasons why some of the men committed offences, we thought it important to find out how the ex-prisoner spent his spare time.

He was asked if he now felt any need for some sort of excitement. About one in three of both groups did. In addition, at one month, 54 per cent of the dischargees and 34 per cent of the parolees mentioned feeling bored, although there were fewer who felt this way at twelve months. For the dischargee, no relationship was found between these two items, whereas the parolee who was bored had a distinct tendency to say that he was in need of excitement. Perhaps this is because there tend to be more dischargees who are unsupported by friends and family and who have little desire to do anything, but are also unhappy; we see them as basically more depressed.

Only 21 per cent had an idea of the kind of excitement they wanted. In that group 22 per cent mentioned a job; 25 per cent a good party; 17 per cent, sports of some kind; 10 per cent, a girl; 10 per cent, getting away for a weekend. The remaining 19 per cent wanted to take their wives out, find some physical and mental outlet, save money, stay on parole, meet people, or just do what they were doing or live well.

At five weeks, three out of five interviewed had spent a night out since release. Dischargees had been out more often and tended to spend more on these occasions although this was not surprising as they were not bound by the terms of a parole agreement. Although there was a group of parolees who went out frequently, the general trend suggests that the majority, at least at the one-month stage, was making conscious efforts to make a go of their marriages, find jobs and stay away from what might be troublesome situations.

How does the ex-prisoner generally spend his spare time? In

response to our question, about 24 per cent said that they usually spent their time at home alone watching television, listening to the radio, reading, or something of this nature. Smaller numbers went out with a girlfriend, or friends, to sports events, took walks alone, or were participating in AA programmes.

On admission to the penitentiary the prisoner was virtually forced by the admitting officer to claim some religious denomination. At the one-month stage he was asked if he currently attended any church. More than 83 per cent said that they did not or had not as yet. 7 per cent had been to Catholic churches, 2 per cent United, and 2 per cent Anglican. Less dischargees (7 per cent) than parolees (19 per cent) claimed to have attended some church.

Indicators of Detachment

It seems important to emphasize that the ex-prisoner lacks a positive attachment to society; he is in a state not of motivation to commit crime, but of lack of motivation *not* to commit crime (or avoid fights, drink in moderation, not use drugs, not get himself into debt, and save). While some of these seem to be related to re-arrest, all of them reflect his general social or personal situation.

FIGHTS

It is difficult to know if ex-prisoners are involved in fights any more than others who live in the same area. However, at both one and twelve months, 20 per cent of the parolees and 45 per cent of the dischargees admitted that they have been involved in one or more fights since release. 44 per cent of both groups thought that they had quick tempers. About one in five at one month, and one in three at twelve months said that they got involved as a result of drinking, although some were justified in terms of the protection of manhood or the reputation of a girl.

DRINKING

A number of questions concerned the ex-prisoner's attempts, if any, to deal with a potential alcohol problem, as well as the extent of his alcohol usage before his prison sentence and at the one-month stage. 25 per cent of the dischargees compared to 37 per cent of the parolees had gone to AA meetings in the institution. In this study we used a scale taken from some work done by Guze *et al.* (1962) in the United States to investigate the extent of their involvement with alcohol or 'alcoholism.' At the time of admission approximately three out of five ex-prisoners were described as having no problem with alcohol. Table 7.1 shows the pro-

TABLE 7.1

Alcoholism classification made on admission to penitentiary, by interview on one-month questionnaire, and by mode of release

	Dischargees						Parolees					
	Not interviewed		Interviewed		Total		Not interviewed		Interviewed		Total	
	no.	%	no.	%	no.	%	no.	%	no.	%	no.	%
Alcoholic	14	15.9	11	8.8	25	11.7	1	5.3	16	8.4	17	8.1
Problem drinker	33	37.5	36	28.8	69	32.4	4	21.0	59	30.9	63	30.0
No problem	41	46.6	78	62.4	119	55.9	14	73.7	116	60.7	130	61.9
Total	88		125		213		19		191		210	

TABLE 7.2

Frequency of drinking outside the home after release, by mode of release (one month)

	Dischargees		Parolees		Total	
Abstain or drinks rarely at home	10	9.3%	31	17.9%	41	14.6%
Rarely	20	18.5%	50	28.9%	70	24.9%
Once or twice a week	20	18.5%	46	26.6%	66	23.5%
More than three times a week	38	35.2%	15	8.7%	53	18.9%
Not specific, or evasive	20	18.5%	31	17.9%	51	18.1%
Total	108		173		281	
No responses available	17		19		36	
Not interviewed	88		18		106	

$\chi^2 = 35.13$; $df = 4$; $p < 0.001$ (one-tailed test)

portions co-operating in one-month interviews by mode of release, and penitentiary service definition of alcohol as problem. The distributions among the three categories are identical for parolees and dischargees. It is particularly interesting, then, that at the time of the one-month interview fewer dischargees (27 per cent) than parolees (42 per cent) saw themselves as having had problems with alcohol before admission. The parole board apparently prefers to parole those who have identified such a problem and have taken steps, such as going to AA meetings, to control it. 11 per cent of the dischargees and only 4 per cent of parolees still felt it was a problem at one month from release, compared to 13 per cent and 28 per cent respectively who said it was not.

Again we see that dischargees tend, perhaps as a result of few family ties, to be involved in behaviour that is thought to be closely associated with crime. 9 per cent of the dischargees and 18 per cent of the parolees said thay did not drink. Table 7.2 shows that 35 per cent of the dischargees compared to only 9 per cent of the parolees went out for a drink more that three times a week. Once again the differences in the distribution of the groups' responses were highly significant.

At six months, one in ten dischargees and one in four parolees said that they did not go out of their homes to drink, and by twelve months one in five of the total had still not done so. On the other hand, at six months, for one in five ex-prisoners, drinking was one of the principal social and recreational activities. By twelve months three out of four dischargees and two out of five parolees went out drinking at least once a week.

At one month, the parolee who goes out drinking is significantly more likely to be accompanied by his wife, whereas the dischargee is more likely to go alone. At six months the parolees were less likely than dischargees to go out drinking, to go out at least once a week, to do so with a friend, and even more likely to be with their wives.

DRUGS

Drug use often has been thought to be a factor contributing to crime and recidivism. 21 per cent of the dischargees, compared to 7 per cent of the parolees, had used some drug other than alcohol since their release. With the exception of one dischargee who had used heroin, all those had used marijuana either alone or in combination with barbiturates, LSD, or morphine, and only a few used drugs with any regularity. However, many more had used drugs after release than before, probably as a result of the general increase in the non-medical use of drugs in Ontario at the time of this study. Still, their use by the sample was relatively infrequent; there would very likely be more users in any prison population studied after 1968 as a concomitant of the increase in convictions for drug offences.

INVOLVEMENT WITH PSYCHIATRISTS

We asked the ex-prisoners about any previous involvement with psychiatrists or psychologists, assistance received from the penitentiary psychiatric services, and suicide attempts.

It is frequently suggested that those who commit crimes are psychologically disturbed. The work of Lombroso (see Mannheim, 1965, 214–21) is often seen as the precursor of the approach that views the criminal from a psychiatric perspective. Looking at the other side of the coin theorists have suggested that the institutions themselves may produce psychiatric abnormalities in their inmates. A number of sociologists have theorized that persons who consult a psychiatrist are almost certainly going to be defined by him as having some psychiatric abnormality, real or unreal, and that this identification may intensify the 'abnormality.' Certain prescription drugs may also be used in an attempt to alleviate the symptoms of 'psychiatric illness.'

Pilot discussions indicated that ex-prisoners often felt that their behaviour was 'inexplicable' and that what they needed was a psychiatrist to provide the 'instant cure.' On the other hand, however, 'madness' was rarely mentioned as a reason for involvement in crime. In this study 45 per cent said they had seen psychiatrists or psychologists at some time before their last arrest. One in five had before age 18, and one in three before age twenty-five. These proportions for the most part reflect the number of ex-prisoners who have served time previously. Some of those who were considered to have had psychiatric problems at an earlier age went on to become penitentiary prisoners at later stages in their life. It is not possible to go beyond speculation on such identification by psychiatric services. It appears that some of the same factors that led the men to psychiatrists at an earlier age may also lead to their arrest. These factors may have more to do with the inability of the family or community to cope with the man, rather than with any 'psychiatric abnormality.'

The ex-prisoner was asked whether he had ever been in the psychiatric unit in Kingston Penitentiary. 85 per cent of the dischargees and 95 per cent of the parolees replied that they had not. He was also asked whether he had ever seen the psychiatrist there, and whether the psychiatrist was able to help him. About half of both groups had seen the psychiatrist. 30 per cent who had asked for help felt they had got nothing in return. For the most part, however, 'help' was seen as the prescription of pills to relieve anxiety, 'therapy chats,' the identification of an alcohol problem, aid in getting permission to transfer from one institution, or one cell block, to another. It seems clear, from the ex-prisoner's point of view, that while the institutional psychiatric services may help the inmate weather his sentence, they are highly unlikely to bring about changes that could affect post-release behaviour.

When asked if they had ever attempted suicide, 11 per cent of those interviewed claimed that they had at some time in their life. Two out of three dischargees, and three out of four parolees who had attempted suicide claimed that they had meant to kill themselves. Over half of these attempts had occurred while the persons were inside. Outside, some reasons were that their wives were with other men, they 'were drunk,' or reasons that could not be recalled because the attempt had occurred when they were considerably younger.

Having explained that everyone has areas in which they feel inadequate or unable to do things as they would like, we asked the men at the twelve-month stage, 'Would you tell me what you think are the inadequacies of the ex-prisoner'? The great majority of the items typified the ex-prisoner as lacking confidence and being insecure. 50 per cent of the dischargees and 40 per cent of the parolees gave these kinds of responses. [5] When asked whether they had similar inadequacies one in two said that they did and one in four denied them. Again, the overriding theme in the way ex-prisoners saw both other ex-prisoners and themselves was lack of confidence.

Returning to Crime

A number of questions we asked were specifically concerned with factors that might be important in terms of returning to crime. Had anyone encouraged them to engage in criminal activities? The following are approximate percentages:

No one had	75 parolees	59 dischargees
Other ex-convicts	18	27
Evasive	4	6
Thought of it themselves	1	6

As might be expected from the general distribution of crimes committed in the first place, the main types of offence considered at this time were 'breaking and entering' or 'armed robbery'; 46 per cent of the dischargees and 41 per cent of the parolees mentioned these two. 9 per cent of the dischargees and 7 per cent of the parolees mentioned various types of white-collar offences, and 11 per cent of the parolees, as compared to none of the dischargees, mentioned smuggling marijuana from the United States.

The ex-prisoner was asked if the police always suspected him when an offence occurred in his area. While two out of three of both groups replied that they felt threatened when an offence occurred in their area, only 43 per cent of the parolees and 55 per cent of the dischargees felt that they would actually be suspected in this particular situation.

Typically, the dischargee was less reluctant to admit that he could get reinvolved in property offences. Those who were not already arrested at the time of the one-month interview were asked how large a pay-off they would need to commit another property offence. The approximate percentage response was as follows:

Not interested, whatever the pay-off	63 parolees	45 dischargees
Would have to be more than $10,000	19	10
Less than $10,000	6	16
Less than $1,000	1	12

Others said that it was not a question of pay-off but rather that the offence be a very sure thing. Another indication of the differential readiness of the two groups to be involved in property offences was whether or not they could think of a situation in which they would steal from a friend. 20 per cent of the dischargees were able to think of such a situation compared to only 5 per cent of the parolees.

Habitual Offender Provisions

The *raison d'être* of the habitual offender provisions in the Criminal

Code of Canada are twofold; first, to protect society by incarcerating the offender for long periods; secondly, to deter (one hopes) potential offenders by making it clear that society can have total power over the offender if he continues in crime.

To be sentenced to preventive detention as an habitual criminal a man must recently have been convicted of an indictable offence; secondly, it must be expedient for the protection of the public; and thirdly, he must be found to be an habitual criminal, in that: '(a) since attaining 18 years of age, he must have been convicted on 3 separate and independent occasions of indictable offences to which he was liable to imprisonment of at least 5 years; (b) he must be persistently leading a criminal life' (Harrington and Devine, 1967). These provisions seem to have been applied consistently only in Vancouver, though there are other cases across Canada (Lynch, 1967). Once under preventive detention a man is held indefinitely with an annual review by the National Parole Board, which, by 1967, had released 42 of the 116 persons convicted since 1947.

On the basis of current offence, previous convictions, and way of life a large proportion of the ex-prisoners in this study could be legally defined by a court as 'habitual offenders.' It was, therefore, of interest to see to what extent they were familiar with the details of these sections of the Code and whether this might affect their behaviour. 49 per cent of the dischargees and 31 per cent of the parolees knew what the provisions were, although 22 per cent of the parolees and 9 per cent of the dischargees did not know them in detail. Although the ex-prisoners generally knew the number of convictions required, they were less clear about how serious the offences had to be. A major element in these provisions is that the accused engages in a life of crime persistently. Only 8 per cent mentioned things that might be interpreted as a 'persistent' life of crime although 12 per cent mentioned never having worked. Of more interest is that only two mentioned that the provisions are only invoked in British Columbia. When asked what the possible sentence for an habitual offender was, 12 per cent were vague or did not know, and 80 per cent specified indefinite or life sentences. The ex-prisoner was also asked if the Act worried him. 80 per cent of the parolees replied that it did not, compared to 62 per cent of the dischargees. With two out of three dischargees arrested within twenty-four months, it seems clear that these provisions are not, in fact, much of a 'deterrent.' (It has been suggested that they may be used to obtain guilty pleas.)

Prison as a Deterrent

Those who sentence offenders are rarely required to provide justifications for action taken; a sentence is probably given because it is consistent with other sentences for similar offences, rather than as a deterrent or a rehabilitative measure (also questionable in so far as prison terms are concerned). Recently, sentencing seminars and researchers have begun to ask sentencers to provide reasons for their sentences. Typical reasons provided by the legal minded are deterrence or rehabilitation, perhaps because they avoid any mention of retribution, a principle which underlies most sentencing practice and legislation, at least in the English-speaking world. While Hogarth (1971) accounts for disparities in sentences among Ontario magistrates that he studied, nowhere does he account for these in absolute terms.

For many ex-prisoners the ideas of going straight, returning to crime, and the fear of prison are all components of their conceptualization of the world. 32 per cent interviewed at one month said that they would indeed be restrained from committing further crime by the fear of returning to the penitentiary; on the other hand, 10 per cent of the parolees and 34 per cent of the dischargees replied that nothing would restrain them.

The parolee is more inclined to mention other aspects of his life situation and experience than prison as reasons for going straight. Positive things that were felt to help keep a person from crime were wife, family, children or persons in a similar relationship (20 per cent); a man's own determination to go straight (10 per cent); money and a good, steady job (10 per cent); finding something so interesting that he would not step outside the law (3 per cent); and common sense (3 per cent).

The ex-prisoner was asked which of the four sub-systems – the courts, police, prison or parole – would restrain him most from committing crime. Of those who did so, 65 per cent of the dischargees and 53 per cent of the parolees said prison first. In contrast, parole was fourth for 64 per cent of the parolees and 67 per cent of the dischargees. Penitentiary, then, is viewed, at least on the verbal level, by the majority of ex-prisoners as an unpleasant experience which would motivate them to avoid returning to crime (or getting caught) whereas parole is of little relevance.

These answers would indicate that the sentencer and sentenced believe in, to some extent, the same myths of our society and, in this case, the myth of the deterrent effect of prison. It could be easily argued, however, that while the sentencer believes that prison deters, the sentenced are deterred, not from crime, but from getting caught.[6]

Why is prison not a deterrent? In offences committed in conjunction with the use of alcohol (a substantial group) or as a result of loss of emotional control, the future potential 'pain' of prison is likely to be forgotten. More generally, however, deterrence may not be a relevant concept for the type of person in a penitentiary. It may be much more important to know what could be done to help the ex-prisoner keep away from situations that are likely to lead to criminal activity. This attempt at containment is possibly a function of parole, where parole helps him find a job or control a drinking problem (although not by means of an Abstinence Clause). This will be considered in more detail in the next chapter.

Zimring (1971) has pointed out that an offender's attitude towards punishment can change in two ways. The punishment may be 'corrective' in the sense that once having experienced it the offender is careful to avoid it in the future. The alternative attitude, however, is a general callousness towards the punishment. There is no doubt that the ex-prisoners see it in both of these ways. Most ex-prisoners in fact experience prison as unpleasant; many of them say that it would have some effect in restraining them from committing crime. But, at the same time, many of them are able to name a pay-off which would justify their reinvolvement in offences. Just as convincing as their own discussion of their attitudes towards punishment are the actual changes in their behaviour, with three out of four dischargees and one out of two parolees being arrested within two years. It is hard to believe that the threat of prison is a very real deterrent for the men in our sample, certainly, and others probably. Actually it is surprising that more ex-prisoners are not arrested earlier. (The chapter on arrest rates implies that arrest is more a function of chance factors associated with policing than of variations in the behaviour of the ex-prisoners themselves.)

Many ex-prisoners with neither wives nor friends would like to 'make it' in terms of such relatively simple things as having the marital and friendly companionship of the ordinary working man. These are quite possibly the very bonds that help prevent re-involvement even in situations where there is 'heat' from police. It can certainly be argued that the ex-prisoner is, to some extent, sometimes, a 'rejected' person, although whether this rejection results from his own characteristics or from having been inside (both of which can be part of a vicious circle) is not clear. It does, however, seem unlikely that it is mainly the result of characterization by the criminal justice system.

Because we cannot know the 'cause' it is difficult to see where changes should be made in the relationship between the rejected and the rest of the world. It might be that a high-paying or otherwise rewarding job and children in a marriage, which would tend to strengthen job, marital and friendship stability respectively, could reduce the probability of rejection. An alternative strategy might be to compensate the employer, or provide some benefit to the wife – to put them in a position where they would be less inclined to reject. Finally, one could make the one who tends to be rejected less likely to be by giving him a job skill and helping him with his interpersonal relations.

NOTES TO CHAPTER 7

1 See Hirschi (1969) for a summary of these points of view and the presentation of an alternative

2 The other problems included: wife ran around while he was in jail; a feeling that marriage was already over; nothing in common; drinking father-in-law; the two partners were too independent; fights; the wife's drinking. One wife had threatened to report her husband to the National Parole Board.

3 There were no differences between the parolees and dischargees with respect to number of children they had. 39 per cent had only one child; 25 per cent had two children; 9 per cent three; 11 per cent four; 9 per cent five; and 7 per cent six or more.

4 Unfortunately the direct probe as to whether this person had been convicted was not included in the question and a number of persons were coded in this category who might have had criminal records.

5 The ex-prisoner has no place to go, no family, no home, is alienated from the outside world, is not accepted, is looked down upon, is stigmatized because of his record, and so is unable to get a job. Some also said that they had no money, were unable to keep jobs, feared going back, were illiterate, bitter, and felt a need to seek revenge on society for the time in the institution

6 Semi-professional offenders who, for instance, have been engaged in planned burglary or fraud, were careful to minimize their chances of getting caught. Some mentioned to us a code of ethics similar to rules required by pilots before flights – no drinking within eight hours of the commission of an offence, gloves to be worn at all times in inspecting and working in the premises, no bragging or ostentatious use of money acquired by offences. Some of these men had stable marriages and tended to be employed during the day as a 'cover' for their other activities. They enjoyed extremely long periods of freedom from both suspicion and finally arrest. Their reasons for involvement in crime were usually financial. With semi-professional offenders the deterrent effect of prison was irrelevant to the commission of offences, but it was strong encouragement to keep the offences fool-proof. They were usually caught for offences where their code of ethics had not been followed. And when these offenders made mistakes they knew of ways of either avoiding conviction or minimizing the sentence.

8

Parole From Prison

One argument 'for' parole is that it provides a control over men released from prison. The supervisor sees the parolee regularly and so the community is protected. How often does the parolee see the supervisor? Do these contacts take place in the supervisor's office? Does the supervisor know what is going on? We will see in the first part of this chapter that control through surveillance is limited in both quantity and quality. It seems, however, that in general the Ontario parole officer sees his function as the provision of assistance, which, hopefully, leads to rehabilitation and ultimately the protection of society. In the second part of this chapter we will look at the 'assistance,' 'service' or 'counselling' provided; the extent to which the parolee establishes a relationship with the supervisor; whether supervisor and parolee agree on the goals of their relationship. In the third part of the chapter we will look at the ways in which the parolee's social situation changes during the course of the first twelve months.

Parolees' Perceptions of Parole

Questions that attempted to find out how parole might have made a difference to the parolee's behaviour were worded in such a way as to encourage the ex-prisoner to mention the parole supervisor or the conditions of his parole. Parolees were also asked specific questions concerning their parole experience. Glaser (1964) has suggested, in the United

States Federal Prison System, that because prospective parolees meet only those who fail on parole there is a negatively biased perception of parole inside the institutions. However, in Canada in 1968, parole occurred within a definite sentencing structure so that only a proportion of inmates were paroled and often only for a short period of time; at least some of the inmates, then, had survived parole previously before being reconvicted after the parole period was terminated. Still, many impressions of parole may have been negative. Whether or not negative perceptions of parole supervisors affect the number who apply, they may affect adjustment on parole, as Skolnick (1960) has suggested.

Of the parolees, 54 per cent had previously been on some form of parole from training schools, reformatories, or penitentiaries. They were asked if anything was different about being released on parole this time. 54 per cent mentioned supervision, police reporting, or both; 9 per cent did not mention anything; the remaining responses were highly individualistic. 11 per cent mentioned positive aspects of parole including 'more freedom,' 'parole supervision being great,' 'having someone interested in him.' 3 per cent said that the parole restrictions were beneficial to them; 10 per cent said there were no similarities, especially as they were not free to quit jobs.

Of the seventy-six men interviewed who were on parole for the first time, two out of three said that there was much more freedom on parole than they had expected. One in four mentioned that it differed from their expectations in that they had not known what to expect, or else they thought that it was better. Only two mentioned that they did not expect so much aggravation from their parole officers.

The general feeling of parolees was that supervision was of little assistance, though a minority disagreed. It could be that parole affects the ex-prisoner's behaviour by the threat of sanctions such as suspension or revocation; alternatively the parole supervisor could act as some kind of intangible 'super-ego' for the parolee.

Parole as Deterrence

In pilot interviews, some parolees said that the existence of the parole supervisor acted as some sort of deterrent from crime: in response to the systematic questions, 33 per cent confirmed this; 49 per cent, however, said that they thought that he did not; 8 per cent thought that he did not because it was up to the parolee himself; 4 per cent thought that the supervisor performed a deterrent function to a degree; 3 per cent did not know.

Some parolees mentioned the threat of suspension or revocation as a reason for not engaging in particular types of behaviour. It will be shown that at least associations, leaving the restricted area and employment are all apparently affected by the parole agreement. It is important to remember that the interpretation of the parole agreement itself is subject to the discretion of the parole supervisor. This interpretation is likely to be a function both of the parole supervisor and the problems that the parolee presents.

We asked the parolee to name the parole rules. They recalled, with few exceptions, reporting to parole supervisor and police, and not leaving the area. More than two out of three of the parolees also remembered buying a motor vehicle, incurring debts or buying on credit; reporting change of address; not drinking (this is not a standard condition – see Appendix A), getting married, and associating with undesirables. When some specific parole rules were read out to the parolees, 20 per cent still said that abstinence was not a parole rule, and 10 per cent mentioned that associations were not. Although 13 per cent of the parolees thought that curfew was in the parole agreement, the majority knew that it was not a parole rule; 4 per cent also thought that incurring debts was not a parole rule. Rules such as informing the parole officer if he was stopped by police, undergoing psychiatric treatment, buying fire-arms, going to work and changing employment, were all mentioned by less than 10 per cent of the parolees.

The parolee was also asked to say which rules were most strictly enforced. One in three said that none were strictly enforced. One in six mentioned leaving the area; another one in six, reporting to the parole officer; another one in six, no drinking; 5 per cent mentioned employment. The remainder mentioned other parole rules.

What rule did the parolees find hardest to keep? Two out of five felt that none of them was; however, one out of five mentioned not leaving the area and one in five mentioned the abstinence rule. 8 per cent mentioned not associating with undesirables; less than 5 per cent incurring debts and buying a motor vehicle. The rest of the responses were spread over the other parole rules that have been mentioned.

More than 90 per cent thought the parole rules were reasonable. Although they were not asked to give reasons if they did see them as unreasonable, one parolee thought it was silly to have rules that were not strictly enforced and another said he felt reporting for five years was unreasonable. In addition 10 per cent of those who thought that, on the whole, the rules were reasonable, mentioned one particular one, that they did not like, such as not being free to leave the area, requiring permission for debts or marriage, and for not drinking. One parolee felt that there should be more guide-lines, particularly for a drug addict; this man was arrested for a drug offence within four weeks of his date of release.

While the dischargee is free to move when and where he wants, the parolee is bound by the parole agreement to obtain permission to move to a different area; for some, staying in the town to which they were released until the end of their parole was a clause given special emphasis. There was a distinct tendency for parolees to plan to stay longer in a certain town probably as result both of the parole agreement and the fact that more parolees were married. Those ex-prisoners not arrested at the time of the one-month interview were asked how long they would like to stay in that town. Parolees were much less likely to plan to move, particularly within the next twelve months. Only 27 per cent of the dischargees interviewed, compared to 51 per cent of the parolees said that they had thought of moving at one month. This implies than many parolees would have moved had they been released without parole conditions. Thus, although some parolees do not mind staying in their town of destination because of family or friendship ties, there are many who feel constrained to live there as a result of the parole agreement.

By twelve months, only 13 per cent of the parolees felt that the parole rules restricted them in associations. While nearly one in two had left the area only with special permission, one in five left without permission. Some parolees thought they would move on terminating parole. In general, more than half the ex-prisoners interviewed were planning to stay in the same town for at least two years; in this case there were 20 per cent more parolees than dischargees. This difference may have been larger but for the bias in the sample interviewed at twelve months. By twelve months, two out of five ex-prisoners had bought a car, although for many this meant going into debt. The restrictions on fire-arms affected less than one in five parolees. Curfew had only been used in the case of two parolees.

As far as reporting to the police was concerned, 70 per cent of the parolees felt that it made little difference, and it did not bother them. 20 per cent specifically stated that they hated or disliked it strongly. The others said something to the effect that it was an inconvenient nuisance or useless. More than 10 per cent had failed to report at some time. In all these cases they felt the action taken was reasonable; usually it was no action, or just an informal warning advising the parolee not to let it happen again.

One in four parolees at twelve months felt that they would *not* have done just as well without parole. 60 per cent said that reporting to the supervisor caused them no problem and that it had some advantages to compensate for its disadvantages. In general, they thought it was a good idea. 23 per cent described it as 'a pain in the neck,' or 'too demanding,' 'a drag,' 'useless,' or 'stupid.' Another 5 per cent thought it was basically a good idea, but not for them. The other comments were similar, often relating to individual problems, for example, that a parolee would not mind reporting to a supervisor if he had a different one; or, theoretically it was fine, but in his case it had become a complete mess; or he did not know as he had seen his supervisor so seldom that he did not even know who he was.

Up to twelve months, approximately 50 per cent of all parole rule violations that the parolee thought the supervisor knew about involved either drinking or leaving the area. Although at six months 34 per cent of the parolees admitted infractions of the parole rules compared to 53 per cent at 12 months, the number of parole rule violations reported increased by nearly 50 per cent. Two out of three infractions resulted in informal warnings by the supervisor; a further one in ten in a written warning.

Suspension and the Parole Supervisor

Does the parolee know who decides when his parole should be suspended? The word 'suspended' was emphasized in this question and explained to the parolee if he did not understand. 16 per cent refused to guess or give an opinion. Under parole regulations the decision to suspend parole was delegated to the regional representative. In practice it is the parole supervisor who is familiar with the parolee's situation and must report what he considers to be violations of the parole agreement to the regional representative, if the police do not do so first. The John Howard Society had a specific policy of forbidding its case workers from providing any recommendation as to whether parole should be suspended or not when reporting possible violations of the agreement. Although this question does not really have a right answer, undoubtedly the parole supervisor is an extremely important link in relaying information pertinent to a parole suspension decision. One in three of the parolees who believed that their parole supervisor decided when their parole should be suspended are in some sense right; similarly, the 10 per cent who mentioned the regional representative. However, one in three mentioned the parole board; unless there was confusion about whether the regional representative is part of the parole board or not, they are 'legally wrong.'

Although one in three were not sure if suspension was used fairly, 17 per cent thought that it was not, for such reasons as re-doing time they had already served on the street; 7 per cent thought that they should have been warned before suspension, or that the parolee ought to be able to defend himself. The remainder thought that, for the most part, it was used fairly.

The parolee was asked how much time he would serve if his parole was revoked. The parolee is very well aware of the time that he has to serve on parole; only three said that they did not know. Their feelings about the time that they would have to serve if their parole was revoked showed that many of the men were seriously worried about this possibility. 62 per cent made such comments as horrible, sick, or scared; 8 per cent thought that it was unfair because of serving statutory remission time; 8 per cent refused to worry about revocation; 9 per cent said they did not intend to have it happen; 3 per cent said 'if he does something that deserves it, that's his own look out.'

The Extent of Parole Supervison

For those released on parole, the parole supervisor was asked to record details of supervision, the parolee's social situation and problems and help offered on a series of seven identical questionnaires sent out by the research centre. These questionnaires covered the first seven days in the community, the first five weeks, five weeks to ten weeks, fourteen weeks to six months, six months to nine months, and nine months to twelve months. The questionnaires were developed from a content analysis of the parole service post-release reports and related information held on files in one of the agencies involved in approximately 50 per cent of the supervision of the parolees in the study. A small cross-check was carried out on information gathered by other major agencies and a brief pilot trial completed using one parolee from each of several offices in Ontario who was not included in the study. The instrument was designed to look at certain selected areas, and obtain *all* the information *all* of the time rather than *some* of the information *some* of the time as parole supervisors normally only mention a few areas.

The sample on which the analysis is based consists of 206 parolees, for 205 of whom at least one of the series of seven questionnaires was available. Some parolees terminated their parole before the end of the twelve months period. In total, less than 5 per cent of the necessary 1168 questionnaires were not returned. The main reason for not returning the questionnaires was apparently simple 'laziness.' However, other reasons included instances where the parolee changed the agency of supervision or where contact was lost because the parolee disappeared. As the missing questionnaires were spread at random over the twelve months they had little effect on the construction of general patterns over time.

Several parolees changed their parole supervisors during their first twelve months, but only a few changed agencies. Comparisons between supervisors were made using the current supervisor, though in general, the parolee's first agency has been used for breakdowns by agency.

Using the definitions of the parole board annual report in this study, 44 per cent of the parolees were supervised by a 'Social Agency,' 51 per cent by a 'Public Service' and only 6 per cent by a 'Regional Office.' 95 supervisors were involved in the supervision of 210 parolees on an average day. Of these, 70 supervisors were in one main agency and 20 in the other, where the workers also had experience with helping ex-prisoners seeking voluntary assistance.

In each questionnaire, the supervisor was asked to record the type and number of contacts made by the parole supervisor either with the parolee himself, the parolee's relatives or friends, or with other persons or agencies relating to the parolee.

Experience of Parole

Parole supervision, as experienced by this sample, was mainly in the form of face-to-face contact with the parole supervisor in the agency office. This was supplemented by occasional visits to the parolee's home and contact with his immediate family and, less frequently, contacts with employers and employment agencies. A parolee starting supervision with either agency would expect, on average, nineteen interviews with the supervisor alone in the office during the first twelve months, twelve of which would take palce in the first three months; less than five other face-to-face contacts for the parolee with family or friends, only two of which would take place in the first two months, and two of which included the parolee; less than two other contacts for the parolee, with Manpower, police or the regional representative. The full details of the types of contact recorded are presented in Table 8.1.

There is a clear pattern of contact with the parolee concentrating quantitatively over the twelve months at the beginning of parole supervision: 17 per cent of the contact took place during the first week; 33 per cent took place within the first five weeks; 63 per cent took place within the first three months. This pattern holds generally true for the other persons with whom contacts were made.

For every two face-to-face contacts there is at least one telephone call to the parolee. The distribution of such calls in terms of time is spread out more evenly than the other activities of the parole supervisor; although a third of the calls took place within the first ten weeks, a third also took place in the last six months. Even though calls were relatively infrequent, the telephone was the main form of contact with the parolee's wife, friends, the various social agencies such as Canada Manpower, the regional representative of the parole service, or the police.

In each time period covered by the questionnaires, between 10 and 25 per cent of the parolees were discussed by the parole supervisor with

TABLE 8.1

Type and number of contacts made up to the end of the twelve-month period, totalled for all parolees during their parole

Person(s) or agency contacted by parole supervisor	Face-to-face interviews: total number to nearest 10	Correspondence outgoing (letters, etc.)	Telephone calls: Total number or	Telephone calls: Number of parolees for whom calls were made
Parolee alone in office	4000	91	2300	
Parolee alone in home	320			
Parolee with wife in office	190	4	30	
Wife alone	90	0		138
Parents with parolee	30			26
Parents without parolee	70	1		44
Canada Manpower	70	3	330	
Employer	120	2	190	
Potential employers	30	1	150	
Friends	180	2		93
Police (other than reporting)	90			77
Regional representative	40			259
Other social agencies*	50			91
Other†	110			85
In-law, uncles, aunts	10			1

* Other social agency includes probation officer, lawyer, family service, welfare, church, nursery school, Clarke Institute of Psychiatry, Workmen's Compensation, Adult Education Centre, Alcoholics Anonymous

† Other includes bank, court clerk, hospital, Indian counsellor, landlord, priest, school guidance officer

a regional representative on the telephone, and between 5 and 10 per cent were the subject of calls with the police. There were minor variations between the two agencies. More of those arrested were the subject of telephone calls with the police, particularly in the six-, nine-, twelve-month period.

It was expected and found that there were differences between the two supervisory agencies, the John Howard Society and the Ontario Probation Service. These were differences in emphasis, with the former giving priority to direct contact with the parolee particularly in the first three months. However, there were no significant differences in the outcome of the paroles supervised by each agency.

Voluntary Referral for the Dischargee

According to John Howard Society information, 43 per cent of the parolees in our sample were supposed to be supervised by the Society on release. 46 per cent, however, said they had approached the John

Howard Society within a month from release. There were thus a few individual parolees who were supervised by another agency who had tried to get assistance from the John Howard Society, who refused it if they were aware of the other arrangements.

Before release a representative of the John Howard Society offers to interview the dischargee, who may refuse. If the prisoner sees the representative, he may then refuse any post-release interviews with community officers. The main purpose of these visits is to make the prisoners aware of the sort of facilities that the Society has to offer and try, if it is thought to be appropriate, to put them in contact with a local branch. Although only 33 per cent of the dischargees requested an interview after release, 46 per cent of the dischargees interviewed at the one-month stage said that they had been to a branch of the Society. Although we did not make a systematic investigation of the reasons at this stage, it was suggested that the main reason was to obtain cash, although some go hoping to find employment and a few to find someone to help them sort out the 'odd' attitudes that lead them to prison.

One of the ways we got in touch with dischargees in this study was by sending lists each month to the John Howard Society to see if they were getting assistance there. Basically, those persons who were not interviewed were those who were not arrested in Ontario, were not seen on a regular basis by the John Howard Society, did not remain in Toronto or contact acquaintances in Toronto who were already known to the study staff.

It is surprising that the proportions of both parolees and dischargees in contact with the John Howard Society is exactly the same. Neither the quality nor the quantity of the relationship, however, is similar. Less than one in four of all dischargees interviewed had been to the Society at least twice since they were released, and another one in four had been there only once. Even though the John Howard Society has a specific policy on trying to avoid giving money without any other form of assistance, it may be inferred from these figures that in fact one in four of all dischargees receives only this or a direct refusal. However, another one in four of all dischargees was voluntarily receiving assistance of the kind provided by parole supervision. Frequency of contact is also associated with the proportions of parolees (84 per cent), and dischargees (70 per cent) who said that their case-workers treated them 'like a man' or 'OK.' It is interesting to note that of those interviewed who reported going to the John Howard Society, 68 per cent were arrested within the first twelve months compared to 57 per cent of those who had not been. 60 per cent of those who had had freqent contact with the Society were re-arrested within the first twelve months compared to 76 per cent of those who had irregular contact. These differences were not significant as neither the numbers nor the implied percentage differences were large.

It was originally hoped, in view of major differences that have been found between parolees and dischargees, that the voluntary referral group would be an ideal point of comparison to see what was the effect of the threat of revocation in addition to the assistance component. However, the numbers of 'voluntary parole' were too small to compare with parolees.

Aspects of Control in Supervision

Other questions put to the parole supervisor asked for details of the parolee's co-operativeness, motivation and obedience to the supervisor's instructions. Violation of the parole agreement and any related action taken by the parole supervisor or the parole agency was also recorded.

Fifty per cent of the permissions that the parolee applied for concerned leaving the area. Approximately 10 per cent related to transferring out of the area, 10 per cent to the purchase of a motor vehicle, and another 10 per cent wanted to assume responsibilities such as marriage. There were no differences between those arrested and those not in the number of permissions requested. The distribution of permissions asked for over the twelve-month period remained constant though there was a tendency in the first week for more of the permissions granted to be concerned with leaving the area. 85 per cent of the permissions were granted for the total population, whereas only 75 per cent were granted for those subsequently arrested.

The parole supervisor was asked to say whether the parolee had abided by any instructions he had given regarding late hours, use of intoxicants, seeing unsuitable companions, operations of a motor vehicle, etc. With slight variations over the twelve-month period, 50 per cent of the parolees were recorded as having been given instructions by the parole supervisor. Approximately 70 per cent of those were general instructions; nearly 20 per cent concerned the use of intoxicants, and other main areas concerned seeing unsuitable companions and operating motor vehicles. More than 80 per cent of the total who received instructions were said to have abided by them. In the first week, nearly 100 per cent reported as keeping to the rules. Approximately 75 per cent of those persons arrested within twelve months, in contrast to 50 per cent of the total population, had been given special instructions of one sort or another from the one-month questionnaire onwards. The proportion not abiding by recorded instructions gradually increased from 30 per cent at five weeks to 78 per cent at 12 months.

Formal or informal reprimands of various kinds were given to 5 per cent of the parolees during the first week; 15 per cent, 22 per cent, and 22 per cent were given during the next succeeding one-month periods; and 34 per cent, 30 per cent, and 24 per cent during the succeeding three-monthly periods. Between 50 and 70 per cent of these reprimands were described as informal, mainly verbal, warnings made by the parole supervisor. There was a gradual increase in formal warnings from the regional representative to the parolee over the first two months to an average of 15 per cent for the remainder of the period. At as early a stage as the first month, the person who will later be arrested was more likely to be given formal or informal warnings. 33 per cent of those arrested within twelve months had received some sort of reprimand within their first month and a similar proportion during their second month.

Over the total twelve month period 1 in 5 of all formal actions taken by the parole agency were associated with questioning, arrest or charges made by the police; 12 per cent involved the parolee not abiding by special conditions of his abstinence clause (usually total abstinence); 12 per cent leaving a designated area without permission; and 11 per cent, not reporting a change or termination of employment.

In some areas of Canada there have been direct attempts by the parole service to nurture a close relationship with the police. In Montreal, for instance, during the course of this study, the regional representatives tried to involve the police in his supervision system, the overt aims being that information about parolees should flow freely between both sources. In Ontario there is little or no contact between the supervision agencies and the police. The police rarely used the parole supervisor to try to control the behaviour of the parolee. Only one parolee was given a warning by the police and only six parole supervisors were contacted by the police to inform them of activities in which the parolee had been involved.

Aspects of Assistance in Supervision

Traditionally parole supervision is seen as having three components; service, assistance, and control. We have seen the extent to which control is exercised. In this section we will consider the other two elements, which, it seems, are almost the same thing to the parolee.

The parole supervisors described approximately 85 per cent of the parolees as being both co-operative and motivated. In each time period over the twelve months, approximately 7 per cent of the parolees were described as non-co-operative or not well motivated. There is a tendency for more of the parolees to be described as co-operative or well motivated a longer time after release. For those who were arrested

TABLE 8.2

Parolee's assessment of closeness of his relationship with his supervisor, by agency at five weeks, showing proportions arrested within two years

Relationship	John Howard Society		Ontario Probation Service		National Parole Service		Total	
Close	37	45.9	27	55.5	2	50.0	66	50.0
Average	35	42.9	53	50.9	5	40.0	93	47.3
Difficult	5	80.0	4	100.0	4	75.0	13	84.6
Missing	15	35.7	22	13.6	1	100.0	38	27.0
Total	92	44.0	106	43.4	12	66.7	172	45.2

within twelve months, however, there was a sharp increase in the proportions who were described as non-co-operative and not well motivated. In this case, they jumped to 25 per cent at fourteen weeks.

Comparatively few parolees formed very close relationships with their supervisors. An attempt was made to measure the closeness of the relationship between the parolee and this supervisor, by asking each to rate the closeness or the difficulty of their relationship on a five-point scale. Both generally agreed on the quality of their relationship which suggests that this crude variable provides a valid measure of this aspect of the relationship. At the five weeks stage, 78 per cent of the parole supervisors described their relationships with each parolee as average, 18 per cent as close, and 12 per cent as difficult. None described them as very difficult and only 1 per cent said they were very close.

At twelve months, as might be expected simply because they had got to know each other better, fewer supervisors, 62 per cent, described their relationships with the parolee as average, while 25 per cent described them as close, 3 per cent as very close, 8 per cent as difficult, and 3 per cent as very difficult. The fewer in the difficult or very difficult categories was due to a tendency for these persons to be re-arrested earlier.

The John Howard Society, which prefers hiring qualified social workers and puts its caseworkers through schools of social work, seems to put more emphasis on achieving a close relationship with the parolee than either the Ontario Probation Service or the National Parole Service. For each time period the parole supervisor from the John Howard Society saw himself as having closer relationships than the supervisors from the other agencies. The same held true for parolees, who saw themselves having closer relationships with supervisors at the John Howard Society than at the Ontario Probation Service and the National Parole Service (see Table 8.2).

Those for whom the supervisory relationship was described as difficult or very difficult were significantly more likely to be arrested within the first twenty-four months (Table 8.2). As there was a high recidivism rate for those without closeness assessments available, there were no differences in the over-all recidivism rate between the John Howard Society and the Ontario Probation Service.

It seemed that certain parole supervisors were more popular than others, usually as a result of their own characteristics, not their agency's. Since there were few Ontario Probation Service officers who supervised more than one parolee it was not possible for any one of them to be termed popular. On the other had, the John Howard Society and National Parole Service officers had generally supervised several parolees. It was found that only one parole supervisor was mentioned more than once in the very close category. He was mentioned three times and had supervised seven parolees.

At both the six- and twelve-month stages the parolee was asked to say what he liked and disliked about his parole supervisor. Nearly 90 per cent at both time periods liked something about their supervisors. 40 per cent said that he was an understanding and friendly sort of guy. Another 39 per cent thought he was understanding, in addition to some other characteristic such as: honest and easy to talk to; does not probe into the personal life of the parolee; asks him to phone only every two weeks; offers help but does not push; good friend, available at any time; gives him his freedom and no restrictions. At twelve months the responses were still similar although 15 per cent said that their parole supervisors left them alone without mentioning other characteristics. At both the six- and twelve-month stages, only one out of three could find things they disliked about their parole supervisors. A quarter of the responses at the twelve-month stage mentioned that the parole supervisor adhered too closely to the rules and was not sufficiently sure of himself. The other responses in both questionnaires included things like 'dislikes the whole parole system,' 'talks too much but does not say anything,' 'parole officer would not allow him to do what he wanted to, like return to Orillia, or Toronto, when he was elsewhere,' 'makes him come too often,' 'prejudiced against the parolee because he was an Indian,' 'hard to communicate with,' 'always talking sex and psychology,' 'tape recording of interviews.'

As a further commentary on the parolee/supervisor relationship the parolee was asked if he felt he would get along better with his parole supervisor if he did not have any legal authority over him. Three out of four did not think they would. 13 per cent, however, stated that they would never have known the supervisor but for parole. A further 8 per cent felt the legal restrictions made little difference as the parole supervisor did not use these in any negative way. 7 per cent said 'yes' without specifying why. Another 6 per cent said that they could be completely free to express their own opinions, which they were not able to do within the present relationship. This question alludes only to the whole problem of one individual having power to deprive another of his liberty and, secondly, whether the individual with something to lose can ever develop an honest confidence in the other. It is probable that this makes the parolee more reticent to communicate information about this 'real' situation to the supervisor, which may force the parole agent to use persons who are close to the parolee as alternative information sources. This in turn makes the adjustment of the parolee more difficult as it becomes harder for him to discuss his 'real' feelings with those close to him. This particular aspect was not investigated in depth in this study. In addition, would a parolee with an abstinence clause in his agreement come to the parole supervisor and say 'I was drunk last night'? when he knows that legally the parole supervisor would be obliged to report this action to the regional representative who might in turn suspend his parole? Of course, it is easy to see that without this information, the supervisor cannot really help the parolee master this (or any other) problem.

TWO VIEWS OF PAROLEES' PROBLEMS HELD BY PAROLE SUPERVISORS

In the survey of parole service files it was noted that parole supervisors regularly used 'catch phrases' to describe the problems of parolees under their supervision. These 'catch phrases' were developed into a list which was included in the questionnaires completed by supervisors. Of the parolees described as having a problem at five weeks, 26 per cent had problems with personality, 20 per cent with unfulfilled expectations regarding work, wife, etc., and 17 per cent limited contact with family and 16 per cent friction with wife, parents, siblings and friends. The numbers seen to have problems increased after the first week, but there were only minor fluctuations over the remainder of the twelve-month period, and in each questionnaire approximately 30 per cent were described as having none of these problems.

As an alternative method of assessing parolees' problems, the parole supervisor was asked to rate the severity of the problem, if there was one, in ten areas. The parole supervisors checked the 'not known' category in less than 3 per cent of the cases for each of the problem areas except alcohol and drugs, where they checked between 8 and 9 per cent. The mean scores were calculated by assigning an integer from 1 through to 5 according to the severity of the problem, 1 representing most severe and 5 representing no problem. 'Not knowns' were omitted. There were also many parolees who were thought to have no problems in these various areas.

From Table 8.3 it will be seen that those men arrested within the first twelve months have consistently more severe problems in each of the areas mentioned than either those arrested in twenty-four months, the total population, or either of the sub-populations supervised by the Ontario Probation Service or the John Howard Society. (Some of those arrested within twelve months were supervised by these agencies.) On all ten items, the John Howard Society tended to identify more problems and to see those identified as more severe. Problems with alcohol and drugs, however, were rated less severely by the John Howard Society than the Ontario Probation Service. There was a marked tendency for the number of 'not knowns' to decrease in the later periods of the twelve months, as the supervisor got to know the parolee better; for instance, for 17 per cent of the parolees supervised by the John Howard Society the supervisor did not know to what extent the use of alcohol was a problem in the first week, whereas all were rated at twelve months. There was also a tendency for problems to be rated as less severe later in the time period.

For both agencies, family and personal relationships featured as the most severe problem. The John Howard Society tended to see more, and as more severe, the parolee's problems with things such as his attitude to authority and his alienation from the community. The Ontario Probation Service, on the other hand, sees alcohol, financial standing and delinquent associations as more important.

As an indication of the severity of the various problems in the population arrested within twenty-four months compared to those not arrested, the difference in the means was calculated. Not surprisingly the largest differences in the means were in patterns of criminal behaviour and of anti-social, but not yet criminal, behaviour. It seems, then, that the parole supervisor was aware of problems and should perhaps have concentrated more time on patterns of anti-social and criminal behaviour and associates in the community. When one considers this in relation to the use of revocation it becomes apparent that supervisors knew, though perhaps not fully consciously, that the parolee was going to be arrested, but were not taking the necessary action either to revoke or help them avoid arrest and new conviction.

PAROLEES' PROBLEMS ACCORDING TO HELP GIVEN BY PAROLE SUPERVISORS

In this study, we placed considerable emphasis on trying to identify what the parole supervisor and the parolee meant when they talked about 'help.' In an open-ended question placed at the end of the questionnaire,

TABLE 8.3

Parole supervisor's rating of parolee's problems – mean severity of problems at three months (on five point scale: 1 = most severe, 5 = no problem)

Rank order for total	Problem area	Total	Arrested within 12 months	Arrested within 24 months	Ontario Probation Service	John Howard Society
1	Family or personal relationships	3.58	2.89	3.50	3.92	3.19
2	Alienation from community	3.86	3.53	3.84	4.23	3.65
3	Attitude towards authority	3.88	3.08	3.66	4.23	3.51
4	Present adjustment in employment	3.95	3.53	3.75	4.20	3.98
5=	Association with delinquent or criminal element in community	3.97	3.54	4.18*	4.15	3.84
5=	Present financial standing	3.97	3.67	3.83	4.09	3.86
7	Use of alcohol	4.06	3.63	4.22	4.00	4.19
8	Pattern of criminal behaviour	4.18	3.61	4.25*	4.27	4.19
9	Pattern of antisocial behaviour not amounting to criminal behaviour	4.24	3.71	4.11	4.34	4.21
10	Use of drugs	4.48	4.11	4.92*	4.37	4.63
N approximately†		169	38	60	90	73

* 9 parolees not known

† Omitting problems not known, and questionnaires not returned

the parole supervisor was asked to list briefly the major problem areas in which he had tried to help the parolee.

The parole supervisor was also asked to record the extent to which he felt he had actually helped. As this question was the only one in which the parole supervisor was given the free opportunity to specify the extent to which he had helped the parolee he was encouraged to record 'yes,' whether or not the problem had been completely eliminated. It was expected that the parole supervisor would state that he had helped the parolee with many more problems than the parolee would be able to identify in the reciprocal question (to be discussed below). A coding scheme was, therefore, developed from the responses of parole supervisors that were suitable for reciprocal comparisons.

Assistance, like the distribution of contacts with parolees, was concentrated in the first three months and particularly in the first week of supervision. There were the equivalent of six problem areas per month where the parole supervisor thought he provided assistance for the parolee in the first week; by twelve months there had been a substantial decline; for each five parolees supervised, the officer had only offered help with one problem area.

The main concentration of problems for which assistance was provided by the parole supervisor were the areas of personal adjustment, employment and family; these accounted for approximately 70 per cent of assistance provided.

Assistance provided in the employment area was particularly concentrated in the first month. In contrast to this, the incidence of reporting assistance with personal problems on each questionnaire remained approximately constant; about one in ten of the parolees reported receiving assistance in each questionnaire. Assistance with marital problems increased during the first three months and reached a peak around nine months, with a sudden decrease in assistance given at the twelve-month stage. It would seem that many of the supervisor's contacts with the parolee's wives result from various problems arising between parolees and their wives, so that the practice of using the wife as a spy to keep in touch with the parolee is only a secondary purpose of the supervisor's contact with the wife.

Much of the parole supervisor's energy was concentrated, particularly in later time periods, on problems relating to personal adjustment such as alienation from the community, loneliness, and a large collection of areas such as 'lack of confidence,' 'lack of motivation,' 'poor self-image,' 'immaturity,' 'lack of insight.' He also tried to make the parolee see that it was necessary to be honest and to discuss sensitive areas. Probems with alcohol were, on the whole, infrequently mentioned.

In examining the proportion of problems identified by the parole supervisor for which help was proferred during the periods five weeks, three months and twelve months, there was a number of expected differences between the John Howard Society and the Ontario Probation Service. The John Howard Society mentioned 50 per cent more problems on which assistance was provided than the Ontario Probation Service. This is consistent with the responses to earlier questions concerned with the identification of the problems where it was found that the John Howard Society had a tendency to identify more problems.

Further, relative to parolees, dischargees not arrested within twenty-four months were more likely to have problems identified for which they received help. In an earlier part it was noted that those men who were later arrested did not receive more supervision in terms of face-to-face contact or total contacts than those who were not arrested. However, parole supervisors tried to provide more assistance to those who were arrested later. A coefficient was calculated which would equal 100 if the assistance given to the total population was exactly the same as that given to those arrested within twenty-four months. This coefficient equaled 111 over all the problem areas, so that those arrested received 11 per cent more assistance. However, this was concentrated more in certain problem areas than others. Nearly 50 per cent was provided for problems associated with alcohol. Help with employment was proferred approximately five times for those arrested within twenty-four months for every four times for the total parolees. The remaining differences were negligible. Though the first part of the question emphasized major problem areas in which a parole supervisor had tried to help a parolee, the second part asked the parole supervisor to specify 'yes,' 'no' and 'not known' in reply to the question – 'Did you help him?' In two out of three of the areas mentioned, the parole supervisor said yes. Of course, he was encouraged to do this.

A table was prepared of the total number of problem areas where the parole supervisor specified 'no,' 'don't know,' 'not stated,' or 'only marginally helped,' under the six main areas of assistance over the full twelve months. The percentages of the total number for each problem area were computed. A similar table was prepared for the five weeks' stage. Of the total problems recorded by the parole supervisor, 12.8 per cent were recorded as 'no help given,' 17.2 per cent as 'not known,' and less than 3 per cent as 'not stated,' or 'marginal help.' These percentages are only marginally different at five weeks, with 19.4 per cent recorded as 'not known.' For employment, marital and family relationships, the omnibus category (including leisure, associates, drugs and alcohol), and personal problems, there is little variation; about 1 out of 3 are not helped with problems. However, for the total, only 19 per cent of 135 cases who needed assistance in the area of finances were mentioned by the parole supervisor as not resulting in assistance. This is markedly lower than for the other areas. The main items to be mentioned under this broad category were management of finances, handling old debt, use of income to reduce indebtedness and, more generally, budgeting or simply giving cash.

The relationship with the supervisor was the other area in which there was a tendency for the supervisor to see himself as giving more help than the parolee. Approximately half of the items coded under this category were concerned with the fact that the parole supervisor had tried to help the parolee adjust to the 'fact of the parole authority.' Involvement with the supervisor to help the parolee obtain 'a deeper relationship,' encouragement of the parolee 'to not avoid sensitive areas,' and not 'to pretend all is well when it is not' were included. Approximately one-fifth of the items included moral support, encouragement, and help in adjusting to difficult situations that were frequently mentioned by parolees.

At five weeks the omnibus group (alcohol, drugs, leisure time, associates, and accommodation) had a tendency to be mentioned more often as an area in which assistance was not successfully given, usually because the supervisor did not know whether or not he had helped.

THE PAROLEE'S VIEW OF HELP IN AREAS OTHER THAN EMPLOYMENT AND ACCOMMODATION

Reciprocal questions to those discussed previously for parole supervisors were put to parolees. The aim of these questions was to see to what extent the identification of problem areas and assistance given coincided for parolees and supervisors. The coding schedule discussed earlier was used to code the responses of the parolees.

There is the expected tendency for the parole supervisor to mention items more frequently than the parolee. In Table 8.4 the frequencies with which parolees mentioned items of assistance have been presented at the one-month stage under six headings. A coefficient of reciprocity was also calculated.[1]

The parolee was considerably more likely to have mentioned aspects of the supervisory relationship than the parole supervisor. The principal item coded under supervisory relationship for the parolee is 'moral support' or 'encouragement'; 43 out of the 138 items mentioned by the parolee, or nearly one-third, related to moral support. Aspects of current finances, welfare or financial responsibilities all grouped under the heading of money, were also more likely to be reported by the

TABLE 8.4

Areas for which help was mentioned with measures of parolee–parole supervisor reciprocity at five weeks from release

Rank order for help mentioned by supervisor	Area of help	For all questionnaires		
		Number mentioning help	Number of parolees and parole supervisors	Coefficient of reciprocity
1	Employment*	—	—	—
2	Personal attitudes and adjustment	27	237	176
3	Family	24	196	145
4	Alcohol, associates, leisure	21	166	123
5	Money	23	104	77
6	Supervisory relationship and moral support	43	40	30
No help		70	—	41
N		138*	135	100

* Items on accommodation and employment were not recorded for parolees – see text

parolee than the parole supervisor. On the other hand the supervisor was considerably more likely to mention problem areas such as aspects of personal adjustment, close relationships, personal inadequacies, and deficiencies. These items follow the earlier pattern of the type and severity of problems, where the parolee's personality was something mentioned most frequently. Other items mentioned more frequently by the supervisor than the parolee were family relationships, associates, drugs and alcohol.

Studt (1970; 1971; 1972), in *Parolees and Agents in Interaction* has computed similar coefficients of reciprocity. She found considerable reciprocity in the identification of help given by the agent. In her report this included the obtaining of a driver's licence (which is not an issue for Ontario parolees), car insurance, and items such as getting a job, family problems, managing social life. The order of Studt's coefficients followed those in this study. The more concrete the help provided by the supervisor the more likely the parolee is to recall it. The more intangible it becomes, the more likely that the parolee will under-report it. In this study it was apparent that there were very few 'concrete' problems that had been solved by the parole supervisor.

In Ontario, as in Studt's study, help with obtaining a job would be important to most parolees. In this study it was not possible for this help to be examined reciprocally from the point of view of both parolees and supervisors because this particular area was investigated using a different format. The parolee was asked to outline the methods that he had used to try to obtain a job and to say which had been successful. Although the John Howard Society was mentioned as a method used to obtain 3 per cent of first jobs, the parole officer was never mentioned. In contrast to this, parole supervisors felt they helped nearly one-third of the parolees with employment in the first week and a similar proportion in the first five weeks. This apparent conflict may result from the fact that the parole supervisor in Ontario does not see himself as being somebody through whom employment is obtained, although often he refers the parolee to the appropriate agency, usually Manpower.

The John Howard Society also ran a service in some of their agency offices where a parolee or dischargee could come to look through the job announcements in the local paper and use a free telephone. He could also be referred through the agency to specific employers. A study done in one large office has shown that many of these referrals in fact take place through Manpower and it is possible that the parolee or the dischargee would not perceive the John Howard Society as being instrumental in obtaining a particular job.

Studt found the same phenomenon of the over-reporting by the parole supervisor of help with medical care, with employers and with welfare agencies; she suggests that this is because the parolee is not totally aware of the parole supervisor's efforts on his behalf.

HELP NOT RECEIVED

There is fair agreement between parolee and supervisor on lack of assistance. Although the parolee was not asked at one month to recall any specific areas in which the parole supervisor had not helped, 42 per cent of the parolees did not say that they received any assistance from him. For 16 per cent of the parolees the parole supervisor did not identify any area in which he had tried to help. In one-third of all cases where he offered help, he felt he was not successful.

24 per cent of the parolees who co-operated in the twelve-month interview said that in the previous six-month period their parole supervisors had not given any help (including in finding accommodation or employment). For those receiving help the most frequently mentioned areas were money or budgeting first, and the supervisory relationship second. Once again the item of moral support or encouragement was important. Personal adjustment and problems were third. The omnibus category (alcohol, associates, education, and leisure time), as at one month, was mentioned extremely rarely by the parolees at this stage.

The parolee was also asked whether his parole supervisor made any difference to his adjustment. 26 per cent stated quite flatly that he had made none at all; 5 per cent said that, in addition, he was an inconvenience; another 5 per cent said that he could make a difference if he tried; 5 per cent said that they did not know. Thus two out of five felt he made no difference. On the other hand, 30 per cent said that he helped give them confidence; that he was someone to whom they could take a problem and talk about it; that he was there to advise and was a man you could reason with. 13 per cent said the supervisor kept them in line and stopped them from doing things that they should not do. The remaining 4 per cent were less specific, but did include the only person who saw him as a middle man or buffer between the parolee and the outside world.

Although the parole supervisor saw himself as providing help to the parolee initially in the area of work and later in the areas of family and personal problems, the parolee did not reciprocate in the identification of areas in which the parole supervisor had helped him. To see if this was because the parolee was expecting some help which he was not given, he was asked if his parole supervisor could help him more. Two out of three of the parolees replied 'no.' 6 per cent said this was the result of the lack of time that the parole supervisor could devote to the parolee, or the supervisor's insufficient experience with people, or because he treated the parolee too much like a probationer. 10 per cent mentioned that the supervisor could try harder to get him a job.

Did the parolee intend to continue his relationship with the supervisor after parole? 43 per cent said that they would and 43 per cent said that they would not; 10 per cent did not know. The principal reason given for continuing their relationships after termination was that the parolee felt that the supervisor was a 'regular' or 'nice' guy. 31 per cent mentioned that he could give him advice and that he was a good person to drop in and talk to. Of the sixty parolees who said they would not continue the relationship, 56 per cent said they only saw their supervisors because they had to. The remaining responses were along these lines: the atmosphere was wrong; the parole supervisor was on his back about a job; he just did not like parole supervisors; he reminded him of prison experience.

FURTHER PROBLEMS RELATING TO THIS EVALUATION OF THE EFFECTIVENESS OF THE PAROLE SUPERVISOR'S ASSISTANCE

Certain parole supervisors, those who conceive their role as that of the catalyst in the adjustment situation, were able to answer a question about the assistance they proffered but had difficulty in saying to what extent they actually helped parolees. To take an example, when the parolee comes to his office, mentions his employment difficulties and possibly asks the parole supervisor for assistance, the parole supervisor's reaction would be to try to force the parolee to solve the problem on his own. The parolee may see this kind of 'solution' as a lack of help. At the one-month stage, a few parolees did see the parole officer as forcing them to find work by themselves. If, however, this was part of the parole supervisor's 'approach,' there were many parolees to whom this conceptualization of help was not explained.

How does one measure the effectiveness of this approach? It would seem that the only way is to compare those cases where there was parole supervision with those where there was none. It is difficult, though, to see how this approach differs from no parole supervision whatsoever.

Although some of parole supervision is devoted to 'practical' problems such as employment, there was also concern about the personal adjustment of the parolee himself, that of the parolee and his wife, and that of the parolee and the supervisor. These kinds of problems were identified by the parole supervisor without prodding from us so that they were probably an important part of his conceptualization of what supervision should be. They may also reflect the real problems that the parolee faces in the community. In the first instance, we see the parolee bringing practical problems to the supervisor. As these are resolved, whether or not through the supervisor's intervention, the parole supervisor then concentrates on the parolee's personality and his immediate environment as he sees these in some sense as 'causes' of the parolee's difficulties. From the second point of view the real problems presented by the parolee are initially those of employment but later those of adjustment in inter-personal situations.

NOTES TO CHAPTER 8

1 The number of times the parole supervisor mentioned the item was divided by the number of times the parolee mentioned the same item (multiplying by 100). Over-all, this gave a ratio of 135 items mentioned by the supervisor per 100 items by the parolee, who may forget or not be as verbally sophisticated as the parole supervisor and thus not elaborate items on which help was received. To allow for this another index (in the fourth column of Table 8.4) was computed. This latter coefficient of reciprocity is calculated to a base of 100 by dividing each of the previous coefficients by 135/100

9

Recidivism of Ex-Prisoners: Recidivism Rates and Parole Selection

Recidivism rates have long been discussed in criminology. The use of numbers or percentages gives to the justification of a penal measure a scientific aura which may prove to be illusory when the basis for the figures is examined. In Canada, those opposed to prison have come up with an 80 per cent recidivism rate; the present Chairman of the National Parole Board, on the other hand, has said in annual reports that only 10 per cent fail on parole.[1] Indeed figures without definitions such as these are used to imply that as a correctional measure, parole is more effective than prison. We will show that these figures are not comparable and that any comparisons using these are meaningless.

A useful rate of recidivism for comparing penal measures takes a strictly defined criterion, such as reconviction for an indictable offence or as in this study arrest recorded on police files, and a controlled period of time, such as two years. The number of persons reconvicted for an indictable offence within two years of the completion of the particular 'treatment' of interest are counted and this number is divided by the total number who had the same treatment at the same time. It is also important for a fuller understanding of the effectiveness of any given treatment to know on what basis men are allocated to it, as selection may account for differences between two penal measures.

Parole in Canada is a selective procedure. First, the prisoner must decide whether or not to apply; approximately half of those released without parole in this study never applied. Automatic review without an application never leads to parole. As we will see in the later stages of this report, those prisoners not applying for parole provide the key to understanding that the effectiveness of parole is an illusion. Secondly, the parole board decides, from among those who choose to apply, who will be granted parole. In 1968, there were 4455 inmates in federal penitentiaries 'eligible' for parole; 71 per cent applied, and of these 47 per cent were granted parole. Parole, then, was granted to approximately one-third of those eligible.

It seems unnecessary, at this stage, to consider in detail what the parole board sees as relevant characteristics for a decision to grant parole. It seems obvious, though, that other things being equal, they will select those who are unlikely to cause further or 'significant' harm to society. The very nature of the decision-making process leads to a lower reconviction rate. The real question, then, about the effectiveness of parole would be answered if we could know the differences in recidivism rates for the same group of men discharged and released on parole.

A further consideration may be that of those 2706 men paroled in 1967, 1664 were from provincial reformatories. It could be argued that in general those sent to provincial institutions (i.e., with sentences under two years) are, at that stage anyway, less committed to a criminal life style and are therefore less likely to recidivate than those sent to federal penitentiaries. In addition to the fact that the parole board grants parole to eight persons from provincial institutions for every five persons from federal institutions, the time a parolee from a provincial institution serves on the street is shorter than the time served by federal prison parolees. These are also factors that could produce a low 'failure rate.'[2] In order to have a meaningful reconviction rate these two populations should be considered separately.

How Many are Re-Arrested?

65 per cent of the dischargees and 44 per cent of the parolees were arrested at least once within twenty-four months from their release (41 per cent of the dischargees and 16 per cent of the parolees were arrested for a second time within the twenty-four month period). Of these, one-quarter were arrested within the first four months, half within nine months, and two-thirds within the first twelve months. Twelve of the 73 dischargees and eighteen of the 128 parolees not arrested within twenty-four months were known to be arrested within thirty-six months. From standard probability theory, it could be expected that within 36 months nearly 24 of the 73 dischargees and nearly 36 of 128 remaining parolees would have been arrested. This would bring the probable number of dischargees arrested within a 36-month period to 3 out of 4. 56 per cent of

the parolees would have been re-arrested; this is nearly 16 per cent higher than expected from the summary of studies carried out on men paroled five years earlier; then, however, the parole granting rate was lower (see chapter 8).

This analysis does not take into account the total number of charges levelled against the sample; in some instances, particularly with 'fraud' there may be ten or more charges associated with each arrest. The later sections of this chapter describe the probability of the occurrence of an arrest in a given month according to various parole selection variables, but first the use of arrest as distinct from conviction will be explained.

Why Arrest?

Many other studies have used reconviction, while the criterion used here is re-arrest. Some argue that arrest, particularly of ex-prisoners, is biased and that it may occur regardless of the behaviour of the ex-prisoner. Others argue that a large proportion of 'guilty' persons are never convicted because charges are dropped at some stage before conviction. A recent study of the operation of the courts in Toronto has supported this latter argument (Hann 1973, pp. 379, 511); for Criminal Code indictable offences only 65.6 per cent of cases, where the key accused was 'secured' by arrest, resulted in a guilty plea. Unfortunately these statistics are not available for persons, nor with tabulations for the number of previous convictions, but it suggests in general that there are many arrests without a final conviction. It will be argued below that whether a person was rearrested or reconvicted for this sample was empirically the same. Further, some of the early prediction analysis was carried out on both arrest and conviction, but the conclusions appeared to be the same, thus additionally reinforcing empirically the notion that as a criterion rearrest is the same as reconviction.

Arrest behaviour has some additional advantages. It may be expected to occur near the time the offence was supposedly committed. If cost-benefit analysis is to be carried out, it is the first point at which police and court costs can be assigned to an ex-prisoner. Lawyers tend to react strongly to this use of arrest as it is not until conviction that one can be sure what happened. However, the proof required to actually sentence a man to long periods of imprisonment is different from what the social scientist and economist needs if they are interested in an indicator of men's behaviour or the costs of a system.

Additionally, in a study concerned with behaviour on the street and time in prison, arrest identifies the point where a man normally starts in jail again and so can no longer be employed, living with a wife or drinking regularly, but instead is suffering the physically debilitating effects

Figure 9:I
Cumulative percentages of parolees and dischargees arrested once or more, by time periods from release

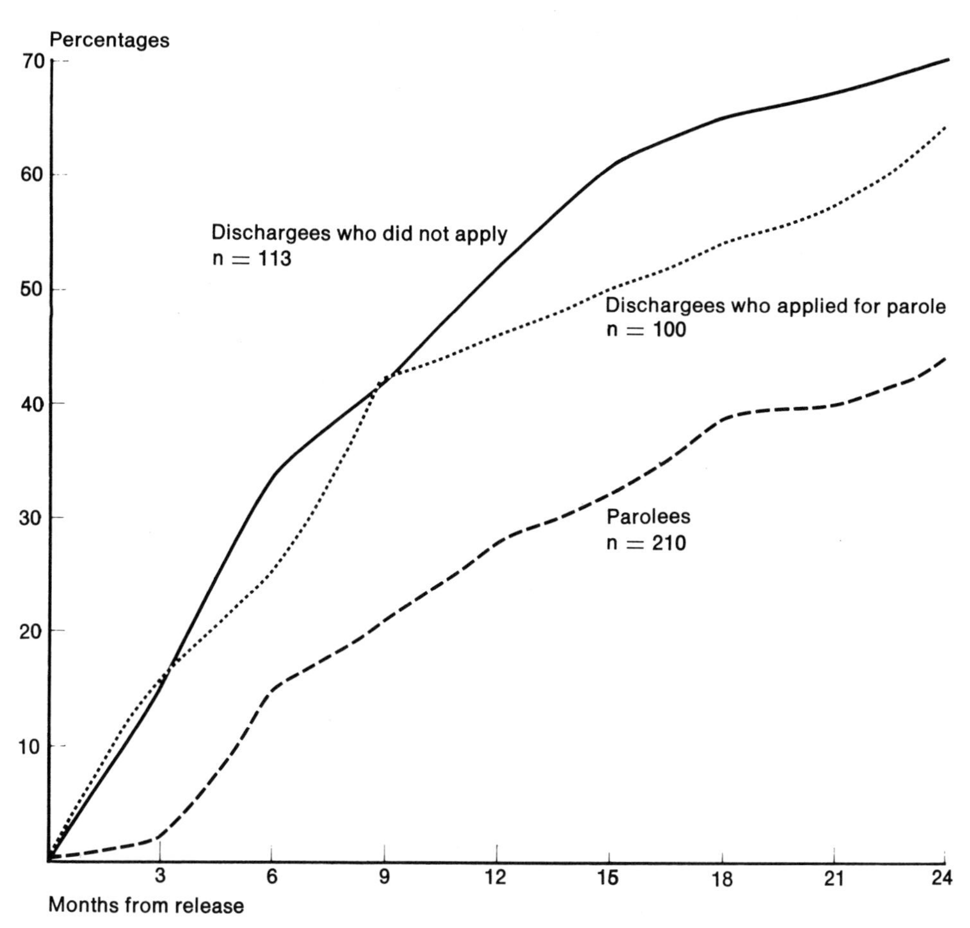

of anxiously waiting in a local jail. Conviction occurs several weeks or months after the supposed crime, so is not useful to questions about time to failure.

Arrest and Parole Selection

Figure 9.1 shows the cumulative percentages of parolees and dischargees arrested once or more in three-monthly time periods from release; the dischargee population is broken down according to whether or not they applied for parole.

In the case of twelve dischargees who were serving new sentences, either in prison or on parole in an area outside that of this study, we did not know whether they had applied for parole as their files had been transferred out of the offices of the Parole and Penitentiary Service in the main penitentiary town in the area. It is important to note in the analysis to follow that were these twelve men or even a portion of them reassigned to the category of dischargees who applied for parole, this would, in general, reduce the differences in arrest rates between dischargees applying for parole and those not, thus making the actual conclusions presented more powerful.

There were significant differences in arrest rates between the parolees and the total group of dischargees and between the parolees and the dischargees who did and did not apply. There was no significant difference between dischargees applying for parole and those not applying. Apparently, then, parole leads to a lower re-arrest rate. (Later chapters will analyse the reasons for this difference and question to what extent it is due to selection, supervision or other variables discussed in Chapter 1.) Even though non-significant, there was a tendency for a higher proportion of the dischargees who did not apply for parole to be arrested within the twenty-four months than dischargees who did apply. At fifteen-, eighteen-, and twenty-one-month periods there was a difference of nearly ten percentage points in the cumulative percentages. If this difference was real, it would only be statistically significant on samples of twice the size used here. (For details see Table F.1.)

An analysis was also carried out for all those arrested to see what parole selection variables were associated in delays in arrest. Although there were no differences noted between dischargees who did not apply and those who did (for details see Figure F.1), it seems that, in general, both groups of dischargees were likely to be arrested earlier than parolees.

Time to Arrest and Length of Parole

In the analysis of arrest rates we found that parolees had a tendency to be arrested less in the first three months and more in the three-monthly period from sixteen to eighteen months. While this could have been the result of random fluctuations, an alternate explanation might be found in the fact that, for a fair number, parole terminated during this period. It was suggested by ex-prisoners themselves that while they may be involved in 'fringe' criminal activities, they avoid anything that could incur an automatic forfeiture of parole. According to this reasoning, and as our figures suggest, parole merely delays arrest for certain people. In fact, the modal parole period was eleven to fifteen months. It was found that seven of the twenty whose parole period was terminated in the eleven- to fifteen-month period had been arrested before the end of their parole; six of the twenty were arrested in the sixteen- to eighteen-month period and nine were arrested in later time periods. The tendency for this particular group to be arrested later when compared to the others was tested for significance. It was found to be significant with probability less than 1 per cent. There is no satisfactory explanation of this, although a plausible one might be that short paroles only 'contain' some parolees. Longer paroles may also 'contain' parolees, but the data are not yet available. (See Figure F.II for details.)

Probability of Arrest in a Given Month for Ex-Prisoners

It is often suggested that most men released from prison are arrested in the first three to six months. In this study, few men were arrested during their first month out. Though the proportion arrested peaks around the fourth month at 6 per cent, after seven months the proportion appears to remain constant until twenty-four months so that on the average 3 per cent are arrested in any one particular month. There was only a slight tendency for more to be arrested within the first few months. (See Figure F.III for details.) Thus, if one were to release an unselected group of prisoners from a federal penitentiary, less than 4 per cent of them would be expected to be arrested in an average month. This finding is particularly significant in terms of leave-of-absence programmes, where the extraordinarily low failure rate is cited as evidence of the efficacy of these programmes. In this case we see that the board could select a group where only 1 per cent would be re-arrested within the first month or 5 per cent within the first three months.

The Most Serious Offences Resulting in Re-Arrest

One in four of the most serious offences for which the men were first arrested after release were offences against the person (see Table 9.1). Two out of three were offences against property. A small number were 'other' (escape, procuring, narcotics and driving offences). For the purposes of this table, robbery was classified as an offence against the person even though the actual event may have involved little personal violence. 4 per cent of these offences were robbery. Similar comments may in fact be made concerning sex offences where little violence may be involved (Menachem, 1971; Mohr et al., 1965). One in three of the offences were categorized as theft (including theft of cars over and under $50 and the associated crimes of possession of stolen goods); 22 per cent, breaking and entering offences; 16 per cent, wounding offences (in-

TABLE 9.1

Most serious offences associated with first arrest by parole selection variables

	Dischargees				
	Applicant	Non-applicant	Parolee	Total	
Offences against person					
Homicide	—	1	—	1	0.4%
Sex offences	1	4	2	7	3.1%
Wounding	9	13	14	36	15.9%
Robbery	3	4	4	11	4.9%
Other*	2	1	1	4	1.8%
Total	15 = 23.4%	23 = 28.8%	21 = 25.7%	59 =	26.1%
Offences against property					
B & E	10	24	16	50	22.1%
Theft	31	20	24	75	33.2%
Fraud	6	9	7	22	9.7%
Other†	—	2	2	4	1.8%
Total	47 = 73.4%	55 = 68.8%	49 = 59.7%	151 =	66.8%
Other					
Escape	—	—	3	3	1.3%
Narcotics	—	—	4	4	1.8%
Driving (except dangerous)	—	1	3	4	1.8%
Liquor	1	—	—	1	0.4%
LCA violation	—	—	1	1	0.4%
Procuring	—	—	1	1	0.4%
Vagrancy	1	—	—	1	0.4%
Violation of immigration laws	—	1	—	1	0.4%
Total	2 = 3.2%	2 = 2.3%	12 = 14.6%	16 =	6.9%
Grand total	64	80	82‡	226	
Percentage of grand total released	64	71	39	54	

* Obstruct justice/resist peace officer; dangerous driving; abduction
† Wilful damage over $50; trespassing
‡ NOTE: A further 11 were arrested as a result of suspension followed by revocation without other specific charge at that time. Previous to each suspension the parolee had been questioned by the police, but not at the instigation of the parole personnel, nor did suspension appear to be actively sought by the police.

cluding assaults against citizens, police officers and one or two possession of offensive weapon offences); 10 per cent were classified as fraud (as defined by the Criminal Code).

Arrests Not Resulting in Conviction

With the exception of the thirteen cases not yet terminated in the courts (because the arrests occurred late in the study) and the eleven paroles revoked, all of the 237 arrested were known to have been convicted of that or a later offence within three years of release. However, seventy-three of the first arrests had not resulted in conviction at the time when the data for this study were coded. Thirteen cases had not yet been brought to court. Sixty did not result in convictions for other reasons (see Table 9.2). 8 per cent of the dischargees and 15 per cent of the parolees had their charges dismissed on their first arrest. 14 per cent of the dischargees and 17 per cent of the parolees had their charges withdrawn or an order of *nolle prosequi* entered.

The figures in the table are supposed to refer strictly to the total group of charges associated with the first arrest; if an ex-prisoner was arrested and charged with (1) breaking and entering and (2) robbery, but if the robbery charge was then withdrawn and he was convicted on the 'breaking and entering' charge, he would not feature in this table as an ex-prisoner for whom a charge had been withdrawn. Even so, 15 per cent is a substantial proportion of ex-prisoners arrested and not tried for that offence. Though this study has not been designed to provide an explanation for these figures, it has been suggested that they partially result from the police *modus operandi*: the ex-prisoner is arrested on suspicion, the police anticipating that it will be possible to substantiate the charges with evidence collected later. Obviously in a proportion of these cases the evidence was not produced so the charges were withdrawn. An alternative explanation is that the man is arrested in connection with an offence for which the police could probably obtain a conviction; the man discloses information about the activities of other persons wanted by the police or about the location of valuable stolen goods; in return for this information the charges are withdrawn.

Although the difference was very small, there was a tendency for proportionately more charges to be withdrawn, to be dismissed, and for more *nolle prosequi* to be entered for parolees than dischargees. (When the three are combined the difference is significant.)

Some authors have suggested that the parole supervisor 'cools' the situation with the police and that this leads to the withdrawal of charges. The evidence collected in this study and general knowledge of the non-relationship between the police and parole supervisors in Ontario do not give much support to this particular hypothesis. It may be, however, that police tend to bring charges against parolees that they would not lay against other ex-prisoners in the expectation that this will result in revocation. The most plausible explanation is probably in the characteristics of parolees which are discussed throughout this report. The parolee is less rejected and more inclined to stand up for himself so that he will be more likely to plead not guilty, can probably get a lawyer more easily and has support, generally, in the courtroom situation. Unfortunately it is not possible to show from our data just what the 'real' explanation is.

TABLE 9.2

First arrests not resulting in convictions, reason for non-conviction, and mode of release

	Arrested	Withdrawn*	Nolle prosequi	Dismissed*	Sub-total	Non-convicted/ arrested	Withdrawn and NP/ arrested	No disposition	Total
Dischargee	144	18 (+2)	2	11 (+2)	33	22.9	15.8	5	38
Parolee	93	11 (+1)	4	14 (+1)	30	32.3	17.2	8	38
Total	237	29 (+3)	6	25 (+3)	63	27.2	16.4	13	76

* Three ex-prisoners (nos. 275, 505, 691) were *not* included in these columns as they had simultaneously one or more withdrawals and one or more dismissals, but they are included in percentages

NOTE: Difference between parolees and dischargees in proportion not resulting in convictions is significant $\chi^2 = 2.78$; $p < 5$ per cent (one-tailed test)

Police Action and Withdrawal of Charges

In the twelve-month questionnaire the ex-prisoner was asked if he had ever got a 'patch' (a term used spontaneously in earlier interviews by several ex-prisoners). He was also asked to imagine a situation where the police knew or suspected that he had been involved in an offence and to say how he would go about getting the charges 'patched.' 15 per cent of the parolees in comparison to 33 per cent of the dischargees said that they had at some stage in their lives got a 'patch.' 45 per cent of the parolees and 32 per cent of the dischargees said that they did not know how to go about getting one. 12 per cent of the dischargees and 14 per cent of the parolees said they did know but were not specific. Approximately 10 per cent of both said it involved the crown attorney, magistrate and defence lawyer; some gave various combinations of these, although magistrates were not mentioned singly. The main contributions of the ex-prisoners mentioned for getting a patch were giving up stolen goods, giving information on the location of other stolen goods, and direct bribing of the appropriate official. These responses suggest considerable bargaining relative to charges, their withdrawal, pleas and possibly sentences.

Parole Action and Arrest

Forty-four per cent of the parolees were arrested within two years of release, 39 per cent of these during the parole period. Table 9.3 presents parole actions and arrest within twenty-four months of release for parolees by the agency of supervision. 20 per cent of the arrests resulted in revocation; 45 per cent in forfeitures with or without revocation; 23 per cent were arrests that occurred during the parole period but where there was no revocation or forfeiture action, and only 12 per cent occurred after the parole period. With forfeitures and revocations combined, 29 per cent of the total had their paroles terminated during their parole periods. One function of revocations is to avoid commission of new offences. An analysis of revocations showed that those of the John Howard Society tended to be more often associated with charges laid than the other agencies, perhaps because they are more concerned with not infringing on the ex-prisoner's freedom until absolutely necessary.

Less than half the twenty-one arrests not resulting in parole action did result in convictions. However the sentences were either fines or short prison sentences. Thus where there was a conviction it is probable that the sentencing judge or police were not aware that these men were on parole at the time; one of the offences, even, was 'uttering,' an indictable offence punishable by two years or more and which should therefore have resulted automatically in forfeiture of parole.

TABLE 9.3

Parole actions and arrests within twenty-four months of release

	John Howard Society		Ontario Probation Service		National Parole Service		Total	Percentage of those arrested	Percentage of total parolees
Suspensions only	2		1		2		5	5.4	2.4
Percentage of total supervised	2.2		0.9		16.7				
Revocations only	6	15.0%	9	19.6%	4	57.1%	19	20.4	9.1
Forfeitures with or without revocation	18	45.0%	22	47.8%	2	28.6%	42	45.2	20.0
Arrest during parole period	11	27.5%	9	19.6%	1	14.3%	21	22.6	10.0
Arrest after parole period	5	12.5%	6	13.0%	—	—	11	11.8	5.2
Total	40	100.0%	46	100.0%	7	100.0%	93	100.0	44.3
Total supervised	92		106		12		210		

NOTE: Charges associated with suspensions: JHS: charge dismissed (1), withdrawn (1); OPS: no charge, offence after parole period; NPS: convicted theft under $50 (1) no charge; offence after parole period (1)

Those revocations and suspensions that were not associated with specific charges did involve police questioning. In four out of five suspensions not followed by revocation or forfeiture, the parolee had been charged with some new offence, although there were other reasons for suspension such as disappearing from the area, leaving the area without permission but returning, undesirable associates, and liquor. (None of these cases was associated with the use of parole suspension to prevent release of an accused parolee on bail.)

Original Offence and Arrest

As in other studies, the rule of thumb held true that the more serious the original offence the less likely the person is to be re-arrested after release (*Newsletter*, 1971). In Figure 9.11 the numbers convicted on the basis of groups of offences are compared showing the proportion re-arrested in the first twelve months. The offence groupings were based on a dichotomy of whether or not the person had been convicted of this offence in the group of offences for which he was sent to Kingston. The offences are laid out in approximate order of seriousness. The narcotics offences referred to a small group of men released on long sentences, who had been involved apparently only in trafficking.

Of the total population, 5 per cent had been convicted of some form of homicide, 39 per cent, of some form of breaking and entering, and 64 per cent convicted of other offences.

A further analysis was carried out on the relationship between the offences for which the person was convicted on admission and those for which he is reconvicted after release.[3] Using the order of offences laid out in this figure, we wanted to see whether post-release offences were more serious than pre-release ones. In the case of those parolees and dischargees arrested within twelve months, only one in four were reconvicted for an offence of similar seriousness, while nearly two out of five were convicted of both more and less serious offences. (See Table F.2 for further details.) Actually a closer examination shows that most of those re-arrested continue to be involved in property offences.

Recidivism, Previous Arrests, and other Variables

Although 13 per cent of the total sample had no recorded adult correctional sentence, only 5 per cent had not been previously arrested. There were only twenty-eight of the ex-prisoners whose arrest leading to their current sentence was their third or less; it was the first arrest for twelve, the second for eleven and the third for five. Three of these twenty-eight men had applied for parole but were refused while the remainder were

Figure 9:II
Numbers convicted of groups of offences
showing proportion not arrested in first twelve months

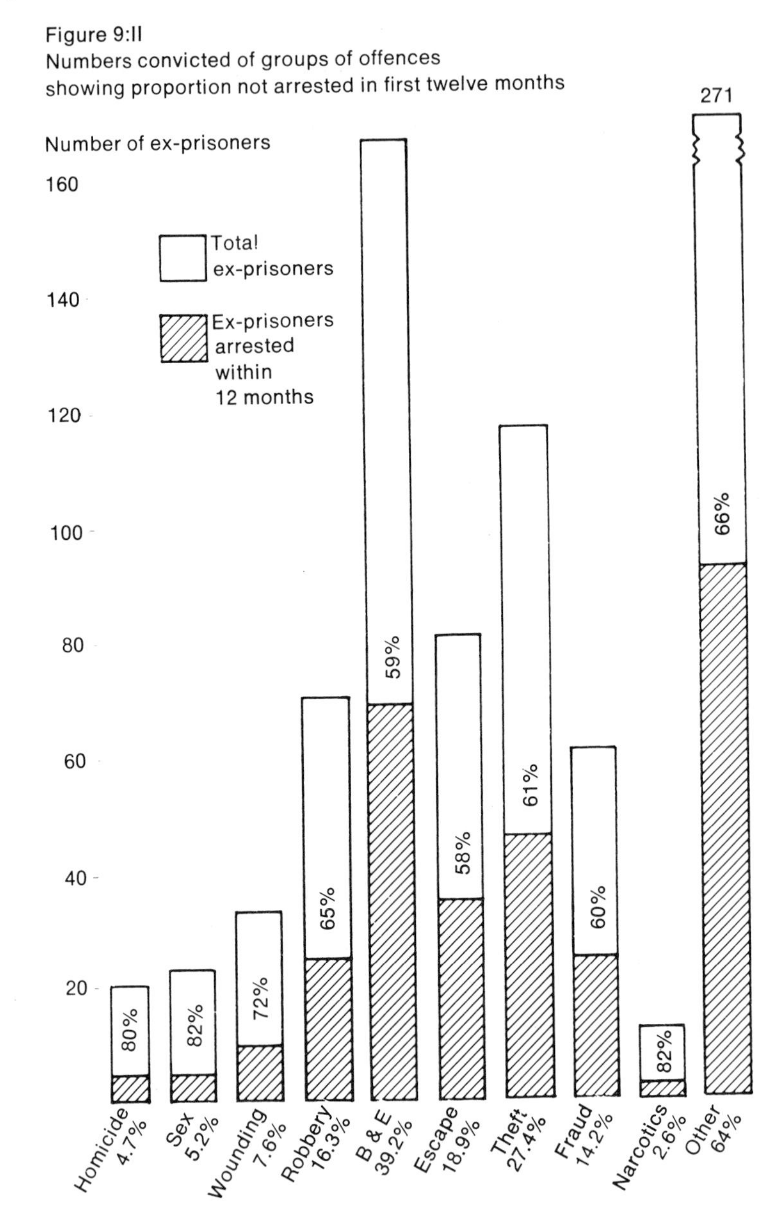

released on parole. The proportion of men in the sample arrested within twenty-four months are shown in Figure 9.III by the number of previous arrests. The median number of previous arrests is seven for the total and eight for those arrested within twenty-four months. This difference is surprisingly small and suggests that, for this population, once a man has started being arrested variables other than arrest are important in a decision to 'go straight.'

A number of analyses were done comparing a variety of variables and previous arrest history. It is a general finding in prediction studies that the best predictive variables of future behaviour are similar past behaviour. This is particularly true of the likelihood of the public to report certain persons to the police and for the police to decide to arrest and charge them. With so few ex-prisoners who had small numbers of previous arrests, this particular variable on its own would have very little predictive power in this study. However, the type of adult penal institutions in which the ex-prisoner had been confined previous to Kingston proved to be a much better predictor; related variables, such as total time in institutions or number of reformatory commitments, predict future arrest about as well as type of past institution and markedly better than the number of previous arrests.

Figure 9.IV presents the proportion arrested within twenty-four months by previous arrests and by age ranges. The considerably higher proportion of those arrested within twenty-four months under the age of twenty-four for all ranges of previous arrests is clearly demonstrated by this table. In a later chapter it will be shown that measures of previous penal record (more serious) and age (younger) combined give the most reliable prediction equation based on background data for arrest within twelve and twenty-four months (arrest more likely). Similar tables were analysed showing arrest to be more likely, if the ex-prisoner was unemployed, meeting with undesirable associates, not living with a wife and children, and had been involved in fights. (The details may be found in Figures F.IV–VIII.) The findings for unemployment are not clear for those with ten or more previous arrests. This result tends to confirm our later conclusion that encouraging employment is one of the small but important contributions of parole in reducing the likelihood of future arrests. Analysis for variables such as having undesirable associates, seeing any children of their own (a measure of family ties), reporting fighting within five weeks of release, against previous arrests presented a similar pattern; for those with comparatively few previous arrests, these variables are definitely associated with higher arrest rates after release. In contrast, there are few differences in re-arrest rates associated with frequency of drinking for those with few previous

Figure 9:III
Previous arrests vs proportion arrested within twenty-four months, and previous arrests for total ex-prisoners

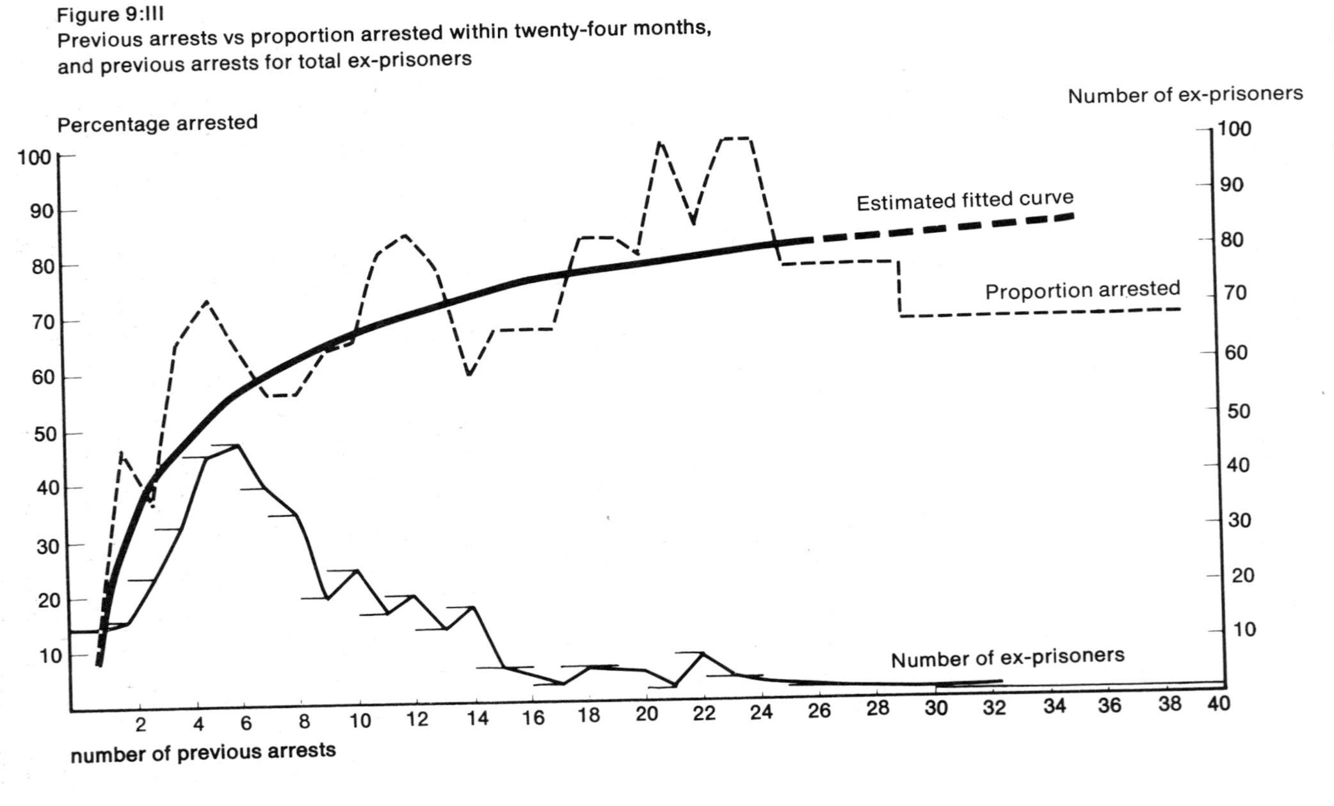

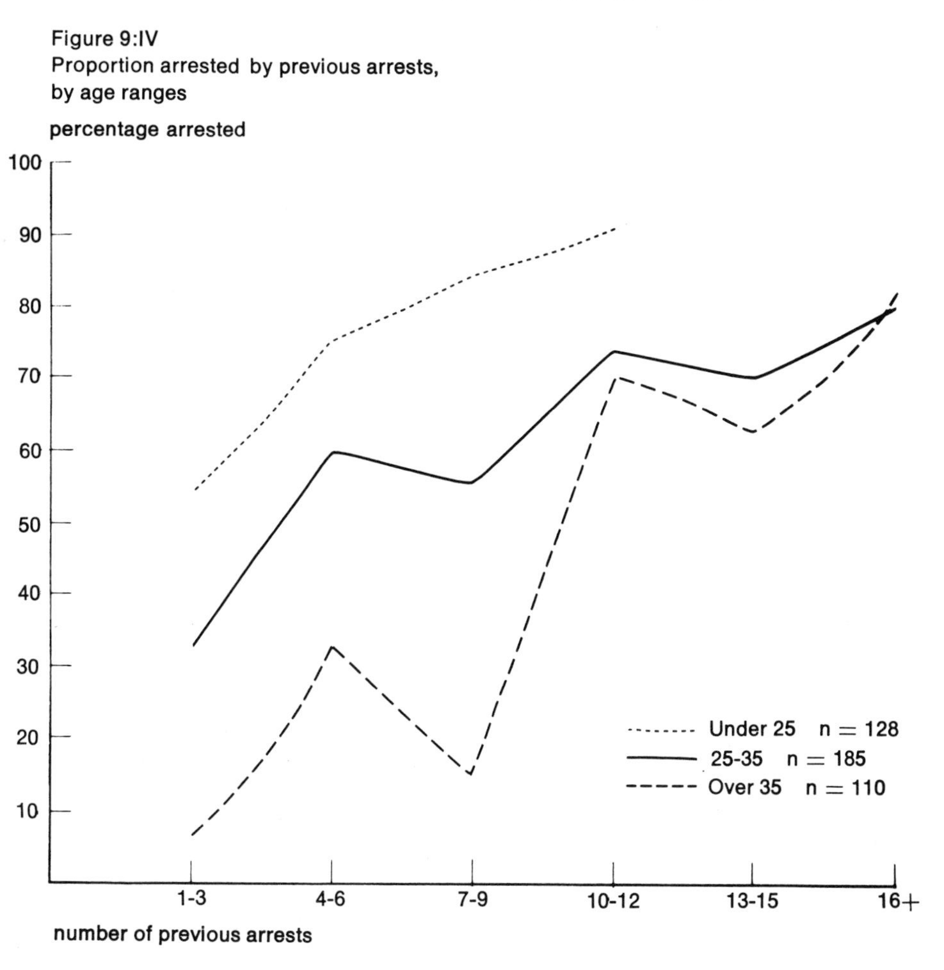

arrests; for those with seven or more previous arrests, frequent drinking is associated with larger probability of being re-arrested.

Time to Arrest

It has been noted by a number of authors such as Blozan and Mahoney and those working in the California Youth Authority, the California Department of Corrections and the Home Office Research Unit in England, that for the total population of men who were going to be arrested within a certain period, the proportion arrested at certain times during that period differs when the population is broken down into different sub-populations (Blozan and Mahoney, 1968; Gottfredson, 1967; Great Britain, 1969b). The tendency for the dischargees to be arrested earlier than the parolees has already been shown. If the parolees and the dischargees who were arrested were similar it would seem that the effect of parole was to delay the arrest of the parolees. This section will look at non-parole variables that were found, in other areas of analysis, to be related to time to arrest, and see whether they differ for parolees and dischargees. The analysis was carried out on ten crucial variables. The details of the period and size of the largest difference for each variable are summarized in Table F.3. The findings will first be summarized and then one of the more clear-cut variables is displayed with a fuller discussion.

Although the employment of a person at the time of arrest for the offence for which he was sent to Kingston was highly correlated with re-arrest within the first twenty-four months, the cumulative proportions of those arrested within given time periods are identical for the two subject populations of 'employed' or 'not employed.' The same basic conclusions follow for the differences between the young, and the combined middle- and old-age group. There is also a tendency for those with more previous arrests to get arrested earlier in the time period.

For some variables, the direction of the differences was opposite for the two modes of release. For those parolees who were arrested the relationships are in the expected direction; those who scored lower on the CPI success scale, those able to name a pay-off, and those having friends in prison interested in how they were doing tended to be arrested earlier. For dischargees, these tendencies were in the reverse direction, although they were in all cases significant. While these may just be chance variations associated with other variables, they may also be due to the concentration among dischargees of an apparently distinctive group of ex-prisoners who would be arrested early. The extent to which these and other associations mentioned here are accidental will become clearer in the multivariable prediction analysis in the next chapter.

The dischargee seeing his children within five weeks from release is arrested later than other dischargees and the parolee seeing his children after release is arrested later than other parolees, who are arrested at about the same time as dischargees not seeing children. The same relationship holds for those ex-prisoners who are employed and not after release.

Principal Variables Related to Arrest

In the later sections of this report, prediction equations will be developed using certain criteria concerned with the post-release arrest of the men involved in the study. As a preliminary to this, it was necessary to consider some of the significant correlation coefficients. It should be emphasized that while the regression equations developed later provide best predictions, the variables included in these equations are not the only variables that might have been used to develop a prediction equation, and are by no means the only ones statistically related to re-arrest.

These correlation coefficients will be discussed first of all for parolees and dischargees combined and will then be broken down by mode of release.

Parolees and Dischargees Combined

The first analysis looked at variables associated with arrest within six months. As for most criterion variables of 'failure,' there were no correlations for arrest within six months with values about 0.3. The relatively higher correlations are associated with post-release variables such as how long money from the institution lasted, and whether or not they were seeing children after release, and whether or not they were involved in fights. The two pre-release variables that were important were the Jesness Combination Score (more 'socially immature,' more likely to be arrested) and the ex-prisoner's pre-release views on the penitentiary's effects (the more ineffective, the more likely to be arrested).

The non-applicant for parole was more likely to be arrested within six months than the man who applied for parole. For parole applicants alone, however, the correlation between parole granting and re-arrest was not significant, implying that many of the differences between the parolees and the dischargees are between those who did and did not apply for parole rather than between persons granted or not granted parole. This would also imply (but not prove) that parole supervision is not an important factor in whether a person is arrested within six months.

Interpreting correlations higher than 0.2, the ex-prisoner was more likely to be arrested within twelve and twenty-four months if he had been involved in fights, if he did not go to church, if he was not trying to avoid friends from before, if he was not seeing children after release, if he was drinking regularly, if the situation in which the crime occurred still existed after release, if the ex-prisoner did not have a steady girlfriend or had no girlfriend at all, and if he was not released on parole. In relation to arrest within six months, the granting or refusing of parole to applicants seems to be as important as whether or not the individual applied for it. Time to arrest for those arrested was associated with similar variables, though those not seeing children were markedly more likely to be arrested earlier.

Correlations with post-release offences against the person were also examined. First it should be emphasized that statistically significant findings are technically less likely as there are comparatively fewer of the ex-prisoners who were reconvicted of offences against the person. Our main conclusion, even after the analysis of the substantial biographical, psychological, and situational information collected in this study, was that men who will be reconvicted on these types of charges were not readily identifiable. However, there is a very small group of individuals for whom prison staff and police could predict *involvement* in violence after release (although even that group would not necessarily get *convicted* of such offences). Moreover, while they could predict for this small group, there would be many for whom they would predict wrongly.

Parolees Only

The analysis was next directed at correlations for only those men released on parole. It was found that a parolee is more likely to be arrested within six months when he sees himself as a 'less successful' person according to the California Psychological Inventory and the Jesness Inventory, and the more he sees the effect of the penitentiary as negative at the time of the interview five weeks before release, if he receives reprimands from his supervisor, if his supervisor thinks he has problems with 'undesirable associates,' if he did not spend his first night at home or with family, if those inside are interested in how he is doing, if his money from the institution lasted less than a week, if he is not seeing children, if he has been involved in fights, and if (providing he had one) his job was obtained through friends and family rather than through impersonal methods or Manpower. A fairly large percentage of these same variables were also associated with arrest within twelve and twenty-four months.

A person with a higher score on the CPI and a lower score on the Jesness is both less likely to be arrested within six months if on parole and is more likely to be granted parole in the first place. It may be recalled from the arrest curves which were laid out comparing parolees and dischargees that there was a lag before parolees started getting arrested. These two findings together imply that the selection process for parole works in such a way as to minimize the number being released with a high probability of being arrested within six months. This is particularly important as the parole board's 'statistic of success' is the failure rate while on parole.

For parolees there are no post-release employment variables that are associated with re-arrest. The variable 'job finding method' reflects a tendency for men who go around with friends from before to obtain a job through them, whereas parolees who identify with the system or do what their supervisor asks are more likely to go to Manpower or use other impersonal methods to find a job.

It will be shown later that equations that predict arrest within twelve months are also useful for predicting it within twenty-four months. There are some extra variables associated with whether a person is more likely to be arrested within twenty-four months; if his original offence was against property but did not include robbery, if he had financial difficulties, if his parole supervisor had tried to help him with undesirable associates; and if he had not gone to a job immediately.

Post-release Offences Against the Person for Parolees

Of the eighty-five parolees arrested for an indictable offence within twenty-four months from their date of release, twenty-one were for offences which involved violence of some sort against a person. This is a legal definition which includes murder, rape, robbery and assault. *If arrested*, a parolee was more likely to have been arrested for a violence offence if, according to his parole supervisor his problem with alcohol was severe, if he spent his first night at home with family or relatives and if he had a job to go to immediately. The first variable seems to be important in offences involving violence both in terms of our statistical analysis and ex-prisoners' self-reports – many said that alcohol was often a factor when they got into fights. The second two variables are ones that are, as we will show later, predictive of arrest within twenty-four months and inversely predict non-violent offences. It will be shown that persons who have been involved in fights within five weeks from their date of release are also likely to be arrested within twenty-four months, though not necessarily for offences against a person.

Dischargees Only

Employment is an extremely important indicator of whether a dischargee will be arrested within six months rather than at a later period. For this group the variables of employment and whether the dischargee tries to avoid people from before (both of which have correlations of over 0.3) are fairly reliable indicators of whether the dischargee intends to return to crime or not. The only real differences within the dischargee group were along the lines of whether they would get arrested immediately after release or at some later time rather than whether or not they would get arrested.

NOTES TO CHAPTER 9

1. Violation rates commonly quoted in National Parole Board annual reports are the number of violations during a particular year divided by the number of persons granted parole during that year. Another statistic used is the total number of persons granted parole since 1959 divided into the total number of persons whose parole has been violated since 1959. While these figures give an indication of the rate at which the parole board takes decisions and the distribution of the amount of time that it may allocate to these particular decisions during a year, it gives no information whatsoever about the effectiveness of parole as is often implied and should not be confused or compared with reconviction rates for other dispositions. See, for instance Street (1968, esp. pp. 82–4), for striking examples of misuse of statistics by the Chairman of the National Parole Board to give the impression of the effectiveness of parole in keeping men out of prison. This use of statistics on returns to prison without reference to parole selection or time on parole for indicating parole effectiveness is common in other parole or probation jurisdictions
2. For example, a reformatory inmate applies for parole at 4 months, after one-third of his one year sentence for breaking and entering. He is released on parole after he has served 6 months, and so he has to serve, on parole, approximately 6 months. He commits an offence 7 months after he was released from the reformatory on parole. An inmate from a penitentiary originally sentenced to 3 years is released after one year. He has to serve on parole a little less than 2 years. He commits an offence at 7 months. The reformatory inmate for the purposes of the parole board statistics is a success. The penitentiary inmate is a failure
3. For comparative statistics in parole agencies in the United States see Newsletter (1970)

10

Prediction of Arrest, Social Functioning, and the Importance of Parole and Prison

The earlier part of this study was concerned with comparing those paroled with those discharged in terms of pre-release variables (penitentiary file information), and post-release variables (the man's behaviour, experiences, and subsequent arrests). Although we drew some implications from the more obvious findings, no attempt was made to combine variables in order to find their greatest predictive power.

Previous prediction studies have all used as data men's experiences before admission or during their prison term. None have used post-release data as a means of predicting subsequent arrests. As we see this distinction as important, these two kinds of information have been dealt with separately.

Arrest is difficult to predict because it results from an interaction of behaviour, that of police, public, and the offender. To what extent is this also true of the ex-prisoner's drinking, employment, or associates? In a later section, negative and positive aspects of social functioning are predicted from the data known before and after release. Can various combinations of behavioural variables predict whether a man was released on parole or not, whether he applied for parole or whether he was released from a maximum security penitentiary?

Prediction of arrest or employment is also important because we will be able to use a person's 'likelihood' of arrest or of getting a job to assess whether parole or penitentiary made any difference to his behaviour after release. If certain groups are classified in terms of their likelihood of re-arrest, it is possible to see whether more are rearrested on discharge than on parole. In the next chapter, the main prediction equations we have developed 'control for risk' in this way and show that those released on parole are no less likely to be arrested than those who were discharged or those who applied for but were refused parole. We did, however, find that those who did not apply for parole had higher probabilities of arrest than those who applied.

The next section summarizes the details of the method used to develop the prediction equations. As in any study collecting data on offenders now free in the community, there are missing data, so we also outlined the method used to allow for this in the equations. The discussion in the text is limited to a summary of what particular equations mean. However, the reader interested in the detailed statistics is referred to Appendix G where some of the actual prediction equations have been set out with statistics on their efficiency and reliability in both the limited and real prediction methods.

The predictive analysis in this part is mainly concerned with attempts to predict arrest within six, twelve and twenty-four months from date of release and to see how these predictions look in relation to claims by supporters of the penitentiary and parole that these dispositions reduce the probability of rearrest. As with the other variables, simple dichotomies were set up for each of the ex-prisoners according to whether he was re-arrested or not within each of these time periods. It is important to note that our criterion was *arrest for an indictable offence and / or revocation of parole, not* conviction for an indictable offence or arrest and / or conviction for a non-indictable offence. In the discussion of arrest in chapter 8, the proportion of first arrests that did not result in conviction was shown. Those not convicted the first time were always convicted on the second or later arrest occurring within the time period of the study. (A few exceptions relate to those arrested late in the study.)

A major emphasis of the study was cost-benefit analysis. In over-all terms, the cost of an individual to the criminal justice system are arrest and time to re-arrest; this refers to the cost in travel and time of the police officers who arrest him, the cost of keeping him in a local jail, and the cost of remand and trial. Also at arrest he normally ceases to function in the community.

SELECTION AND DICHOTOMIZATION OF VARIABLES

The second step in the analysis was to select from the large range of variables created at the data collection stage, those related to arrest that would be used in the prediction equations. The only variables included were those measuring an 'objective' aspect of the ex-prisoner's situation or a score measuring an aspect of personality derived from one of the attitude instruments (CPI, MMPI, or Jesness). 'Objective' here is used to describe an aspect on which two independent raters might be expected to agree such as whether the man was employed or not. It thus excluded variables based purely on subjective evaluations. The personality variables, however, do measure aspects internal to the parolee.

In other parts of the research the emphasis was on giving an idea of the depth of the different responses given by the ex-prisoners. However, it has been noted in many studies that a great proportion of the information can be reduced to dichotomies such as 'yes'/'no,' 'married'/'unmarried,' 'young'/'old,' 'better off in prison'/'not better off in prison.' While it is not denied that some information is lost in the dichotomization of each variable, the information gained using none/some/other or an alternative scaling procedure would not be justified in terms of the increased variance that would have to be accounted for, as it was not possible to define a variable that would measure the concept in a more sophisticated manner.

It should be realized that most scales are use-specific; although some variables have a natural scale already, this particular scale may not meet a particular need. While it is true to say, for example, that chronological age has a built-in scale, in terms of understanding behaviour the changes that take place between sixty-one and sixty-two are probably not of the same order as those that take place between sixteen and seventeen. What scale, then, should be used for variables like age? Scaling can be carried out on the construction sample by considering the relationships between the variable and some criterion variable to be used later in prediction analyses. This procedure should be avoided as it results in inordinate shrinkage later.

The researcher who wishes to use his carefully collected large range of categories for each variable is left with the choice of simple guesswork, the development of scales from the work of others or some objective rule. The combination of the last two approaches was used in this study. Age, for instance, was dichotomized around twenty-five years (a round number) in line with findings from studies showing marked changes in the probability of arrest taking place between seventeen and thirty. However, our consideration of arrest rates by age showed that the optimum cut-off in terms of maximizing predictive efficiency was one or two years earlier.

All these decisions should contribute to considerable reliability in the use of the equations in the sample. Finally some variables had to be excluded because they were not 'well balanced,' meaning that at least 10 per cent of the sample had to be in each category of a dichotomy.

THE METHOD

The basic techniques used centre round a step-wise multiple regression analysis programme which is applied initially to a construction sample. The loadings are estimated from the construction sample, using strict objective criteria defined before the analysis started. The standard procedure involves the addition of a variable to the development equation if the regression coefficient associated with it has a t-value with $p < 0.01$. The developed equation is then applied to a validation sample to estimate the extent of shrinkage. The construction sample consisted of a one in two random sample of the combined parolees and dischargees. The 'validation' sample consisted of those not selected in the construction random sample.

Regrettably, the construction-validation method is not the simplest. It is, however, extremely important as it is the only way to test the reliability of the production equations. Step-wise multiple regression analysis, like the non-parametric methods that might have been used, is a technique that maximizes predictive efficiency on the construction sample, and so it could be that high correlations found are merely chance ones. From this point of view, the importance of a second 'validation' sample is obvious theoretically; this was given empirical proof in our study by the shrinkage found when any of the equations was used on the second sample.

The prediction equations were to be used simply to understand what variables are related to arrest and, in the analysis of variance, to see the impact of various aspects of prison and parole on arrest and after release. Were prediction equations to be used for administrative decisions such as the selection of certain parole cases for a second review, samples of between one and two thousand would seem to be essential. Some experimentation in this regard is being carried out by the National Parole Institutes in the USA.

A number of other methods such as predictive attribute analysis, association analysis, factor analysis, and combinations were systematically tried, but as a result, apparently, of the sample sizes involved in this study, gave both less reliable and less efficient predictions of arrest from pre-release data. These methods were abandoned and are, therefore, not reported in the following analysis.

MISSING DATA AND VALIDATION

One type of missing data was found to be empirically unimportant. There were some individuals for whom particular pieces of information were not known. The basic reasons for these 'occasional' missing data were discussed earlier. Some of the analysis was specifically run to compare results for selected variables where all the information was known with those having and not having particular pieces of 'occasional' data missing; no differences, or even tendencies, were found.

The main difference between the analysis carried out on the background data and the prediction analysis carried out using the information known after release is the extent of the missing data on the dischargees. For a variety of insurmountable reasons, only 125 out of the 213 dischargees were interviewed concerning their first five weeks in the community. Those interviewed were more likely to be arrested than those not, which indicates a considerable bias.

Because of these missing data, it was necessary to test the validity and reliability of prediction equations in two ways. The regression equation was developed using the sub-sample of the construction sample on whom all the variables read into the particular correlation matrix were known. There were two methods that could be used to test the validity of this equation. The first model – 'Limited Prediction' – measures reliability and validity only on those members of the construction and validations samples who had all the original variables in the correlation matrix available for analysis. For the second model – 'Real Prediction' – the mean scores from the construction sample are substituted for missing scores in both the construction and validation samples; then the necessary statistics are calculated.

Conclusions based on the Limited Prediction model would be reliable only if the equation was used on a third sample where all the information was known. The Real Prediction method has the advantage in that one can substitute where information is not known. This method thus gives a conservative estimate of the *validity* of the prediction equation, enabling it to be applied to all members of the study.

DYNAMIC DATA

The prediction equations developed using post-release data are said to be using 'dynamic data' as these variables generally describe statuses that could change markedly over time; thus a person could be unemployed at five weeks but employed by ten weeks. A penal record, on the other hand, is a 'static' variable; a person who has been to prison cannot change the fact that he has a penal record. The use of the word 'dynamic' is also used for areas where aspects of parole supervision such as enforcement of a particular rule or assistance by the parole supervisor may change the parolee's situation.

'Dynamic data' were only available for 128 of the 204 subjects in the construction sample as a result of missing occasional variables and the number who were not interviewed concerning their first month in the community.

The Prediction of Reconviction and Re-Arrest: The Limits of Pre-release Data

This chapter now turns to the attempts to develop a regression equation to predict re-conviction and re-arrest within specified time periods from release using the information known at release, that is, biographical and psychometric data. In the previous predictive literature, it has been noted that age, penal record and seriousness of original offence combined enhance the predictive power of each separately. Accordingly, these were the basic variables in the equation, sometimes called the base expectancy score; others were added to these later.

According to one equation, then, an ex-prisoner is more likely to be convicted on an indictable offence if he was under 25 at release, the more he had previously been committed to reformatories or penitentiaries and if he was unemployed at the time of the arrest leading to admission to Kingston Penitentiary.

PSYCHOMETRIC DATA AND MODE OF RELEASE

To see whether reconviction within 12 months could be better predicted when psychometric variables were taken into account, we included the Jesness Combination Score as the third variable. This score was developed from an analysis of the means of parolees and dischargees on a variety of background and psychometric variables. Because the score did not result in a large enough improvement in predictive efficiency, it was excluded from the standard prediction equation. The results of the analysis, however, suggested that 'personality' cannot be totally overlooked.

The equation developed by the Real Prediction model gives satisfactory differentiation on validation though the predictive efficiency and reliability are small. A similar analysis was run for both reconviction within twelve months and arrest within twenty-four months. This latter could be much more efficiently predicted at twenty-four than at twelve months.

The next question to ask was what difference does parole make? At this stage it is important to remember that this question was in reference to background and psychometric data, the information that other studies have shown to be most relevant. Our results at this point, and were the study to stop here, suggest that parole is correctionally effective in reducing the probability of reconviction. However, when post-release data are added to the question, we see that the effects of parole are, for the most part, illusory.

Attempts to Predict Re-Arrest Using a Dynamic Model

In the first section, using background data only, we developed prediction equations (base expectancy scores) to predict arrest within twelve and twenty-four months, the best two of which were added to the data set; dynamic prediction equations were developed from these to predict arrest within the limited time periods – six, twelve, and twenty-four months. For each criterion, two tests were done, one using only dynamic data and a second using this and the base expectancy score.

ARREST WITHIN SIX MONTHS

A man is more likely to be arrested within six months the more reformatory commitments he has, the higher his Jesness Combination Score, the less time he is employed during the first twelve months, if he got a first job through Manpower, if he does at least a fair amount of drinking, if he spent time in the psychiatric unit in Kingston Penitentiary. There is a slight improvement in the predictive efficiency when the base expectancy score was included (the variable combining age, penal record, and Jesness Combination Score which predicted arrest within twenty-four months). If a man has spent time in the psychiatric unit in Kingston Penitentiary, the more reformatory commitments he has, and if he often went to drink with friends after release he is more likely to be arrested within six months from his date of release.

ARREST WITHIN TWELVE MONTHS

In an equation developed omitting background base expectancy scores, an ex-prisoner is more likely to be arrested within twelve months if he has been involved in fights within his first five weeks from release, the shorter his longest job within the first twelve months, if he does at least a fair amount of drinking, if he was not seeing his children. With base expectancy scores included, the ex-prisoner was more likely to be arrested the lower his base expectancy, if he had been involved in fights within the first five weeks from release, the shorter his longest job within the first twelve months from release.

It is interesting to note that the predictability of arrest within twelve months is based on information known after release. The variable concerned with fights is of particular significance as this has not been noted in the previous literature; other studies, however, support the findings that employment, drink and family relationships are variables all related to re-arrest.

ARREST WITHIN TWENTY-FOUR MONTHS

An ex-prisoner is more likely to be arrested if his parole supervisor or the interviewer described any of his associates as 'undesirable,' if he was involved in fights within five weeks from release, the more serious his record of institutional commitments and the younger he is. The only difference between this equation and the one including background base expectancy score was that the variables previous commitments and age at release had been replaced by the base expectancy score comprising those two variables and the Jesness Combination Score. As in the prediction of arrest within twelve months, the equations omitting background base expectancy scores shrink less on validation and result in more efficient predictors. In fact, this equation was the most efficient predictor of any of the three arrest criteria.

One might have expected information collected at five weeks to be a better predictor of arrest within twelve months than within twenty-four months as the time span is shorter, thus allowing for less change in the dynamic situation. Additionally it must be noted that post-release variables predict better, but only marginally better than pre-release variables. So, it is not surprising to find that the equation at twelve months included four post-release variables, whereas the equation at twenty-four months contains only two. This suggests that a change in the employment situation at one month would only have a significant impact on arrest up to twelve months. Other post-release areas and at later points after release may be more important for twenty-four months.

DISCHARGEES

It was found impossible to predict from background data which of the dischargees in this particular sample would be arrested. The analysis of recidivism rates has shown that two out of three of the dischargees were arrested within two years and it was expected that three out of four would be arrested within three years and that more than 80 per cent would be arrested within five years. Being discharged, then, indicates an extremely high probability of being arrested and so technically makes it difficult to locate dischargees who will not be arrested.

PREDICTION EQUATIONS FOR PAROLEES ONLY

A prediction analysis was also carried out for the parolees only. First of all, an equation was developed that included the base expectancy score and parole supervisor information. In the earlier prediction equations for the parolees and dischargees, some variables were used for which the parole supervisor was the source, although in that case they were treated as attributes of the parolees. However, in these equations we used two additional variables, the parole supervisor's perception of the parolee's employment situation and the variable concerned with the closeness of the relationship between parolee and supervisor.

The best prediction equation developed for *arrest within six months* included only the base expectancy score and omitted parole supervisor variables. The parolee was more likely to be arrested within six months the more he had previously been committed to reformatories and penitentiaries (penal record), if he did not spend his first night at home, if he was unemployed for more than five weeks and the higher his background base expectancy score. For parolees, then, penal record is particularly important in relation to short-term recidivism. The person who is going back within six months is likely to be one with low family support, without a job, with a serious penal record and having a non-successful personality type as measured by the base expectancy score.

The best prediction equation developed on a construction sample for *arrest within twelve months* included both the base expectancy and parole supervisor variables. This equation was extremely simple and consisted of the base expectancy score plus whether the parolee received any reprimands within his first five weeks of release.

The prediction equation developed on a construction sample for *arrest within twenty-four months*, omitted the base expectancy score and included parole supervisor variables. Once again reprimands by the parole supervisor within the first five weeks indicated that the parolee was more likely to be arrested within twenty-four months. Problems with financial standing during the first five-week period and seriousness of his previous commitments to penal institutions were the other two variables.

It is particularly interesting that 'financial standing,' which was something dischargees mentioned before release as one of their principal concerns (and we should remember that dischargees have a higher expectation of arrest) should also be an important predictor of re-arrest for parolees within twenty-four months.

SUMMARY

The basic equation, taking into account the ex-prisoner's age at release (under 25 or not) and his penal record, provides a reliable, statistically significant but extremely inefficient equation that predicts reconviction within the first twelve months. This is similar to the findings of other studies. This equation was not improved by including other pre-release variables, such as type of offence; an alternative equation starting with whether the ex-prisoner was employed at the time of the original offence gave similar results on validation. The addition of personality characteristics as measured by the Jesness inventory marginally improved the equation, suggesting that they are important. Finally, knowing the mode of release also increased predictability; parole, then, for some unknown reason makes a difference.

With post-release (dynamic) data, using the limited prediction model on the construction sample, we got fairly high multiple correlation coefficients for prediction of arrest within twelve and twenty-four months; however, these shrank considerably (to 0.3) on validation. The equation using dynamic data resulted in marginally higher correlation coefficients on validation than those equations based on background data only. Post-release information does seem to improve predictive efficiency and is, for the most part, available within five weeks from date of release. However, our study has also shown that this information is extremely difficult to obtain; unless it is collected for other reasons, then, perhaps it is not worth collecting such information for the small improvement in predictive efficiency alone.

The real value of the dynamic prediction equations is in helping to understand the way in which structural variables operate; that is, the sort of behaviour that young offenders with long penal records engage in after release before re-arrest. This is primarily the subject of the next section which looks at the extent to which other levels of functioning in the community can be predicted from the data bank used here.

Before leaving the interpretation of the predictive equations, it should be emphasized that those containing a mixture of pre- and post-release variables illustrate the importance of the post-release situation in relation to a man's chances of re-arrest. This analysis has used dichotomies, which are important indicators of underlying variables but do not tell us all that such a variable might. Even so, this analysis suggests that a method that aims to be correctionally effective should be concentrating on controlling fights, employment and associates. Ideally, also, more should be done to find out what these variables really mean. As only one step towards this, in the next section these three variables themselves will be predicted and so it will be possible to see how much these are independent of the other characteristics of the ex-prisoners. If, for example, being employed or not is simply a result of being young and having a long penal record, not much can be done. If, however, ex-prisoners were 'unlucky' in terms of 'chance' factors that affect the job market, then there is a number of recommendations that could be implemented to help them find employment, the result being, hopefully, that the proportion of ex-prisoners being reconvicted would be reduced.

Social Functioning

Why is it that we can predict arrest with only marginal efficiency? Is it because there are too many factors unrelated to the ex-prisoner's behaviour that affect his arrest or because his behaviour is itself largely unpredictable? In this part we shall first consider the prediction of certain aspects of social functioning, family, friends, employment and drink that were themselves found to be related to re-arrest.

Then we will be looking at the same variables, but in relation to whether a man was discharged from a maximum security institution, whether he applied for parole and whether he was granted parole. It seems that the decisions made by the parole board are more predictable than any of the others considered in this or the previous chapter. We also find the parolee's behaviour not much more predictable than his arrest.

THE NEGATIVE SITUATIONAL VARIABLES

(i) Fighting

For parolees, fighting was significantly correlated ($p < 0.01$) with 11 variables (men not co-operating in a one-month interview were not included in the analysis). A parolee was more likely to be involved in fights the younger he was when he first left home, the younger he was at release; the heavier he was; if he had been reprimanded by his parole supervisor, if his parole supervisor had tried to assist him with drink and associated problems; if the situation in which the crime originally occurred still existed; if his penitentiary money lasted less than a week; if he drank regularly and with friends; and if he saw his chances of staying out of prison as low. This relationship between fighting, alcohol, age and associates was also found for dischargees.

In another analysis done on the same data, we found that the parolee who fought was more likely to be released on minimum parole, to be single or not have a steady girlfriend, for his original offence to be against property, to have been in the psychiatric unit at Kingston Penitentiary, and, also generally speaking, to have a psychometric profile similar to a dischargee's.

As early as five weeks from release, younger parolees, particularly those under twenty-five, are already going around with their old friends and getting involved in fights. It has been suggested by some authors that this may be a reaction to steps taken by the parole supervisor. The evidence from this study would suggest that the parole supervisor has little effect on this vicious circle, although we know from his formal or informal warnings to the parolee that he identifies it.

Using only background information for this equation, an ex-prisoner is more likely to be involved in fights the younger he is, if he was released from Kingston Penitentiary, the lower his CPI combination score (that is less like the successful person, and more like the average dischargee), and if he had not applied for parole.

These relationships suggest that fighting is just a proxy for some underlying personality trait. Statistically, however, fighting was more closely related to arrest than any psychometric variable collected in this study. A parole supervisor concerned with changing a 'fighter' into a 'non-fighter' by working on personality or the situation should still direct his work closely towards fighting, until detailed analysis has been undertaken to explain this variable more fully.

(ii) Undesirable associates

An ex-prisoner was more likely to have undesirable associates, if he spent his first night away from home; if his intentions had not changed; if he was drinking regularly; and if he was a parolee he was more likely to be described as having problems with employment. Two equations combining these variables were developed to predict whether or not a man would have undesirable associates. The first, based on the two pre-release variables, reformatory commitments and the ex-prisoner's perception of the penitentiary's effectiveness, validated, but only at a very low level. A more reliable one, however, was developed from post-release data. According to this one, a man was more likely to have undesirable associates if he spent his first night away from home, if his intentions had not changed, if he did not go to church, and if the situation in which the original crime occurred still existed (typically lack of employment or money).

Spending the first night away from home appears to be a proxy for lack of persons attached to the ex-prisoner in the first few weeks. It thus implies a process whereby certain ex-prisoners 'filter' from a detached state to having undesirable associates. The first night for ex-prisoners is very important. Dreams and fears are built up around what will occur. It is suggested that making suitable supportive arrangements for the ex-prisoner may make considerable difference as to whether he gets involved in situations which later will lead back to re-arrest.

(iii) Regular drinking

As one might expect from the previous analysis, drinking regularly is linked with unemployment, fighting and undesirable associates with correlations between 0.2 and 0.3. However, a regular drinker is also more likely to be a bad risk on CPI scores, not go to church, to be able to name a payoff for involvement in a new offence and to feel his intentions had not changed. This analysis would suggest that a typology taking account of these relationships would have considerable predictive power.

THE POSITIVE SITUATIONAL VARIABLES

(i) Length of time employed within twelve months

The main findings were that parole is importantly associated with whether the person obtains employment or not. Once again, it is not clear whether this results from parole selection, the parole agreement or both. There was a relatively high correlation between whether the ex-prisoner was paroled and whether he was employed. This implies that there is something about parole supervision that leads to longer periods of employment in the community. It will be shown below that this appears to explain the delays in arrest associated with release on parole.

(ii) Seeing children or not

A man was more likely to be seeing his children within five weeks of release if he was released on parole, if he applied for parole, if he was not released from a maximum security penitentiary, if he was over twenty-five years old, if he was a more 'successful' type of person on the CPI and Jesness, if he thought he would succeed, if he was close to his supervisor, if he intended to go straight, and if the situation leading to arrest no longer existed after release. The cluster analysis showed that he was also unlikely to have offences against staff or inmates and to have made his money from the institution last.

This variable is a classic example of the kind that influences parole board selection. A prisoner with a wife and children to whom he could go on release, is more likely to be in a medium or minimum security institution and to apply for, and be granted, parole. We have already seen that marital status on admission is only marginally related to arrest; yet 'family status' on release is important not only by itself but also because it is related to a wide range of variables positively related to non-arrest and selection for parole.

It is also clearly related to closeness of relationship with the parole supervisor, the tendency being that the 'good' parolee has a close relationship with his supervisor and the 'bad' parolee a not so good relationship. Perhaps, too, the supervisor gives more help with family problems to those parolees with whom he has a good relationship. This variable appears to delay arrest. Speculating on the trends in the data, those marriages with children may contain the parolee for about twelve months and then start to deteriorate; this is consistent with the parole supervisor's identification of problems in the six-to-twelve month period, which come to a head some time after the twelve-month period.

The main conclusions from this section must be that the behaviour of the ex-prisoner in the community is only as predictable as his probability of getting arrested. Whether he will find a job, get into debt, save, be involved in fights, go around with undesirable associates, drink, are all criteria which can be predicted with about the same efficiency as whether he will be arrested within twelve or twenty-four months. Individual variables like 'seeing children' are more predictable because they are dependent on such things as whether he was married at the time of admission. We are left with the conclusion that there is no simple key to knowing what the ex-prisoner will do or what will be done to him after release. Basic tendencies can be forecast but there are so many unforeseeable contingencies that may arise where it is impossible to predict with much accuracy which way he will go.

However one should not allow these contingencies to return us to clinical predictions or the assumption that ex-prisoners' behaviour has no common factors. The variables used here were dichotomized, and all this analysis was carried out as a construction sample and retested on a validation sample. Thus the estimates are systematic and conservative. As a result one can have considerable confidence that the variables identified from the pilot and qualitative work preceeding the quantitative analysis, which were then found to contribute at high levels of statistical significances in the prediction equations, are important in most ex-prisoners' careers. While changing an ex-prisoner's situation on one of these variables would not guarantee that he would not be arrested, it should lead to identifiable changes (statistically significant) on samples of the size used here (about 200) which could have major economic significance on a parole system where National Parole alone releases 5000 men each year.

Parole, Maximum Security: The Selection Component

We have now looked at arrest and the social functioning of the men after release. Throughout the report we have seen that parolees differ from dischargees in many ways. It is evident that selection for parole is a principal element in those differences. What sort of variables are associated with that selection? Are those variables the same as those associated with arrest? Even though institutional behaviour is not related to arrest, is it related to parole?

The ex-prisoners generally felt that the parole board was fair, although 10 per cent said the board pulled the names out of the hat, 15 per cent that 'the guys who deserve it don't get it and the guys who don't do,' and 3 per cent said that they were made to wait too long for parole. More than one-third of the ex-prisoners mentioned the nature or character of the man as one of the things that the parole board took into consideration. Some aspects of employment, family life, or the relationship with the wife were mentioned by 20 per cent; 16 per cent mentioned the past record of the applicant; 9 per cent mentioned his background before coming to the institution; only 8 per cent mentioned his behaviour inside; and 13 per cent described what people had to say about him on the outside.

Are these indeed among the criteria used? Our pilot interviews suggested that the institution in which a prisoner was held affected his

TABLE 10.1

Totals released, by parole selection variable and released from maximum security or not, showing proportion arrested within twenty-four months

	Kingston Penitentiary		Lower security institutions		Total	
	Released	Percentage arrested within 24 months	Released	Percentage arrested within 24 months	Released	Percentage arrested within 24 months
Parolee	21	38.1	189	45.0	210	44.3
Dischargee applying	21	66.7	79	63.3	100	64.0
Dischargee not applying	33	75.8	80	68.8	113	70.8
Total	75	62.7	348	54.6	423	56.0

chances for parole. Let us first try to answer this question and then try in retrospect to predict who would apply for or have been granted parole.

PAROLE, ARREST, AND RELEASE FROM KINGSTON PENITENTIARY

Some believe that it is harder to get parole from maximum security only because it is there, where the worse risks are held. However, the analysis suggests that being in maximum security has an additional negative 'labelling' effect over and above being a worse risk. Several other studies have shown the importance of recommendations to the final decision (Leveillé, 1970; Macnaughton-Smith, 1973; Robison, 1971) in parole decisions. The analysis here suggests that the classification decision to keep in maximum security is a proxy for a negative recommendation for parole.

Those selected for parole from Kingston Penitentiary had a lower re-arrest rate than parolees released from less secure institutions (see Table 10.1). The tendency is reversed for the dischargee, who is more likely to be arrested if he was released from Kingston Penitentiary as opposed to one of the other institutions.

Our findings also suggest that the final application rate is directly related to the institutional granting rate. Table 10.2 presents the non-application rate and the final granting rate by institution for the year 1968. The proportion of releases not applying for parole in Kingston Penitentiary was nearly twice that of Collins Bay and at least 10 per cent

TABLE 10.2

Proportions of parole: final decisions in 1968, by institution of release

	Kingston Penitentiary	Joyceville	Collins Bay	Warkworth
Non-application rate*	42.2%	29.9%	20.5%	7.9%
Granting rate†	35.3%	46.8%	50.8%	70.8%

* Non-application rate is defined as parole denied on automatic parole review without application divided by all those eligible to apply

† Granting rate is defined as those to whom ordinary parole was granted divided by all those who applied, but were not deferred

SOURCE: Parole board

more than Joyceville's. In contrast to this the granting rate for Kingston was lower than that for the medium security institutions, and half that for Warkworth.

A man was more likely to be released from Kingston Penitentiary as opposed to lower security institutions, the earlier he was admitted, if he was under twenty-five at release, if he was single, if he had several offences against staff, and if he was refused parole. If granted parole, however, he was likely to have more contacts and phone calls with his supervisor, was more likely to be unemployed in the first five weeks and to have received help with employment, so that he apparently gets more intensive supervision from his parole supervisor. While three Kingston ex-prisoners were later involved in the only post-release homicides, it is interesting to note that the men released from Kingston were not in general those who were dangerous to society, but those serving long sentences who were dangerous to the prison authorities.

SELECTION FOR MINIMUM PAROLE

Minimum parole is a system whereby a prisoner can trade a month of prison time (up to six months) for each year of his sentence; a person with a two-year sentence could be released two months early. He would then serve those two months including his statutory remission time in the community under parole supervision, making a little less than ten months under supervision. This, of course, was also the additional time he would have to serve were his minimum parole revoked or in addition to the new sentence (if his parole was forfeited). A prisoner who applied for parole might also have been offered this type of minimum parole instead of a complete refusal. The parole board claims to use this for persons considered to be poor risks. Many of those offered this type of parole refused it, although some prisoners made specific applications for it.

In relation to the average 'regular' parolee, more of the 'minimum' parolees in our sample tended to be under 25, to have more pervious commitments to penal institutions, and to have been sentenced to Kingston for assault or fraud. (See Appendix E.) What is surprising in view of the reasons for the implementation of this programme which enables the parole board to grant parole to persons who are bad risks, thereby providing more 'protection' for the community, is that there were no apparent differences in the over-all recidivism rates between the two groups, particularly since minimum parolees tended to be younger and have a more serious penal record, both factors which are indicative of a greater likelihood of re-arrest. In view of the fact that minimum paroles generally have a higher failure rate than ordinary paroles, our finding for this sample probably reflects a higher arrest rate for ordinary parolees associated with the more liberal granting of ordinary parole in 1968.

According to statements by the parole board, minimum parole was almost always offered when a prisoner who had applied for 'parole' was turned down. 24 of the parolees interviewed at one month had been released on minimum parole. Why had they accepted it? 12 said simply that they wanted to get out. Of the remainder, 4 wanted to get back with their family and 2 that their family wanted them although they would rather have stayed in. The remainder said they intended to go straight anyhow. No more sophisticated analysis was carried out on minimum parole, partly because the numbers were so small and partly because the arrest rate was so similar to that of regular parolees.

PAROLE SELECTION

In the next chapter it will be shown that parole is apparently effective. However, we will suggest that this is an illusion resulting from differences between those granted parole and those refused, but more importantly between parole applicants and non-applicants. This section continues to look at the data on characteristics of the ex-prisoner in an attempt to provide further understanding of differences between applicant and non-applicants, parolees and parole refusals, and, parolees and dischargees.

Throughout the early sections of this report there has been extensive analysis using *t*-tests, contingency tables, and other methods which have pointed out the similarities and differences between parolees and dischargees. What emerges from this is the peculiar importance of the psychometric and self-concept variables. At the time these particular questions were asked the men were aware of how they would likely be released. It is suggested that responses to the two questions concerned with the effects of prison and the perceptions of chances of failing after release may in fact be affected by the granting of parole; that is, a 'halo' effect could result from being considered for parole which may later become a self-fulfilling prophecy. This cannot be due to parole board selection, as the board would not know or get a truthful answer about the man's beliefs about his chances of succeeding after release. The correlations with these variables are higher than with any other variables which are apparently related to the parole board's decision. It could be, however, that the various recommendations made by institution staff or parole service employees are highly correlated with the prisoner's own perception of his chances of failing. As these variables are related to arrest, it is unlikely that they are simple artifacts of the interview situation. Certainly the high correlations (as high as some of the validated background prediction correlations) between arrest rates and ex-prisoner's own perceptions of their chances of success would indicate that they have a fairly realistic view of the situation.

If an ex-prisoner loses his parole through revocation he serves a longer total time in the institution than if he had been paroled. This probably helps to separate some sheep from the goats. However it was not possible to quantify its importance. It is clearly possible to produce a reliable prediction equation based on our data to predict who the parole board will release on parole; such equations are more efficient than those predicting arrest. However, it is difficult to predict who would have applied for parole. Non-applicants are often those who spend long periods of time in penal institutions, do not obtain jobs after release, do not have a family with children to which to go, and run into continuing problems as a result of drink. In an earlier chapter, where breakdowns against arrest criteria were carried out, these variables were among those more closely associated with arrest.

There is marginal support for the view that a person applies for parole because he wants to get back to his family and because he is planning to go straight. A person is more likely to have applied for parole if he spent his first night with a family, if he saw his chances of succeeding as high at the time of the pre-release interview, if he had personality characteristics similar to a parolee (i.e., a more 'successful' person), if he had debts within five weeks of release, if he was unable to name a pay-off to commit another crime after release, if he was not involved in fights within five weeks from his date of release, and if he found a job during his first twelve months in the community. In spite of this the most reliable equation was based solely on perception of chances of succeeding.

How do those granted parole differ from those refused both before and after release? The best equation developed from the construction sample relating variables to the granting or refusing of parole for those persons who made application is this: a person is more likely to be granted parole if, at the time of the pre-release interview, he saw his chances of succeeding after release as high, the shorter his longest job in the first twelve months from release, if he obtained a job within the first five weeks, the shorter his time in the penitentiary and the more he was like the 'successful,' adjusted person (CPI combination score). Among applicants those selected are likely after release to get jobs immediately, although their longest job is usually shorter.

RELEASE AS A PAROLEE OR DISCHARGEE

A person is more likely to have been released on parole if he thought before release that he would succeed and if his penal record was less severe. This analysis was based on information that has been used earlier to predict arrest, the two variables concerned with perception of the effectiveness of the penitentiary and perception of chances of post-release failure. The prediction equation developed on the construction sample against release as a parolee or a dischargee using pre-release background variables only was, compared to many of the other prediction equations that have been developed, an efficient predictor.

Another equation was developed using all pre- and post-release information to predict release as a parolee or dischargee. This emphasized the characteristics that most differentiated the two groups after release. Pre-release perception of chances of post-release failure is once again the most important and clear-cut variable in the equation, although employment, penal record, where they spent their first night, whether they went on nights out, whether drink was a problem before or after the time in the penitentiary, were also important.

The final equation developed omitted the two variables concerned with the effectiveness of the penitentiary and the chances of failing. A person was more likely to have been released on parole the less serious his penal record, if he said no-one in prison was concerned about him, if he could not name a pay-off and if drink was not a problem before and after the penitentiary. The predictive power of this equation is similar to the predictive power of the equations to predict arrest. It is difficult to say whether drink is not a problem and that is why he was selected for parole or whether it is not now because he conforms to parole rules or a supervisor's threat that parole will be revoked if he drinks.

COMPARISON BETWEEN PREDICTIVE EFFICIENCIES

It appears that men who do not apply for parole tend to have many characteristics in common with those who apply for but are refused parole. It may be, too, that non-applicants can correctly second guess the parole board decision. In general this study was not designed to predict these criteria,[1] but rather to show that the selection component certainly accounts for, in some measure, the effectiveness of parole.

Selection and its relation to success can operate in several ways. First, the parole board tends to grant parole only to those who will be released to a family and job and who are less likely to drink and go around with undesirable associates (the average successful parolee). Secondly it may be that those men with these attributes are, in the main, the ones who apply, thereby selecting themselves. Thirdly, it could be that being granted parole makes the man think that, in fact, he can succeed, in terms of getting a job, not drinking, etc.

We have found that it is easier to predict the decisions of a small group (at the time of this study the parole board was composed of only five members with similar backgrounds who worked in the same building) with some kind of consistent philosophy than it is for a larger, more diverse group who come from a wide range of institutions and on whom more 'chance' factors can operate.

Selection for or Rehabilitation by Prison or Parole

Men selected for parole by the National Parole Board are a population that differs from those released at expiration of sentence in terms of a wide range of characteristics; these include both variables concerned with the original offence, sentence and previous convictions and also variables relating to the type of adjustment made by the prisoner in the institution. The analysis of the psychometric data indicated that the parolee was a relatively more successful, better adjusted person than the dischargee. Some of these variables are themselves related to re-arrest, although, after controlling for one or two, we still found a tendency for the parolee to have a smaller probability of re-arrest. In this chapter the base expectancy techniques (i.e., controlling for risk) that include post-release information will be used to show that such a difference exists, although it mainly results from differences between dischargees who applied for parole and those who did not, rather than parole selection itself.

There are a number of possible explanations for the differences in arrest outcome between parolees and dischargees that cannot be accounted for by prediction equations. Such explanations include the following.

(1) There were factors not included in the prediction equations but used consciously or unconsciously by the parole board in selecting better risks for parole, meaning that the parole board can improve on the ability of a base expectancy equation to select. *Or*

(2) the conditions of parole deterred some of those released on parole from behaviour that would have led to their arrest. There are two important ways in which this may operate: (*a*) the parolee commits no

offences, deterred by the threat of the extra 'time' to serve if his parole is revoked or forfeited; (*b*) as a result of the parole agreement, the parolee gets a job or does not drink to excess (assuming that these are related to going straight) or does not engage in other behaviour conducive to reinvolvement in crime. *Or*

(3) the parolee benefits from his association with his parole supervisor. It could be that: (*a*) the parolee is counselled or 'converted' into going straight; (*b*) the parole supervisor helps or encourages the parolee to get a job, not drink, etc. *Or*

(4) selection for parole labels the parolee as a better risk and therefore, creates some kind of self-fulfilling prophecy; alternatively, being refused parole may have a negative effect on those refused parole. *Or*

(5) early release may provide more chance for the family to stay together and mitigate harmful effects of longer imprisonment. *Or*

(6) there are important differences between those who apply for parole and those who do not. *Or*

(7) suspension of parole, followed by continuation, is used to protect society by imprisoning the parolee before a new offence occurs, but releasing him without revoking his parole.

Let us try to narrow down the issues. First, a brief review of the literature on the clinician's ability to predict a person's behaviour shows that statistical methods of combining information, which may have been originally collected by a clinician, are more efficient than the clinician working on his own. From this point of view, then, it would seem that the clinician, or in this case, the parole board, does not have 'divine insight' (Wilkins, 1969).

Secondly, we saw in the first chapter that where randomization was used to avoid the selection of more 'suitable' offenders for certain treatment, there were few differences in the apparent effects. We also know that when the intensity of parole supervision is varied in experimental studies differences in outcome are found; however, these can be accounted for satisfactorily as effects of differential decision-making by parole supervisors and the parole revocation authority.

Thirdly, we have contradictory evidence from two non-experimental studies. One was a study carried out in Quebec that used prediction methods to control for risk (Landreville, 1967). When type was controlled for, their results suggested that parole was associated with lower recidivism rates as their parolees had a significantly lower tendency to be re-arrested than their dischargees. The other study is one that compares the alternatives in traditional dispositions for convicted offenders as summarized briefly in a manual for persons holding judicial office in the United Kingdom (Home Office, 1969, 69–73). Absolute discharge, fine, probation, borstal and prison are compared by means of a base expectancy table. Some of their conclusions were that: '(1) fines were followed by the fewest re-convictions compared with the expected numbers for both first offenders and recidivists of almost all age-groups; (2) at best the results (of probation) were only about equal to expectation. Probation produced relatively better results (in comparison with the calculated expectation) when used for offenders with previous convictions than when used for first offenders.' The prediction equations were restricted to three variables and so it is highly likely that factors were omitted which might explain these differences in the failure rates. In a sense, then, we are no further ahead as it is not possible to tell whether these differences resulted from some aspect of the fine and probation or some completely different selection factor. However, because we know that the clinician cannot predict more efficiently than a good prediction equation, we are forced to conclude, at this point, that parole does indeed have some effect (Sawyer, 1966).

Given this apparent confusion, we tried to find out which of the various explanations was 'correct.'

Earlier in the report a number of different prediction equations was developed to facilitate comparisons between dischargees and parolees with similar 'base expectancies' or chances of recidivating. The conceptual model is simple. An equation is developed which enables the researcher to say that individual A or group A with certain characteristics has an X per cent chance of recidivating. A comparison is then made between members of group A's behaviour on parole and on discharge. If group A does better than predicted on parole, then parole is 'more effective' for this group. The widely used and statistically efficient method for doing this is called the 'analysis of co-variance.'

The analysis, on which this section was based, is divided into three sections. First of all six prediction equations that were developed to predict arrest within six, twelve, twenty-four months were considered. The *co-variants* to be discussed first were parole selection variables; (i) whether the ex-prisoner was released on parole or discharge, (ii) whether the ex-prisoner applied for parole or not, and (iii) whether he was granted parole or not. The *criteria* are arrest within six, twelve and twenty-four months. In all cases the analysis of variance was carried out on the validation sample using the original regression coefficients developed in the construction sample. If an effect was present, it was therefore more likely to appear as statistically significant.

The analyses of co-variance were carried out within both the limited and real prediction models, although all co-variants were more likely to be significant in the limited prediction model. This is due to a technical differential selection factor; dischargees interviewed were more likely to be arrested than those not interviewed.

THE EFFECT OF PAROLE SELECTION ON ARREST

The first of the parole selection variables is concerned with the simple comparison between persons finally released on parole or not. All we know from this is that the apparent effectiveness of parole results either from selection by the parole board, applications by 'good' inmates or from some aspect of parole supervision or the threat of revocation. The other parole selection variables were added to provide some further clarification. The second variable would indicate whether there was a selection factor associated with not applying for parole. The third variable concerned with whether parole was granted would bring us closer to assessing the results of the parole board's ability to select from applicants, though it would not be able to discriminate between effects of selection and those of parole supervision or threat of revocation.

Although it appears that magistrates and parole boards do not have 'divine insight' (they cannot select better than prediction equations), parole did seem to have some effect often controlling for risk in the non-experimental studies cited. Either some selection factor was still operating or, despite the conclusions in chapter 1 on the general lack of effectiveness of most sentencing dispositions, these measures did have some effect (as some claim).

Our results suggest that if anyone has 'divine insight,' it is the inmate. Using the limited prediction model, we found, after accounting for expected probabilities of re-arrest, that the two variables, mode of release and application for parole, were very much related to re-arrest within six and twelve months, although not twenty-four months. The variable concerned with the granting of parole, on the other hand, was not found to be related. These findings can probably be understood when we remember that a man whose parole is revoked will have additional time to serve in the penitentiary.

When parole selection variables were added to the base expectancy equation (with or without psychometric data) predictive efficiency was increased for arrest within twenty-four months. When post-release information was included in the equation all three parole selection variables were non-significantly related to arrest, implying that application for parole was independent of whether the man would have undesirable associates or be involved in fights after release.

In the real prediction model no parole selection variable could be added to an equation within the significance criterion of 1 per cent. Using a 5 per cent level of significance, applying for parole would have been included in equations against six and twelve months but not twenty-four months. Being released on parole would only have been included against arrest within twelve months. In relation to arrest within twenty-four months mode of release was significant when pre-release variables were added, and began to approach significance used with the equation based on post-release variables such as associates and fighting.

We do, however, show that when the parole supervisor gave help with employment, the probability of arrest within six months was significantly reduced. However, this was the only aspect of parole which seemed to have any impact on the probability of arrest within any time period.

The effectiveness of parole in terms of reducing recidivism within twelve and twenty-four months, or in the long run generally, is an illusion. First, those selected for parole are no less likely to be re-arrested than predicted based on such relationships as those between age, initial employment and re-arrest, though parole is, however, granted in the first place to those with lower probabilities. Secondly, those who do not apply are more likely to be re-arrested than predicted. More generally, neither the length of imprisonment nor release from a maximum security institution have any important impact on the probability of arrest. It does appear that parole delays the arrest of a parolee from the first six months to a later period within twenty-four months, perhaps by getting the parolee employed or possibly through help from the supervisor with his associates and drinking.

THE DIFFERENTIAL EFFECT OF PAROLE ON PAROLEES

Much of the experimental research carried out in California has been concentrated on controlled experiments to investigate the effects of 'more' parole rather than the effects of parole or not. Even in the well-known San Francisco project offenders supervised through minimum case-loads were still under the threat of revocation of probation or parole and could get some help from the federal probation office if they wanted it. Rarely have analyses been carried out to see whether any particular component of intensive supervison was in any way related to outcome.

This we have attempted to do. The parole supervisor's help with employment was associated with non-arrest and no help, with arrest. This was the only variable that resulted in a significant contribution to the explanation of the criteria.

Although the preliminary analysis suggested relationships, once the type of men released on parole was statistically controlled the number of contacts between the parolee and the parole supervisor was found not to be related to arrest within any time period from the date of release. This was also true of variables such as reprimands by the parole supervisor, the closeness of the relationship between the parolee and the parole supervisor as seen by the parole supervisor and help with problems such as drink or associates.

THE EFFECT OF PRISON ON LIKELIHOOD OF ARREST

We carried out a similar analysis for two prison variables, length of time in prison (admission year) and effect of security level (maximum security institution or not).

When talking to prison administrators or prison staff, one often hears remarks such as 'we keep trying, they may just happen to take notice of some piece of advice I mention one day.' More sophisticated arguments of the same genre are that imprisonment provides an opportunity for education and work training to be undertaken or that the prison experience will motivate the ex-prisoner to go straight or release.

It has been suggested that a man reaches an optimum release point during his imprisonment, perhaps when the sentence is really 'biting' or when institutional advice is being heeded. If the man was then released, prison would be effective. However, when is this point reached? Would this make any difference in terms of the problems a man will face with respect to drink, unemployment, friends or a wife, or simply surviving after release? We simply do not know.

Another argument put forward particularly by opponents of prison, is that the longer a man is inside, the more likely it is that he will be affected by harmful aspects of prison such as associating with other criminals, and 'prisonisation.'

Although our detailed analysis has suggested already that length of imprisonment is not related to re-arrest, we carried out the analysis anyway to strengthen our conclusions and, hopefully, to rebut these types of 'myths.' Admission year was so unrelated to arrest within six, twelve and twenty-four months that the computer would not even compute a t-value in either the limited or real prediction models.

We did the same kind of analysis for the variable, release from a maximum security institution. The arguments, both pro and con, used for length of imprisonment also apply here. In addition the man who was not in maximum security was more likely to have received some kind of further education or job training. After controlling for risk an offender interviewed who was released from maximum security was more likely to be re-arrested within six months although the relationship did not hold up for the total sample. There were some significant differences in the limited prediction model. Release from a maximum security institution was significantly related to arrest within six months and marginally related to arrest within twelve months. However, in the real prediction situation this variable was not related to arrest.

The analysis in this chapter has brought us both new insights and disappointments. We have been able to develop and test an empirical theory as to why men are re-arrested. We have found that if we know certain aspects of their early post-release behaviour, we can predict longer term re-arrest behaviour, although not very efficiently. Although this may result from the fact that this behaviour is, to some extent unpredictable, it may also very well be that we do not, at this point, know which indices of behaviour to use.

We have looked at both prison and parole only to confirm the conclusions of other studies that they are ineffective in terms of reducing the likelihood of re-arrest. We have also looked at some components and with one notable exception, help with employment, have not been able to show an effect. We did, however, find that parole apparently had a delaying effect.

Our findings on lack of effectivness are also particularly powerful as we compared men released on parole with those released without supervision or threat of revocation.

Finally we were fortunate to have a situation where the prisoner by his application for parole gave us his own assessment of his chances of succeeding on parole. In fact this may have been quite accurate as we know that he very definitely has something to lose if his parole is revoked.

NOTES TO CHAPTER 10

1 See research reports by James (1971) for a discussion of information on parole and the decision to apply for parole, and the research report by P. Macnaughton-Smith (1973) for an interesting perspective on prediction of the parole granting decision compared to prediction of 'failure' on parole.

11

An Overview of the Findings

Introduction

In this study, subjects were a representative sample comprising 423 ex-prisoners released from Ontario federal penitentiaries in 1968: 210 were paroled, 113 never applied for parole and 100 applied but were refused; these last two groups then, were unconditionally released at expiration of sentence.

The investigation began while the men were still inmates, and included group interviews, administration of several standard psychological tests, and the collection of data from the institutional files. The most important sections of the study were based on an intensive analysis of the progress of the ex-prisoners during their first twelve months in the community 'measured' by interviews held with female interviewers concerning their experiences during the first five weeks after release (98 per cent of parolees and 60 per cent of dischargees were interviewed; arrest and background data were used to allow for non-representativeness). For each parolee, questionnaires were completed by his parole supervisor at seven predetermined stages during the first twelve months. Also, data on arrests and reconvictions within the full twenty-four-month follow-up period from each man's date of release were collected from the police.

Of those discharged, 68 per cent were re-arrested in connection with an indictable offence within two years from release; similarly 44 per cent of those paroled were re-arrested or had their parole revoked within this time. It was expected that by the end of thirty-six months the respective proportions would exceed 75 per cent and 50 per cent.

We have given considerable emphasis in this study to gaining a well-rounded picture of the ex-prisoner's social situation in terms of his family circumstances, his handling of alcohol, his financial resources, associates, fights, the way he spent his leisure time, employment difficulties and adjustment, and his attitude to life in general. Our operational definition of his 'integration into society' consisted of an assessment of these variables.

The study has also concentrated on the extent to which the experience of penitentiary alone, compared to the experience of penitentiary and parole, affects the probability of recidivism, and, more generally, the men's integration into society. Only when these things are known can we assess, first, the effectiveness of the peniteniary or parole in terms of protection for the public and rehabilitation of the offender, and second, the extent to which money so spent is well spent.

Ex-Prisoners' Behaviour and Experience

Compared to an unselected sample of the adult male population, proportionately more of the men in this study were English Canadians (unlike in other parts of Canada), from urban areas, of low socio-economic, occupational, and educational status, and young. Nearly half were defined by themselves or by others as having a problem with alcohol. Most were single or faced with marital break-up. Their scores on personality, but *not* intelligence, tests differed markedly from the norm. Nearly every man had been arrested several times previously and most had been to a penal institution; one-third had been to a training school for juveniles. Many came from families with a brother or possibly a father with similar histories. Most had been convicted this time of one or more property offences.

Before going to the penitentiary this time, more than three out of five ex-prisoners had held a job for at least a year, and more than 80 per cent of all jobs held were in the unskilled or semi-skilled categories. More than three out of four ex-prisoners, then, arrived at the institution with no real skill.

Most often, the ex-prisoners saw themselves not as deliberate criminals but as men overcome by a variety of circumstances. One-third said that some aspect of employment, or money, was the primary reason for their offence, and another third mentioned sudden passion.

Although those selected for parole differed from the combined group of those refused and those who never applied for parole on a number of variables, these differences were usually small in comparison to those between the total group of men studied and an unselected non-imprisoned adult male population. Moreover, there were few large dissimilarities, on these biographical and psychometric variables, between men arrested within twenty-four months of release and those not arrested. Where such differences existed they were usually not as large, and the total pattern of disparities between those later arrested and those not arrested did not seem as consistent as the differences between those granted parole and those not.

On release the prisoners were issued with a 'prison suit,' and for most this was the only clothing which they had at this time. Although about half the group wore this suit after the first day, almost as many disposed of it as fast as possible with great pleasure as an expression of their freedom, or in order to get a job. Certainly, a good many of the men had to buy clothes when they got out, even just to work. In common with other prison systems, the men here were released with relatively little money, little enough to make it difficult for a man without family, friends, or support to survive for a month without recourse to welfare.

Although most ex-prisoners were not actively rejected by their families, they were usually left to face the problems of the free world on their own. The lack of interest and support by others is typified by the suggestion that the police may be the persons most actively interested in the man released from prison. Very few were met at the bus or train terminal. For the minority who were, the parolee was more likely to be met by family, the dischargee by friends. Few parolees were met by their parole supervisor.

Most ex-prisoners remembered the first day out and their feelings, of exhilaration at being free and of anxiety at the problems of finding food, accommodation, drink, or a girl. Even parolees typically faced these alone. However, one in three said that seeing their families was the most important thing they did the first day, though after the deprivations of the prison as many others mentioned various 'indulgences' such as getting drunk, girls, new clothes, a good meal, or a good bed.

They experienced many of the expected symptoms associated with other transition statuses, such as depression, anxiety, difficulty getting used to things, loneliness, trouble talking to people, and feelings of looking like an ex-con. Most ex-prisoners felt that others reacted to them negatively because of their record, particularly police and neighbours. On the other hand, a few said that sometimes the Manpower and welfare people went out of their way to help them because of their record.

During the period soon after release, many ex-prisoners met other ex-prisoners. While most were friendly enough at the time, they really did little more than pass the time of day. At five weeks from release, some ex-prisoners still felt lonely, perhaps because they had difficulty in making friends. Many were already going around with friends described as 'undesirable,' although there were also others who deliberately avoided such company. Many had already been involved in fights; quite a number, particularly dischargees, were drinking regularly after release and mentioned problems associated with this.

There was considerable variation in the methods used by the ex-prisoner to get his first job, although usually these did not include friends, family, or previous employers. About half of the employers contacted asked for, or had, information about the applicant's criminal record. Where such information was known, less than half of the ex-prisoners were turned down immediately. During the whole period of the first twelve months, a smaller proportion of dischargees was actually employed. Although this may have been partly the result of the methods they used to try to obtain jobs, it may also have been associated with lack of effort and the fact that dischargees are usually less employable on the basis of previous employment history. On the other hand, the greater effort made by parolees to obtain jobs probably had something to do with the way parole supervisors interpreted the parole agreement.

Parole itself seems to make little difference to the actual employability of an ex-prisoner though the job-seeking methods used by parolees were probably less likely to lead to refusal. Although only a minority had difficulty getting a job because of bonding, it tended to be a problem for those in types of employment that they liked and were qualified to do.

Two out of three ex-prisoners felt that they had to lie about the time missing in their employment histories in order to obtain jobs, although they did not have a very good lie to tell. While some who did admit to having a record were turned down immediately, about half were not even asked for such information. Comparatively few expressed any job satisfaction; what they did like was often the setting and freedom of the job.

We asked quite a number of questions about budgeting. The main problem with money seemed to be not the handling of it, but the lack of it generally. First, the ex-prisoners were released with very little money (and not surprisingly, some of this went on 'indulgences'). Secondly, quite a number had difficulty obtaining jobs and getting welfare. In fact about a third of the ex-prisoners had spent all their money from the institution within a week, and half had borrowed by the two-week stage.

Only a minority of ex-prisoners said they had not been drinking since release; over half the group went out for a drink at least once a week, often with a friend, although compared to dischargees, parolees were more likely to go with their wife and less likely to go alone. More parolees than dischargees identified themselves as having a problem with the use of alcohol on admission to the penitentiary. At five weeks from release this was still the case. However, parolees were more likely to have involved themselves in Alcoholics Anonymous in the penitentiary.

A small proportion of both groups (although again there were more dischargees) had used some other drug since release. With the exception of one dischargee who had used heroin, they had mainly used marijuana either by itself or in combination with barbiturates, LSD, or morphine.

One in five of the ex-prisoners had seen a psychiatrist before his eighteenth birthday. Such a high proportion is primarily a reflection of the number of ex-prisoners who had previously served time in institutions. During their current sentence most ex-prisoners felt that the psychiatric help they had received was concerned with weathering their sentence. Other than that they did not feel the psychiatrist had been of much assistance. 11 per cent of the ex-prisoners interviewed claimed that they had attempted suicide at some time in their lives. Two out of three of these said they seriously meant to kill themselves. Over half the suicide attempts had occurred while the men were in institutions.

Parolees could identify various 'stakes' in the community which might keep them away from crime. In addition, they agreed with sentencers that the fear of return to the penitentiary was an important element in keeping them straight. We know, however, that two out of five parolees and two out of three dischargees were arrested within twenty-four months, so that in terms of efficacy, this fear was not very great. Besides, many of them could name a pay-off large enough to re-involve them in crime. Some ex-prisoners had been positively encouraged to return to crime, particularly by other ex-prisoners. Most said that if an offence occurred in their area, they would feel threatened and suspected by the police.

In line with findings of other studies, age and criminal record were found to be the pre-release variables which, in combination, made the best, most reliable, though not very efficient, predictor of post-release arrest and conviction. Post-release variables such as employment, undesirable associates, fighting, and seeing children, all at five weeks, were found to have an independent relationship to arrest within twenty-four months for those with few previous arrests. Frequency of drinking was important in the same way for those with several previous arrests. Generally such variables were related not only to the variable of whether or not arrested, but also to the time elapsed before arrest. These variables and a psychometric variable combined into prediction equations that were marginally more efficient on validation than age and criminal record.

Impact of the Penitentiary

The principal benefit of the penitentiary is thought to be the opportunity to get further education. However, only one in five of those ex-prisoners who had taken some form of training in the penitentiary (one in ten of the total) had used this in some way during their first five weeks in the community. At the same time, it is arguable that the men probably learned more sophisticated criminal techniques during their time inside.

In terms of the effects of imprisonment, neither the type of institution nor the length of the current sentence were found to be related to reconviction. A few of the men who had spent more than ten years in the maximum security penitentiary did appear to suffer gross debilitating effects transforming them into 'prisonized inadequates' almost totally unable to function outside. In general, however, the debilitating effects of imprisonment were not so extreme: many said they lost weight or were unable to sleep during the time they were in a local jail awaiting trial (Two out of three ex-prisoners had not received bail, either because they had no money or no hope. One-third had also spent two months or more in a local jail). But there were few identifiable effects of imprisonment at six or twelve months though several questions probed this.

Many ex-prisoners felt that the most serious deprivations were in terms of their employment, family, and friendships. Yet we have shown that these are among the most important aspects of life outside, and that if they are maintained, they lower the likelihood of re-arrest. Although we did not interview the families of the ex-prisoners, we did try to get an idea of what happened to the family during the period of incarceration. Very often the ex-prisoner's wife had to move as a result of his imprisonment. The wives of parolees usually continued to live by themselves, whereas the wives of dischargees often lived with other men or moved in with friends during this time. A large proportion of ex-prisoners who said, on admission, that they were married were not visited while they were inside. Only half of the 37 per cent of the parolees who said they were married on admission were still married and living with their wife at five weeks from release. While quite a number of parolees got married or started living with a woman during the first twelve months, even eliminating those arrested, the proportion living with someone at the end of twelve months did not equal the proportion doing so immediately before admission. In only a minority of cases, however, did the prisoners hold the prison responsible for the break-up of the family, although many said it was a contributing factor.

Though the penitentiary experience was seen as a hardship, some ex-prisoners still felt there were moments when they were better off in prison. A small group of parolees felt this way as a result of pressure from their parole supervisors, particularly about employment, and others experienced this in crises of various kinds. Generally, they saw the time inside as a chance to think about things. Some felt bitter as a result and others more mature, though there were widely different meanings attached to their use of the word 'mature.'

Although there were people in the institution that the men could talk to about release problems, most prisoners felt they received little real help other than a sympathetic ear. Their main pre-release concerns were about family, employment, and finances. During the period after release many worried about not being able to talk to people, about looking like an 'ex-con,' and felt quite lonely, problems, however, which usually faded with time.

Men released from maximum security institutions differed from the general population of prisoners, particularly in regard to offences against guards. Men committing offences against guards were less likely to be granted parole but were not more likely to be re-arrested although if they were, it was often earlier. While such men pose problems to the prison administration, they are not necessarily more violent or dangerous after release.

Impact of Parole

Sixty-eight per cent of the dischargees and 44 per cent of the parolees were re-arrested within twenty-four months and eventually reconvicted. Two factors seem to account for this difference; first, the selection procedure of the parole board, and second, the differences between those who apply for parole and those who do not. The results would be the same if all those paroled were over twenty-five; or had minor or no previous commitments to penal institutions; or possessed positive characteristics on a number of other variables. The use of a prediction score would probably make a difference of about 30 per cent, but not more unless the number paroled was reduced drastically.

When one allows for the fact that better risks are selected for parole, parolees are no less likely to be arrested than those who are discharged, but who had applied for parole. Although the actual re-arrest rate for non-applicants was the same as for parole refusals, we found that the non-applicant was more likely to be re-arrested than predicted. This was closely related to how he saw his chances, at the time of the pre-release interview, of being re-arrested later. As parole revocation would result in a longer total period of time in prison, inmates not intending to go straight were apparently less likely to apply. Other authors have suggested that inmates, clinicians, judges, and parole boards cannot select those who will not be reconvicted any better than prediction scores. We found the same thing, although it did appear in this study that, relatively speaking, the inmate could do so, though only through his behaviour in not applying for parole.

On the whole, dischargees tended to get arrested earlier than parolees. Some parolees in this study were arrested later than expected, but often these were men on short paroles (less than fifteen months); parole, then, had a delaying effect. Many of the paroles in this study were too long for this possible delaying effect to be investigated further.

On the whole, those parolees intending to go straight saw parole as a benign imposition. For others, it was a more serious imposition in that they had to do things differently than they would have in the absence of parole supervision. Nearly all parolees reported as required to their parole supervisors and the police. Some parolees felt physically restricted to the area to which they had been paroled; others did not, but felt threatened by possible sanctions. These kinds of modifications in behaviour, however, were not, in general, related to reconviction, although in cases where the parolee was pressured to get employment (or 'given help' with employment, depending on the point of view) arrest did seem to be delayed.

Parole supervision is concentrated in the first three months; it averages out over the first twelve months to an office interview about once or twice a month supplemented by the occasional visit to the parolee's home or employment situation. Such as it is, the supervision is individually oriented. Some parolees also felt their parole supervisor was understanding and supportive.

In the majority of cases parole supervisors knew some, but not all aspects of the parolee's social situation. In the case of debts and associates, he often did not become aware of these until three months after release. Those who would be arrested tended to be less well known to their supervisor, to be reprimanded more often, and generally to have a worse relationship. A good relationship in the early months of parole did not apparently have an effect on the probability of reconviction, usually because such relationships were with parolees not expected to be reconvicted – good risks.

Parole revocation in this study always involved, in addition to one or more technical violations (though *not* necessarily charges or arrest), questioning by the police; it appears that parole revocation is used as a control where there is a possibility of new offences being commited. Because of the small numbers involved, this result can only be generalized cautiously.

One of the main things parole supervision does is to 'encourage' the parolee to get employment. (Compared to the dischargee who obtained employment, the parolee changes jobs more often, is employed for a higher proportion of the first twelve months, and earns less.) From the second month onwards, approximately 80 per cent of the parolees were usually employed. In contrast, at no point over the full twelve-month period were more than 30 per cent of the dischargees interviewed employed.

The main areas in which parole supervisors felt they provided assistance were employment, marriage, and personal attitudes or problems. In response to a reciprocal question, parolees said that the help they received was mainly in the way of 'chat' therapy and, in individual instances, concrete help.

One of the greatest disadvantages of institutionalization is that it removes the man from his family, work, and community, and possibly engenders more bitterness against society; yet these are precisely the factors connected with re-arrest. The only way in which parole counters this separation is by early release, hopefully before these bonds are irreparably broken. Parole supervision is, at most, a temporary antidote.

The Findings and Changes in Legislation

Before we turn in the next chapter to reflecting on these findings and to suggest directions for improvement in the way we manage offenders, we should review the recent changes in the organization of the penitentiary and parole. Despite these modifications and changes likely to follow in the future, the findings of this study will be germane as long as such institutions exist. Though the ideal research situation is removed, for example, by the introduction of mandatory supervision, the force of the conclusions is unaffected. At the time of this study few men had been released from prison following sentences for trafficking or possession of marijuana. If prison sentences continue to be used for such people and if they are found to have different characteristics from the men studied, modifications in our conclusions would be necessary.

Mandatory Supervision: Over-filling Empty Institutions

Under revisions of the Parole Act made in 1968–9,[1] mandatory supervision was introduced for all dischargees and affected men sentenced after August, 1970, and expected to be released in early 1972 or thereafter. This means that dischargees are subject to conditions similar to parole for a time equal to that of their earned and statutory remission.[2] According to the findings of this study, approximately one in three dischargees will be arrested for indictable offences within six months of release. The men first released under this regime had only short penitentiary sentences of two years. As a result, because their supervision will last for only six to eight months, and because there may possibly be a delaying effect of the kind noted for parolees with short paroles, this programme may at first give the illusion of success. After 1972, however, the group of men sentenced to between three and five years who in this study were less likely to be granted parole will be released on mandatory supervision. These men will be 'at risk' for longer periods. There is no reason to suppose that the outcome for those on mandatory supervision will be much different than those in our study, where two out of three dischargees were arrested for indictable offences within two years. In the case of forfeiture, approximately one-third of the previous sentence of the dischargee would be added to the new sentence which he received as a result of the offence committed after release from the institution (unless the sentencing judge takes this remnant into account); this would lead to protection but only by additional imprisonment.

This study has shown that the threat of revocation does affect behaviour of parolees, but only marginally. The same would probably be true, only more so, for dischargees; it seems even clearer in their case that prison is not an effective deterrent. Most, but not all, dischargees interviewed in this study would probably report to their parole officer and to the police. As a result, those who did report to their parole officers would be more likely to find employment, and possibly the date of arrest might be later than expected had they been released without mandatory supervision. However, the parole service may, in some cases, be placed in the dilemma of issuing warrants for the arrest of men not reporting, then either cajoling the police to locate and arrest them or, alternatively, waiting for the men to commit a new offence and then be arrested.

If there are no changes in sentencing and parole policy, the effect of the introduction of mandatory supervision may be drastically to increase the prison population. Costs to both the offender and taxpayer would go up, although benefits would not. To make matters worse, the current trend is to reduce the proportion of paroles granted (possibly associated with shorter paroles) and not of the parole failures are by forfeiture, so that it appears that unless new alternatives to incarceration are developed the criminal justice system will face prison overpopulation and construction (see Appendices B and C). This might lead to revisions of the parole system itself, particularly the conditions of mandatory supervision. The alternatives arising out of our findings will be detailed in the final chapter.

In this study we found that dischargees differed from parolees in a number of ways; these characteristics may mean that they are less likely to live within the boundaries of a parole-type agreement. If this were the case it could mean that over time the parole supervisor's role could change from 'counsellor' to 'law enforcement officer.' At the present time, parole supervisors in Ontario generally have a passive 'helping' orientation. In order to avoid this change it might be better to leave the police to enforce the law and initiate revocation proceedings.

There are also many arguments to support the introduction of mandatory supervision; three of these are discussed below.

1 The threat of supervision after release will persuade more prisoners to apply for ordinary parole during their imprisonment.

It would seem from this study and the parole board statistics, that the principal determinant of the number of applications is the proportion of offenders to whom parole is granted. The problem is, therefore, how to get more prisoners out of the penitentiary earlier. One suggestion to be discussed later is *directed supervision* within an evaluated demonstration experiment. This might be one way to continue the high parole rates of 1968–71 or to release even larger proportions of these men, without 'endangering' the community.

2 By its very nature parole is selective so that those who would benefit most from its 'effectiveness' do not get it.

Parole is indeed selective; but our overriding conclusion, consistent with previous findings around the world, is that parole is not correctionally effective. There is no reason to suppose that mandatory supervision would be any different. On the other hand, the man released on parole may be partially contained during parole in that his reinvolvement in arrest is delayed (the possible strength of this effect is not clear from this study). However, the provision of special employment programmes could be just as effective in terms of containment, and probably cheaper.

3 Parole is necessary to aid all prisoners during the period after release from the institution.

This appears to be partially true, but Canada has long been renowned for its voluntary after-care. The effect of mandatory supervision is to 'buy out' these after-care agencies. Because the government provides contractual funds for mandatory supervision, these agencies are left with little choice but to supervise such men. Even if they were to remain as private agencies, the dischargee compelled to accept a parole supervisor is not likely to go out looking for voluntary assistance. Besides, many dischargees do not co-operate with classification officers or workshop instructors and rebelliously reject compulsory action. Moveover, few take advantage of voluntary after-care, but this could be changed if these agencies reconsider the kind of services they provide as well as how to sell them to the inmate before release.

Suspension and Revocation

A further recent amendment to the Parole Act[3] enables a member of the parole board, or any person designated by the board, to suspend a parole 'whenever he is satisfied that the arrest of the inmate is necessary or desirable in order to prevent a breach of any term or condition of the parole, or for the rehabilitation of the inmate, or the protection of society.' The suspension can be canacelled by the person who introduced it within fourteen days from the time of such remand. Effectively this gives the parole supervisor and his immediate superior, as the person designated by the board, the power to impose sentences of up to two weeks without any review of the basis for such a decision. Such arbitrary administrative powers are not new in North America. In all cases where suspension was used in this study, society might have been equally well protected by the arrest provisions in the Criminal Code or other statutes; each case was associated with police questioning which suggested that the men were at least suspected of committing, or being about to commit, an indictable offence. The problem here is not that arbitrary powers are used arbitrarily, but that could be. Indeed, if Canada were to follow the trends in California, the misuse of such powers would become a central concern. At the moment, however, it seems difficult to justify such powers for parole supervisors without better procedural safeguards, especially in light of present police powers to arrest (see Hugessen *Report*, 1973). At the very least such powers would seem to compound the already difficult role of the parole supervisor. He becomes at once prosecutor, defender, and judge.

The experience of release has now been dissected and related to prison and parole and to some changes in legislation since 1968. Our findings in some areas were expected, in others they were not; but this project was designed to suggest answers to the question 'What should be done?' The final chapter will go beyond the task of interpreting statistical analyses to speculate on possible alternatives.

NOTES TO CHAPTER 11

1 Ottawa, Canada, *Parole Act, SC 1968/69*, c. 38, s.101, 11(b) (1) and (2), p. 948; *Parole Act, RSC 1970*, p.2, 15(1) and (2), p. 5683

2 For an understanding of remission, see Glossary

3 Ottawa, Canada, *Parole Act, SC 1968/69*, c. 38, s.101, 12(1–5), pp. 948–9; *Parole Act, RSC 1970*, p.2, 16(1–5), pp. 5683–4

12

Understanding and Alternatives

Our main concern in this study has been to demonstrate the extent to which various modes of treatment are correctionally effective, not to question the morality of these treatments. Moral considerations, or 'humanitarianism' if you will, are not irrelevant. But one of the most common confusions is between the goals of humanitarianism and those of social defence. Granted, it is not only nice to treat offenders decently, but also 'moral' to do so. The confusion lies in thinking that by being nicer to the offender (for example by making prisons more livable, more democratic, or by building them closer to large cities) one is also reducing the likelihood of his re-arrest. This idea is, in a large part, the rationale behind current trends in penal reform. The findings from this study, however, indicate that the proper way to assess the effectiveness of any innovation is to look at actual changes in behaviour according to carefully defined criteria. As yet, few alternatives have been shown to be effective, which would indicate the necessity of reconsidering the effects of reform innovations. Treatment reorientations should be made in the knowledge that, for the most part, they are justified only in terms of humanitarian concerns; most probably they will not result in dramatic decreases in criminal behaviour.

Through the use of statistical techniques we have shown that neither prison or parole, in part or in total, are correctionally effective. They appeared to be at first, but this was an example of the fallacy of the 'fly-on-the-axle-who-thinks-he-is-raising-a-big-dust' (England,

1956–7). While parole may have other functions, such as the mitigation of severe sentences or the relief of overcrowding in prisons, it is not, nor indeed is the prison itself, effective in terms of the primary aim of reducing the likelihood of future criminal behaviour. Certainly, there are ways in which the $10,000 or more required to maintain one inmate for a year could be better spent.

Of course, one cannot simply abolish prisons. Aside from incapacitation, the constructive results of such a system are 'intangible.' It is important to remember that we are dealing with a bureaucracy and that bureaucracies tend to perpetuate themselves, especially when they have large budgets. Still, the problem is a bit more complicated than this. Prisons tend to be built in areas needing economic stimulation; in addition the government has an obvious obligation to prison guards to continue their employment. However, it should be possible to redirect these resources in ways that would be of more benefit to both offender and community.

Although one of the overt aims of the system is rehabilitation, practically it is geared to merely 'managing' the offender, perhaps because on some less articulated level the underlying theme is one of retribution. The idea of 'management' is convenient, too; the public feels protected and can forget about these offenders, although this general apathy probably results partly from the lack of realistic alternatives.

The men in this study were not unlike the 'ordinary citizen'; many of them wanted a good job, a stable marriage, or close friends. Yet they were rejected persons, although whether this was part of the reason they went to the pentitentiary in the first place, or a result of being inside, is not clear. It is clear, however, that having been inside made it harder for them to achieve these aims afterwards, and that they were more likely to be re-arrested as a result. Frustrated, therefore, many rejected their earlier goals.

The released prisoner is in a 'detached' state. Though not necessarily motivated to commit new crimes, he also has little reason not to. The penitentiary probably does little to oppose this; it might even be argued that the way offenders are treated inside makes them more detached. The entire prison and parole system is in the business of trying, eventually, to lessen future criminal behaviour and to help reintegrate the offender into society, but on a practical level the system defeats its purposes for quite a large number of prisoners. If this vicious circle could be broken by a successful relationship or a good job, this might increase the ex-prisoner's chances of developing other attachments to the 'straight' world.

If this perception of the process is correct, then the repercussions in terms of changes or modifications to the system are important. Prison, like transportation, prevents crime during the time a man is removed from society. One should not, however, be looking only for ways to stop a man from committing offences (which, in the long term, penitentiary sentences, with or without parole supervision afterwards, do not) but one should also be examining alternative ways of handling men whom, to a greater or lesser extent, nobody else wants.

The Search for Alternatives

There are no obvious alternatives. This means that the first step must be rational experimentation followed by adequate evaluation. The alternative should be compared, both in total and by components, with the situation as it stands in the non-experimental state. There is plenty of room for innovation because, in terms of reducing the probability of re-arrest and improving social functioning, it would be hard to find anything less effective than the present system. Presuming that rational, and hopefully effective, alternatives might exist, one could begin experimentation by spending at least $5000 per inmate, a figure not out of line with the Solicitor-General's cost quotes of $10,000 per inmate and $500 per parolee excluding the cost of prison construction. In the end, much of the innovation may simply be in reducing *cost*. The rest of this chapter will examine directions in which such rational innovations might begin, while remaining within both economic and humanitarian constraints.

Our findings suggest where innovation might begin. The first step would be to redirect the efforts of parole supervisors, and those of the prison and parole system generally, to those areas found in this study to be related to re-arrest. There should also be a review of the type of people involved in working with offenders.

We should be looking for cheaper and more humanitarian ways of handling the offender through *containment*. This idea involves three important elements: to help the ex-prisoner find a positive stake in the community, to control the man's behaviour during the day by means of employment, family, semi-custodial means, and differential supervision, and to introduce 'prisons' whose role is literally to 'contain' the offender without further weakening his ties with the community. The last two points place more emphasis on what Walker (1969) calls precautionary measures, that is, measures intended to prevent an individual from committing an offence by making it physically difficult for him to do so. Here we are referring to several full and partial alternatives to prison, though, in extremes, imprisonment itself may be the only choice.

In addition to changing the social situation of the offender, some effort should be directed towards the general public who refuse to help offenders for various reasons: some believe in retribution, others, in treatment; some are basically apathetic about the whole problem, while others believe no problem exists as long as they have the apparently absolute protection of the prison. The public must be educated to accept and help these men, especially since many of the ex-prisoner's problems seem to stem from not being accepted by straight society.

Directed Policies

This study discovered that certain 'intervening variables,' employment, drinking, fighting, associates, and family situation, were related to the probability of re-arrest. New efforts to reduce re-arrests should concentrate on these areas. An alternative might be to find ways in which police or parole-service discretion to arrest and to revoke might be better used. Thirdly, as Jeffery (1971) has cogently argued, another alternative is to reduce the opportunities for crime.

EMPLOYMENT

The proportion of parolees employed is convincing evidence that the ex-prisoner's record, lack of skill, and lack of experience do not preclude his finding a job although it may be difficult to obtain, less well paid, and less long lasting than the 'average' man's. Encouragement and suggestions by parole supervisors in this respect were apparently not wasted. This could be reinforced at the systems level, not just by providing sheltered workshops where the offender passes his day or prepares to face the job market, but also by affording some kind of subsidy to employers who hire offenders.[1] This compensation would, for example, cover the employer's losses were the offender to quit after less time than the 'typical' employee.

Despite each compensation, some employers undoubtedly will still refuse to employ offenders on purely emotional (but nevertheless, real) grounds. But, if compensation could be implemented for some, it would raise the offender's probability of finding employment, an event which our findings indicate might delay his arrest and which would certainly result in considerable savings for the taxpayer who must otherwise foot the bill for new offences and prison sentences. More sensible use could be made of the time served in the penitentiary by providing work opportunities or realistic training programmes. After release, schemes like the 'Local Initiative Programme' or 'Opportunities for Youth' could be set up for men coming out of penitentiaries.

UNDESIRABLE ASSOCIATES, FIGHTING, DRINKING

If the ex-prisoner were described as having undesirable associates, if he said he had been involved in fights, and if he were drinking regularly, all within five weeks of release, he was more likely to be re-arrested within twelve months. These are perhaps the three clearest characteristics of men who have spent, and will spend, much of their lives in institutions. These men are usually rejected by the community, often unemployed, and unmarried. The special problem they pose may only be solved with time and, hopefully, maturity; in most cases the vicious circle of prison, arrest, prison, arrest, eventually weakens as they grow older.

It may be necessary to break away from traditional casework and work with groups of offenders in the community in order to try to deal with their problems *in situ*. For instance, it may be that to handle undesirable associates an adaptation of the detached-worker concept could be used to divert these men away from activities in which they lay themselves open to arrest and conviction; another alternative may be to get men into ex-offender groups where they might develop new interests.[2]

In one pilot study (Gallant, 1968), the compulsory attendance of criminal (*not* skid row) alcoholics at a clinic resulted in dramatically more regular employment careers and lower reconviction rates. Clearly, the abstinence clause does not 'work.' A better alternative would be for parolees to make more use of such clinics in southern Ontario, a practice which might result in some reduction in drinking and frequency of re-arrest.

There does not seem to be any obvious antidote to fighting. Its occurrence may reflect personality characteristics such as low frustration tolerance, recklessness, or a strong adherence to lower socio-economic group norms. Those who fought were usually young and often drank regularly; they were, in fact, the men likely to be arrested. It may simply be a symptom that suggests more intensive efforts be exerted on one of the other intervening variables.

DIRECTING PERSONNEL

Personnel in this field must be not only motivated, but also able to provide the parolee with real help. Simply recording 'man-months supervised,' for example, a variable which by itself does not seem to affect the parolee's behaviour, is not very helpful. Instead, achievable and clearly identifiable goals should be set and maintained. One might ask the parole supervisor to record the number of parolees employed and earning over $90 a week; persumably such reporting could be extended to the areas of fighting, associates, and family. Such recording would be not additional superfluous red tape, but information essential to the supervisor for setting objectives and so ensuring that his skills were used effectively.

While recording such information would probably help the supervisor, it would also make the task of evaluation easier. When a high proportion of parolees who previously had low chances of getting jobs become employed, it would then be possible to see if this change were related to a partial reduction in the probability of reconviction. In this way the hypothesis of a relationship between employment and reconviction can be tested. At the same time, one can show the extent to which changes on the intervening variable were associated with the parole supervisor's efforts. This would provide the feed back vital to effective development of parole supervision.

Of course, identifying problems (including difficulty of who makes the identification) and doing something effective about them are two different things. That is where our findings can help by suggesting alternatives. It might be possible to redirect, and give help with, supervision in some of the obvious trouble spots we identify. On the other hand, one might take an over-all systems approach by advocating the use of special workshops and volunteer groups or the organization of ex-prisoners' groups to supplement or replace individual case-work relationships. It might be argued that these efforts are only directed at 'symptoms'; again, we repeat that these symptoms were found to have a much closer relationship to the probability of re-arrest than various measures of personality. If a programme involving the specialization of parole supervision were implemented, it would have the advantage, not only of helping the parolee, but also of telling us more about these symptoms and in the long run, about how to deal with them more effectively. Finally, if supervision were geared toward the individual's problems, it would be possible to release more people on parole without increasing the danger to society.

Personnel

The rationale of supervision is that the supervisor could create a close relationship with the parolee which might then be used to modify the parolee's behaviour. While we do not deny the importance of having people to whom parolees can take problems or simply chat, it is nevertheless important to remove from its pedestal 'the relationship' as a rehabilitative tool and to discard the assumption that people doing this kind of work must have the professional skills and psychological training represented by postgraduate degrees. Warmth and empathy are not granted with degrees. While it may be desirable to have some workers with further education, we cannot afford not to consider others with perhaps equally valuable qualifications of a different sort. The sex of the workers seems not to be an entirely irrelevant factor. Parolees often felt that they were more at ease with, and got more help from, an older, perhaps middle-aged, woman.

'Satisficing' is essentially the sacrifice of the optimum solution in order to avoid the pain of achieving it. Parole supervisors who remain detached from the parolee in a personal sense, but who continue to fulfill job requirements by using the dictaphone and recording man-hours supervised are satisficing. Certainly the parole officers found to be most helpful and understanding were not like this, but rather got involved on some level and moved to help the parolee when needed. These characteristics are important simply in terms of providing a friend to look after the ex-prisoner during the anxious transition period, when he may be having difficulty finding a job.

The Policy of Containment

For some of the subjects in this study it appears that little can be done except temporarily change them or their situation. The police may be persuaded to concentrate on other offenders, jobs may be found, but in the final analysis what is needed for these men are measures not to rehabilitate but merely to contain them. Because of the lack of correctional effectiveness of any type of 'treatment' for certain offenders, we are suggesting that the 'precautionary' philosophy should be given prime emphasis in the case of many of those sent to penitentiary. To be consistent with our humanitarian and economic constraints, however, we must try to find alternatives to prison within this framework.

First, we should look at what have been variously called 'bond,' 'control,' or 'stake in the community' theories. Sinclair found that the behaviour of probationers seems to be influenced by the warm, firm, and consistent regimes within hostels; where those were not present, the effect was negative. Davies found the same thing in his study of the family environment. Secondly, the influence of the hostel wore off after return to the community (Davies and Sinclair, 1971).

An alternative interpretation of the effect of hostels and families on delinquents is incorporated in a theory of 'containment': the family restrains the delinquent. This view has been put forward by Hirschi (1969). When a person's ties to the conventional order have somehow been broken he is free to commit delinquent acts (Hirschi, 1969, 1). Studying the importance of attachment to parents, school, and peers, Hirschi sees a stake in the community as an ultimate restraint.

In this study it is not possible to resolve conflicts between bond and containment theories because almost any variable we might look at could be either a bond or a restraint. Important variables such as drinking or fighting may, in that framework, be the result of both a lack of any stake in the community and a failure of the parole model to contain. There are two factors to consider: the cost of imprisonment and the need to protect society. The obvious choice, then, is semi-institutional programmes where a man spends the night in an institution or house but is free to work or to educate himself during the day. Belgium is renowned for its systems of semi-detention and weekend-arrest.[3] These are used principally for short sentences as alternatives to harmful (and ludicrously expensive) short prison terms. Though these programmes create staff problems, they deserve to be developed and evaluated as potential solutions to the problem of managing many of the men currently kept in penitentiaries. Programmes could vary from private houses, hostels, and half-way houses to centres such as the Montgomery Pre-release Centre in Toronto already opened by the penitentiary service itself.

What we are suggesting is a two-pronged approach. Men should go out to work during the day, for example, from the beginning of any sentence but be 'contained' by bringing them back to the hostel-prison at night, the warden having discretion to control their evening activities by means of a curfew. Efforts should be made to find them jobs and to locate (and perhaps compensate) ordinary citizens with time to take an interest in them. Such volunteers would probably themselves need support of the kind supervisors in this study were expert at giving.

In spite of such programmes some are still going to be re-arrested. As a result, there would still have to be sanctions which could, and should, be carried out, perhaps by means of various deprivations within the semi-detention centre. Full containment prisons will still be needed for certain offenders. These, however, should be as humane as possible; a small group-living situation would be desirable because more pleasant and easier to manage. It is important to realize that, in this situation, the aim would not, and could not be to rehabilitate the inmates.

For a 'dangerous' minority convicted of serious offences – probably less than 5 per cent of those now in federal penitentiaries – containment would involve very long periods of time.[4] In these cases 'restricted access communities' might be created in various remote areas of Canada where containment would result from the geographic situation. This would amount to 'transportation' – with a difference. Prisoners would be paid for working, though a part of this might go in restitution; they could have wives, girlfriends, ordinary clothes, television, with them if they wanted, provided that their wages were used to cover part of the cost of living. Eventually they could be released on parole. Although this may seem far-fetched our findings showed that it makes little difference to many prisoners that Kingston is 150 rather than 1500 miles from Toronto: they are just as unlikely to be visited, keep up contact with their families, or find jobs in the local community.

Restitution and Prevention

In thinking about social defence we must take into account the victims' losses and the reduction of the number of criminal acts occurring, but within reasonable humanitarian and financial boundaries. The system as it stands now almost totally ignores the victim and prevention while concentrating on the offender. Any man on trial has, hopefully, the full protection of 'due process,' but justice seems to break down after the pronouncement of 'guilty' because no rationale is ever provided, or asked for, in relation to sentences given. Sentencing practice is, at best, informed speculation as to the most effective use of the taxpayers' money. Little thought is given to the possibility that a sentence may not achieve its supposed goals. One can be sure, however, that the victim will be forgotten (or possibly given a nominal grant), that a similar offence is just as likely to occur again in the future, and that the individual offender will only be further degraded at taxpayers' expense.

As we have seen, the vast expenditure on catching, convicting, and punishing the offender is, for him, a waste of money. Though imprisonment is feared, the experience does not seem to lower the probability of his re-arrest (Prison may deter other groups: see Zimring and Hawkins, 1973). We should certainly take a longer look at developing further preventive measures in the hope that they would make it more difficult for such socially undesirable behaviour to occur. Take burglary, for example: the development of burglar alarms, requirements in local housing standards for door locks or, more generally, the design of buildings, regulatory law to keep doors and windows locked, and the improvement of outside lighting – all these things could contribute to lowering the rate of 'breaking and entering.' These measures may require research into the components of offences themselves. Probably the typical and most frequent crimes of the future will be cheque forging, cheque passing, or credit card frauds, all of which could be substantially reduced by wider use of thumb-print identity cards.

Reported burglary is on the increase in Canada as well as the UK and the USA (USA, 1970). In 1965 in the United States this offence alone (of index crime) accounted for more than one-third – $820 million out of $2100 – of the estimated criminal-justice system direct operating costs. 72 per cent of this was spent on police operation and 16 per cent, on adult 'corrections' (USA, 1967a). This money could be much better used, first, on the development of preventive measures, and second, on providing restitution to the victim since offences will still occur. Smigel and Ross (1970) pointed out that one reason companies do not call in law-enforcement agencies after discovering an offence is that they are more concerned with reimbursement than retribution. If there were more ways to compensate the victim, there would probably be less insistence on punishing the offender. Without the increased use of preventive measures and restitution, we will go on 'dealing' with the problem in a way that probably insures its recurrence.

Assessed Demonstration Projects

The public has believed for a long time in the myth that prison protects, not only in the present while offenders are inside, but also in the long run by deterring potential criminals. In moving towards a more rational and efficient system, proposed changes must be demonstrated to be effective in order to allay public anxiety.[5] This study was designed to show how this might be done by new experiments in which practical hypotheses are tested against actual behaviour.

The next step would be a *demonstration* project. Such projects have been carried out in California, for example, where it was shown that juveniles previously thought to be manageable only in institutions could be cared for in the community. Our findings suggest that if a man had a wife and children, if he were to get involved in Alcoholics Anonymous or clinic treatment in order to control his drinking problem, if he could be helped and encouraged to find a job and 'desirable' friends, he would be contained in the community by virtue of these 'stakes' and the probability of his re-arrest would consequently be lowered.

In view of the fact that a very large proportion of the men in this study did not have positive stakes in the community, it is not surprising that such a large number were re-arrested. Indeed, it is astonishing that there were, relatively speaking, so many still free at the end of twenty-four months. If this were so, it was in spite of the system, not because of it.

NOTES TO CHAPTER 12

1 Bribing California counties to put more offenders on probation is a classic example of how this might be achieved: see *California* (1968).

2 N. Christie has referred me to the organization of ex-prisoners in Scandinavian countries concerned with political reforms of the handling of offenders. T. Mathiesen has written a book, called *The Knot Completed*, about their operation.

3 Belgium also has a system of semi-freedom, which parallels the leave-of-absence programmes or gradual parole current in Canada.

4 Discussions of the concept of dangerousness are contained in Morris (1967–8) 529–36, and Price (1970) 241–64.

5 See Courtis (1970). This work on personality characteristics associated with particular attitudes to crime and police suggests that demonstration would be more complicated than discussed here.

Appendices

A PAROLE AGREEMENT

The following is a typed copy of a certificate of parole as carried by one of the parolees in the study; only the names, dates, and identification numbers have been changed.

NATIONAL PAROLE BOARD
Ottawa, Canada
CERTIFICATE OF PAROLE

PS CK 9876
FPS 123456

To Whom It May Concern

It is ORDERED by the NATIONAL PAROLE BOARD that *SMITH, John #9876* an inmate in *Kingston Penitentiary* who was convicted of *Attempted robbery at Toronto, Ontario*

on *February 29, 1963* and was then and there sentenced to imprisonment for the term of *12 years from January 12, 1963*

be PAROLED, upon the conditions given hereunder, on the *30th* day of *May 1968* or within *14* days thereafter at the discretion of the Custodian, and until unless the said *SMITH, John* shall before the expiration of the said term commit an indictable offence punishable by imprisonment for a term of two years or more, in which case his parole is thereby forthwith forfeited, or unless there is cause for the National Parole Board to alter, suspend or revoke the present Order.

Given under the hands and seal of the National Parole Board, this *sixth* day of *May* nineteen hundred and *sixty-eight*

NATIONAL PAROLE BOARD

Secretary

PAROLE AGREEMENT

I clearly understand that I am still serving the sentence imposed but I am being granted parole to permit me to resume my activities as a citizen at large in the community, under supervision. Therefore, in consideration of parole being granted to me, I solemnly agree:

1 To remain, until the expiry of my sentence, under the authority of the National Parole Service Regional Representative or his successor in *Toronto, Mr. A.B. Jones, Room 902, MacKenzie Bldg., 36 Adelaide Street East, Toronto, Ontario*

2 To forthwith proceed directly to *Toronto, Ontario* and, immediately upon arrival and at least once a month thereafter, to report faithfully to *the chief officer of police nearest to my place of residence*

3 To accept the supervision and assistance of my supervisor or his successor *The John Howard Society as represented by Mr. M.N. Orlando, 168 Isabella Street, Toronto 5, Ontario.*

4 To remain in the immediate area of *Toronto, Ontario* or as designated by the Regional Representative and, if I have good cause to leave this area, to obtain permission beforehand through my supervisor.

5 To endeavour to maintain steady employment and to report at once to the Regional Representative through my supervisor, any change or termination of employment or any other change of circumstances such as accident or illness.

6 To secure advance approval from the Regional Representative, through my supervisor, if at any time I wish to:

(a) purchase a motor vehicle;
(b) incur debts by borrowing money or instalment buying;
(c) assume additional responsibilities, such as marrying;
(d) own or carry fire-arms or other weapons

7 To abide by all instructions which may be given by my supervisor or by the Regional Representative through my supervisor, and especially with regard to employment, companions, hours, intoxicants, operation of motor vehicles, medical or psychiatric attention, family responsibilities, court obligations.

8 To abide by this special condition: *To abstain from intoxicants*

9 To forthwith communicate with the Regional Representative, through my supervisor, if I am arrested or questioned by peace officers regarding any offence.

10 To obey the law and fulfill all of my legal and social responsibilities.

I have read, or have had read to me, and fully understand and accept the conditions, regulations and restrictions governing my release on parole. I will abide by and conform to them strictly. I also understand that if I violate them in any manner, I may be recommitted.

(name) *(number)*

Witnessed: *(title)*

Date of leaving

(official stamp: NATIONAL PAROLE BOARD, May 9 1968, KINGSTON OFFICE)

B THE PENITENTIARY IN CANADA: CURRENT STATUS AND FUTURE GROWTH

It is sobering to those in research that there is still dispute concerning the conclusions to be drawn from the manipulation of simple published statistics on the rate of imprisonment. Before our brief discussion of future rates let us reconsider how Canada compares with other countries on one definition of this rate based on, (i) *the daily average number of persons in prisons or correctional institutions* (which ignores persons involuntarily detained in mental hospitals or institutions for the mentally retarded, but includes short jail terms and pretrial detention),[1] and relate this to the simple, readily understood, and reliable statistic, (ii) the total population of the country (*not* the total male population; *not* those over 16 years).

In the USA in 1965 there were 404,049 persons known to be held in correctional institutions; 342,523, or 72 per cent, were defined as adult; *in addition*, 'many thousands more [were] serving from a few days to a few weeks in a variety of local lock-ups and jails not included in this survey' (USA, 1967b).

In *Canada*, the population in correctional institutions as of 31 December, 1970, was 21,475; of these, 19,232 were not held in training schools.[2] These figures include those remanded pre-trial.

In England and Wales, the average population in prisons, borstals, and detention centres was 30,421 in 1965, but was 39,028 in 1970 (Great Britain, 1969; Sparks, 1971, 385; Great Britain, 1971).

In Holland, there were 1800 men and youths in prison serving sentences and another 1800 on remand (Stockdale, 1967, 100).

Table B.1 brings this information together and relates it to estimates of the total population. Accordingly, the rate for the United Kingdom is only 85 per cent of that for Canada, whereas the rate for the USA, adding crude approximations for pre-trial detention and jail sentences of less than thirty days, is twice that of Canada, while that for Holland is one-quarter of that for Canada.

In 1970 the truth was therefore not as bad for Canada as we were led to believe. However, by 1975 the rate for Canada may have increased markedly and certainly the differences between the relative rates for Canada and England and Wales will be significant. To provide justification for this view it is necessary to return to the official statistics in England and Wales and draw on some of the

TABLE B.1

Rates of adults held in prisons relative to total populations for USA, Canada, England and Wales, and Holland

	Estimates of average nos. of adults held in prisons or correctional institutions	Pre-trial detention included	Sentence less than 30 days included	Total population in millions	Rate per 100,000	Canada = 1.00
USA	342,523 (1965)	No	No	199 (1967)[3]	172.1	1.78
Canada	19,232 (1970)	Yes	Yes	20 (1966)[4]	96.2	1.00
England and Wales	39,028 (1970)	Yes	Yes	48 (1967)[5]	81.3	0.85
Holland	3,600 (1966)	Yes	Yes	13 (1967)[6]	27.6	0.28

findings of *Men Released from Prison* and the literature on the effectiveness of dispositions.

In a disastrous attempt to reduce the prison population, the Criminal Justice Act 1967 (UK) introduced the discretionary suspension of terms of imprisonment of two years or less for between one and three years. However, where the offender was sentenced to six months or less, this sentence was *mandatorily* suspended (previous to the act of 1967, 60 per cent of those sent to prison were sent for terms of less than six months). Immediately following the coming into force of the legislation the population of prisons, borstals, and detention centres dropped to 32,461 (1968) and grew slowly to 34,667 in 1969. Yet in the first six months of 1970, the population grew from 35,965 (15 January 1970) to 38,644 (15 April 1970) to 40,137 on (15 July 1970).

The earlier conclusions of *Men Released From Prison* suggest that, from the date of release into the community, the probability of reconviction of an offender within a specified time from his release is unaffected by the type of disposition selected by the court or the length of imprisonment as determined by the parole board. Thus, those given suspended sentences would be expected to be reconvicted at the same rate as they would have been after release from an immediate prison term; but being released immediately, the delay in the arrest due to the time in prison is lost. At first this reduces commitments to prison. However, on reconviction the offenders previously given a suspended sentence may get a new prison sentence to which will be added the previous suspended sentence. Possibly also in giving suspended sentence, which may be expected not to be served, the court may give a longer sentence than it would have done for immediate imprisonment.[7] Thus the offender may go to prison for longer. This particular measure also attracted sentences away from fines, which do not have the prison build-up effect, and probation, which of course may have.

In Canada, absolute figures for prison populations have remained constant from 1966–70. In later years these were associated with a steady growth in the use of fines and recently a rapid growth in the use of probation and parole, all of which, for similar reasons to the suspended sentence in England and Wales, would result in a brief and temporary respite in the growth of the prison population, followed by a surge a few years later. This upsurge has only recently begun.

There are several factors in Canada that make matters worse, however. First, parole is now being used less liberally, so that longer prison terms are served. A less liberal parole policy may mean not only fewer paroles granted, but also paroles for shorter periods of time and fewer re-paroles. However, the growth in the use by courts of fines and probation disproportionately associated with the rising crime rate may be levelling off so that, other things remaining the same, prison populations would have grown disproportionately faster than the crime rate.

Second, revocation of National Parole results in a total time spent in the penitentiary longer than that spent without a grant of parole (the extra time equals one-quarter of the time spent before parole was granted). When there is a sudden rise in the use of parole, this will result later in a bulge due to longer mean times spent in prison. The same is true of parole forfeiture, though the person gets an extra sentence (unlike the suspended sentence case), earlier than he would have done. Revocation in place of reconviction for new offences thus may result in less prison time. However, a new emphasis on revocation, while possibly providing better protection for the public, might be used where no conviction could be obtained, so that the exact balance is not clear.

Third, mandatory supervision adds one-third of the previous sentence to all those whose mandatory supervision is revoked or who are reconvicted during such supervision. Yet court sentences are unlikely to have made allowance for such time either in the original or in the new sentence.

In these few comments no attempt is made to predict the actual size of the prison population in Canada. However, it would appear to be feasible to provide estimates of this population given estimates of expected time to reconviction, expected growth in crime rate, and parole release policy.

Undoubtedly, the fast growth in the prison population will necessitate major re-assessment by sentencer, legislator, government official, and the public on the aims of imprisonment, its cost, the alternatives, and attempts to reduce crime through prevention.

NOTES TO APPENDIX B

1. This note ignores the question of the number of persons put into prison during a year, as the problem of identifying the number of admissions is beleaguered by finding out how many times the same individual was admitted during one year, whether the admission was really a transfer from one prison to another, or for how many charges the indivudual was consecutively or concurrently sentenced.
2. Canada (1970). Population of provincial institutions were expressed as of March 31, except for Quebec, which reported as of December 31.
3. USA (1967d)
4. Canada (1970–71, 213)
5. Quoted in Newspaper Enterprise Association (1968) as a government estimate for mid-1967
6. Quoted in *ibid.* as UN estimate for 1967
7. For a fuller discussion of the sentencer's actual behaviour, see Sparks (1971).

TABLE B.2

Number of inmates in federal penitentiaries by level of security of institution, fiscal years 1966–7 to 1970–1

Type of security	1966–7		1967–8		1968–9		1969–70		1970–1	
Maximum	3876	54%	3576	51%	3490	49%	2843	39%	2782	37%
Medium	2066	29	2416	34	2615	36	3477	47	3757	50
Minimum	1243	17	1065	15	1056	15	1055	14	925	13
Total	7185	100%	7057	100%	7161	100%	7375	100%	7464	100%

SOURCE: Proceedings of the Senate Standing Committee on Legal and Constitutional Affairs, Wednesday, March 8, 1972, excerpt from appendix D, prepared by W. Bellman, 10 Feb. 1972.

TABLE B.3

Average maintenance cost per inmate by security type based on actual expenditures for federal penitentiaries, fiscal years 1966–7 to 1970–1

TYPE OF SECURITY	1966–7	1967–8	1968–9	1969–70	1970–1
Maximum					
Male	6229	7580	7597	10393	11040
Female (Kingston)	6706	9860	9570	11388	10491
Average cost	6240	7625	7636	10410	11027
Medium					
Male	10929	11284	10218	8456	8480
Female (Matsqui)	—	—	—	13026	32745
Average cost	10929	11284	10218	8521	8594
Minimum					
Male	3721	4106	5448	3814	5361
Average cost	3721	4106	5448 (see Note 2)	3814	5361
Average cost per inmate, all types of security (excluding administration)	7380	8492	8389	8659	9140
Administration overhead includes Ottawa HQ, RHQ and CSC[1]	535	390	257	630	580
Total average cost per inmate	7915	8882	8646	9289	9720

1 The administration base varies due to changes in grouping of components over various years

2 The high average cost per inmate in minimum institutions for 1968–9 is primarily due to the opening of the community correctional centres with high opening costs and low occupancy rates

SOURCE: As Table B.2, excerpt from appendix G

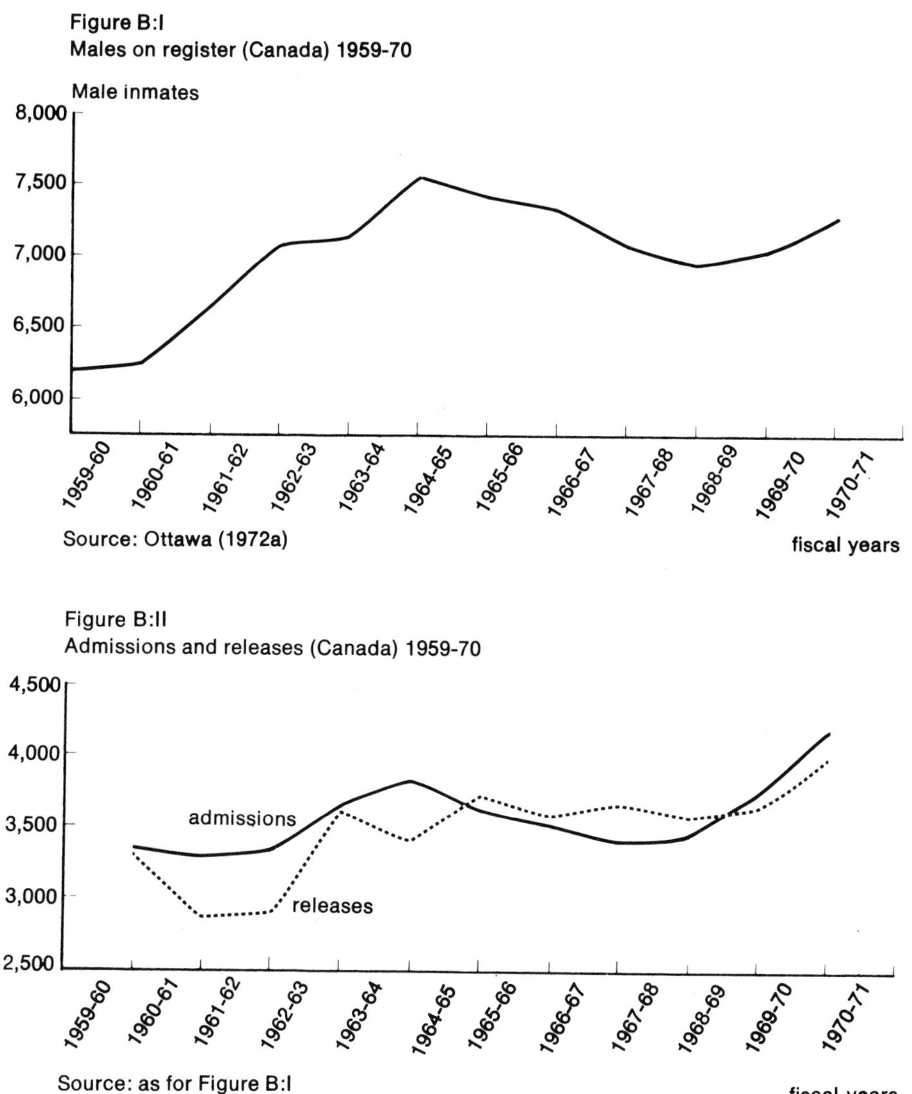

Figure B:I
Males on register (Canada) 1959-70

Source: Ottawa (1972a)

Figure B:II
Admissions and releases (Canada) 1959-70

Source: as for Figure B:I

Figure B:III
Population in training schools, provincial adult institutions, and federal penitentiaries in Canada 1966-70[1], and percentage change

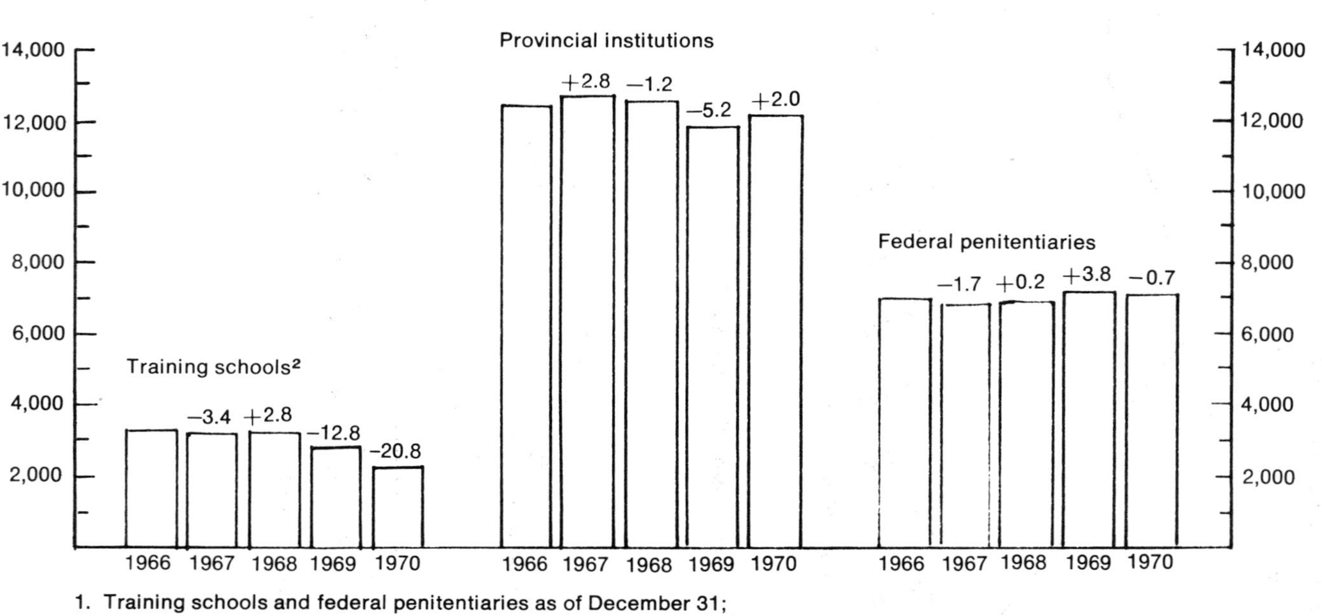

1. Training schools and federal penitentiaries as of December 31; provincial institutions as of March 31, except Quebec
2. British Columbia ceased to report in 1969 and Alberta in September 1970

Source: Canada (1970)

C PAROLE STATISTICS

Statistical trends in applications, granting, and termination (for violation) of National Parole in Canada since its inception, 1959–71 (all paroles)

Year	1959	1960	1961	1962	1963	1964	1965	1966	1967	1968	1969	1970	1971
Federal													
Percentage eligible applying	—	85%	64%	64%	57%	56%	61%	62%	66%	71%	75%	83%	89%
Number granted during year	994	1192	1005	885	663	751	1127	1114	1328	1331	2030	2852	2785
Granted as percentage of applicants	44%	34%	35%	32%	26%	29%	37%	41%	47%	42%	62%	64%	61%
Provincial													
Number granted during year	1044	1333	1292	987	1126	1101	1170	1382	1760	2187	3062	3071	3493
Granted as percentage of applicants	41%	51%	32%	30%	31%	29%	31%	39%	46%	54%	70%	74%	71%
Total													
Granted during year	2038	2525	2297	1872	1789	1852	2297	2496	3088	3518	5092	5923	6278
Granted as percentage of applicants	42%	41%	33%	31%	29%	29%	34%	40%	46%	49%	66%	69%	66%
Revocation during year	60	97	115	97	122	111	107	127	141	176	212	365	367
Forfeiture during year	58	94	141	114	114	95	85	116	151	206	339	639	1142
Total during year	118	191	256	211	236	206	192	243	292	382	551	1004	1509
Number on parole 31 Dec. 1971:	5374												

SOURCE: Hugessen (1973)

D DEFINITIONS OF CRUCIAL VARIABLES IN EQUATIONS TO PREDICT ARREST

ARREST WITHIN A CERTAIN TIME PERIOD – SIX MONTHS, TWELVE MONTHS, TWENTY-FOUR MONTHS

1 Arrested and finger-printed for an indictable offence; the date, for charges discontinued or conviction, occurred within the certain time period.
2 No such arrest recorded within the certain time period.

AGE AT RELEASE UNDER TWENTY-FIVE OR NOT

1 Age at release, under twenty-five, computed by subtracting birth date from release date.
2 Age at release, twenty-five and over.

BE AGE/PENAL RECORD/JESNESS COMBINATION SCORE

A continuous score derived from the equation predicting the probability of arrest within twenty-four months. This equation included the weighted sum of age at release, penal record, and the Jesness combination score.

DRINK OR NOT

1 Told the interviewer that, within five weeks of release, he had drunk alcoholic beverages out of his home rarely or never.
2 Told the interviewer he drank at least once a week out of his home, or did not state.

GOT FIRST JOB THROUGH MANPOWER

1 Within five weeks of release the first job obtained was through the public employment agency – Manpower.
2 Job not obtained or the job obtained through another method.

JESNESS COMBINATION SCORE

A continuous score calculated from individual scale scores on the adult version of the Jesness inventory. The scales were selected as those having significant t-values for the parolee-dischargee comparison. Actual score calculated as $(Smx + Vo + Au + Ae + Ma) - 30$.

OFFENCE AGAINST PERSON

1 Original offences before going to Kingston included murder, manslaughter, wounding, sex offences, assault, or robbery.
2 No such offences recorded.

PENAL RECORD/TYPE OF PREVIOUS COMMITMENTS TO ADULT PENAL INSTITUTIONS

An eight-point scale taken from penitentiary admission form: 1 no recorded adult commitments; 2 jail only; 3 reformatory only; 4 penitentiary only; 5 (2) and (3); 6 (2) and (4); 7 (3) and (4); 8 (2), (3), and (4).

REFORMATORY COMMITMENTS

A nine-point scale reflecting number of previous commitments to a reformatory (sentence of two years less a day)

REPRIMANDS (PAROLEES ONLY)

1 Parole supervisor recorded a reprimand within five weeks of release.
2 No such reprimand recorded.

SEES CHILDREN OR NOT

1 Has seen his own children within five weeks of release as told to supervisor.
2 Has no children or not seen them.

SPENT TIME IN PSYCHIATRIC UNIT

1 Never spent time in psychiatric unit during current sentence as told to the interviewer at five weeks, or nothing recorded in reply to question.
2 Told interviewer that he had spent time in the psychiatric unit.

UNDESIRABLE ASSOCIATES

1 For parolee, associates described by parole supervisor as undesirable or desirable at five weeks; for dischargees, friends described to interviewer at five weeks and interviewer coded undesirable on the basis of friends' implied or known involvement in crime.
2 No such undesirable recorded.

E TABLES ON MINIMUM PAROLE

TABLE E.1

Type of parolees by birth year (or age at release)

		Minimum parolees		Ordinary parolees		Total
Year of birth	Age (in years)	No.	%	No.	%	No.
1943 and after	(–25)	13	39.4	43	24.3	56
1933–1942	(26–35)	11	33.3	95	53.7	106
Before 1932	(36–)	9	27.3	39	22.0	48
Total		33	100.0	177	100.0	210

TABLE E.2

Type of parolees by adult sentences of incarceration (previous penal record)

	Minimum parolees		Ordinary parolees		Total
	No.	%	No.	%	No.
Recorded sentence to jail, reformatory or penitentiary	30	90.9	139	78.5	171
No recorded adult sentence of incarceration	3	9.1	38	21.5	39
Total	33	100.0	177	100.0	210

TABLE E.3

Type of parolees by type of offence on admission to penitentiary

	Parolees			Ratio of
	Minimum	Ordinary	Total	ordinary to minimum
01 Homicide	1	13	14	2.4
02 Sex offences	0	11	11	
03 Wounding, assault	2	4	6	0.37
04 Robbery	3	33	36	2.0
05 Breaking and entering	11	49	60	0.8
06 Escape	4	22	26	1.0
07 Theft	3	19	22	1.2
08 Fraud	8	14	22	0.3
09 Narcotics	0	5	5	
10 Drunken driving	0	0	0	—
11 Other	1	7	8	1.3
Total	33	177	210	1.0

TABLE E.4

Type of parole release by arrest within twenty-four months

	Minimum parolees		Ordinary parolees		Total
	No.	%	No.	%	No.
Arrested within twenty-four months	15	45.5	78	44.1	93
Not arrested	18		99		117
Total	33		177		210

F TABLES OF ARREST

TABLE F.1

Cumulative proportions, arrested to total population, by three-month periods and by parole granted, refused, or no application

Months from release	Parolees (%)	Dischargees who applied for parole (%)	Dischargees who did not apply (%)
3	3.80	15.00	15.04
6	15.22	25.00	33.62
9	20.93	42.00	41.58
12	27.59	46.00	52.19
15	31.87	50.00	61.03
18	38.06	54.00	65.45
21	39.96	57.00	67.21
24	44.24	64.00	70.74
N =	93/210	64/100	80/113

TABLE F.1a

Kolmogorov-Smirnov tests

	Range	$K - S\chi^2$ ($df = 2$)	P (one-tailed test)
(i) Parolees versus dischargees applied	3	12.00	0.005
(ii) Parolees versus dischargees not applying	5	24.98	0.000
(iii) Dischargees applying versus not applying	6	2.78	not significant
(iv) Parolees versus dischargees	6	24.53	0.000

TABLE F.2

Seriousness of post-release offence relative to that of pre-release offence, by mode of release

		Less serious	Same	More serious	Total
Discharges	No.	33	19	30	82
	%	40.3	23.2	36.6	
Parolees	No.	13	10	15	38
	%	34.2	26.3	39.5	
Total	No.	46	29	45	120
	%	38.3	24.2	37.5	

TABLE F.3

Largest differences for cumulative proportion arrested within eight, three-month time periods of twenty-four months, by crucial variables and by mode of release

	Mode of release N = number arrested/number released					
	Dischargees N = 139/213		Parolees N = 93/210		Total	
	Time period with largest difference	Percentage difference	Time period with largest difference	Percentage difference	Time period with largest difference	Percentage difference
Employed or not at admission arrest	3	7.5	4	4.54	5	3.15
Age at release (middle vs old)	1	8.33	2	27.69	2	15.45
Previous arrests (3 arrests or less/more than 3 arrests)	5	21.3	3	52.37*	3	35.10
CPI success (low score/high score profile)	1	15.03	2	25.9	2	15.32
Employed or not after release	2	36.7†	3	24.9	3	30.1
Able to name a pay-off for reinvolvement in crime	3	14.0	5	26.6*	5	12.0
Man in prison interested in how he is doing after release	2	17.6	2	35.1†	5	14.49
Sees children	4	21.3	3	44.3‡	4	36.8†
Drinking frequency	2	12.5	4	26.1*	4	20.1*
Fights or not	2	13.6	3	26.4	3	18.9*

* $p < 0.05$; † $p < 0.01$; ‡ $p < 0.001$

Figure F:I
Cumulative proportion arrested by mode of release and three-monthly period from release

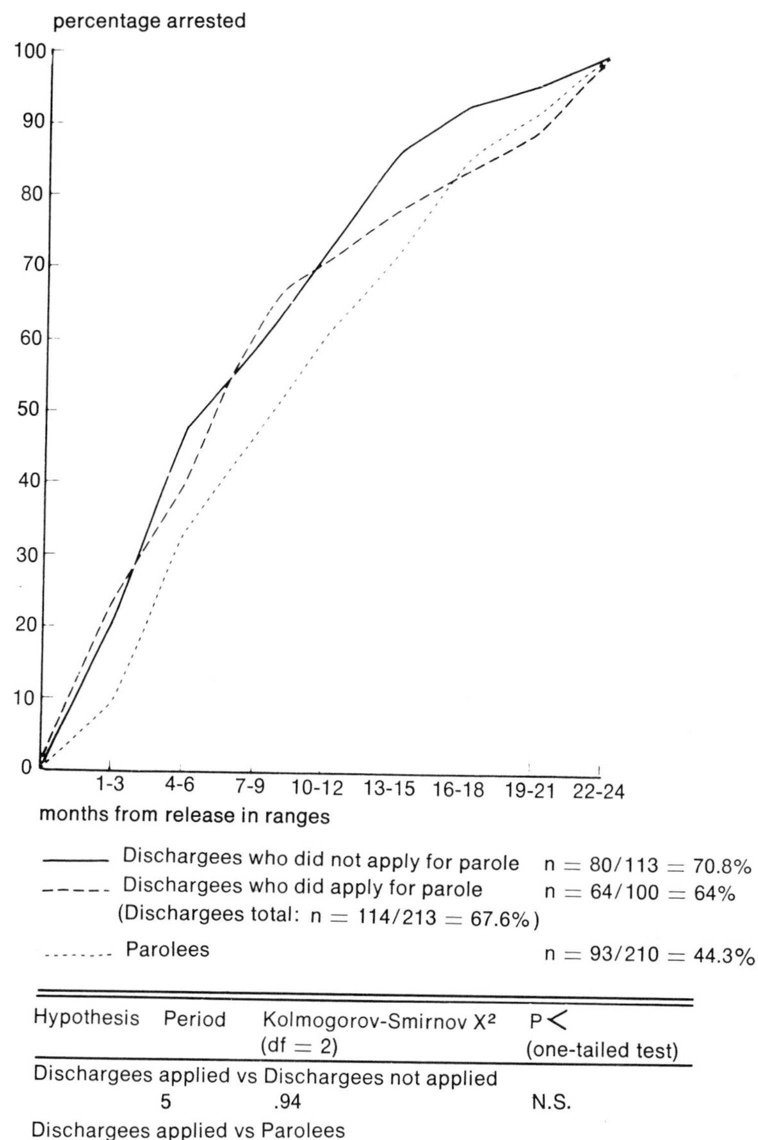

Hypothesis	Period	Kolmogorov-Smirnov X^2 (df = 2)	P < (one-tailed test)
Dischargees applied vs Dischargees not applied			
	5	.94	N.S.
Dischargees applied vs Parolees			
	3	5.08	.05
Dischargees not applied vs Parolees			
	5	3.47	.10
Dischargees vs Parolees			
	1	5.71	.05

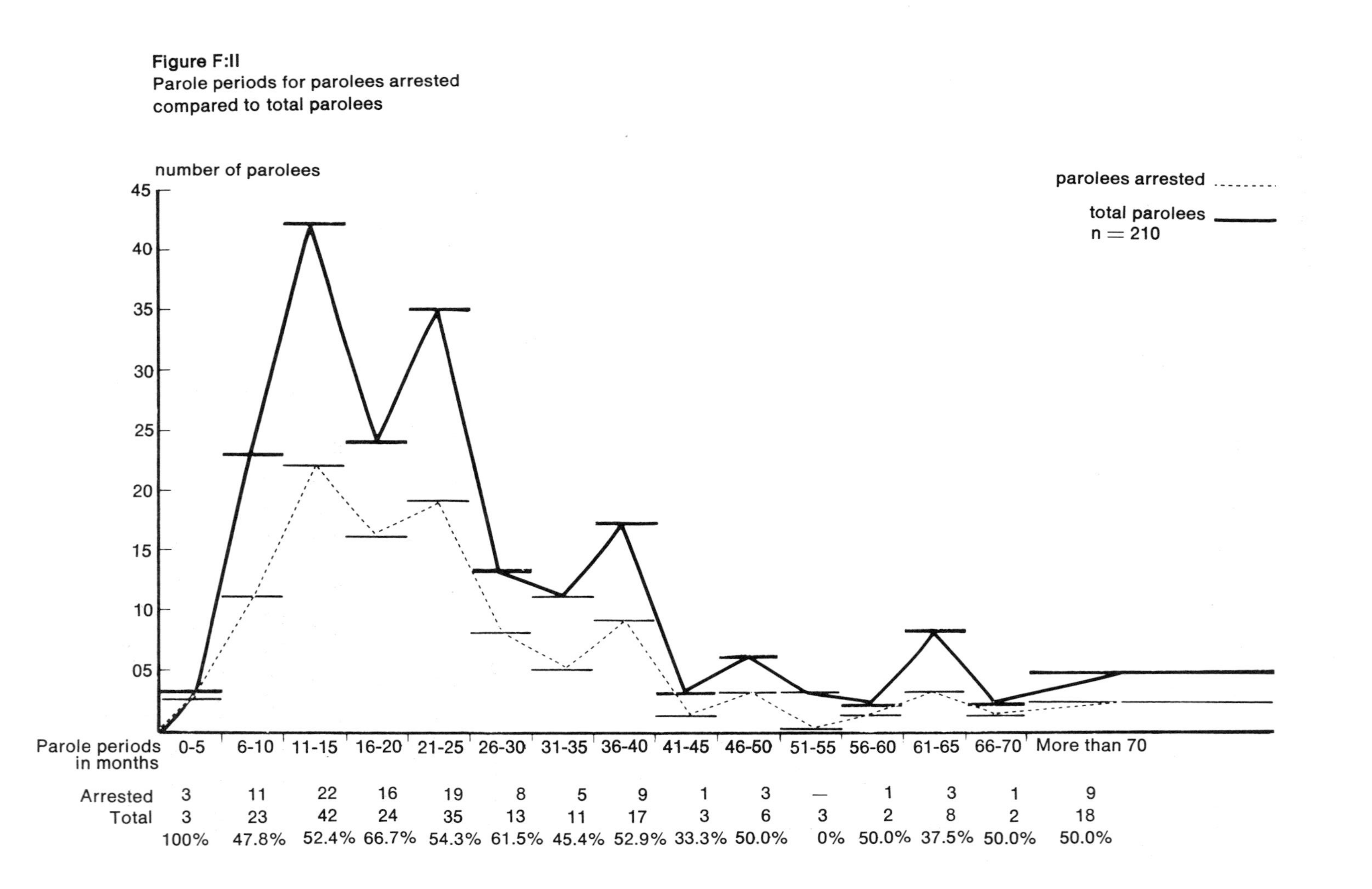

Figure F:II
Parole periods for parolees arrested compared to total parolees

Parole periods in months	0-5	6-10	11-15	16-20	21-25	26-30	31-35	36-40	41-45	46-50	51-55	56-60	61-65	66-70	More than 70
Arrested	3	11	22	16	19	8	5	9	1	3	—	1	3	1	9
Total	3	23	42	24	35	13	11	17	3	6	3	2	8	2	18
	100%	47.8%	52.4%	66.7%	54.3%	61.5%	45.4%	52.9%	33.3%	50.0%	0%	50.0%	37.5%	50.0%	50.0%

Figure F:III

A. Three-month moving average of the proportion of the total arrested in each month

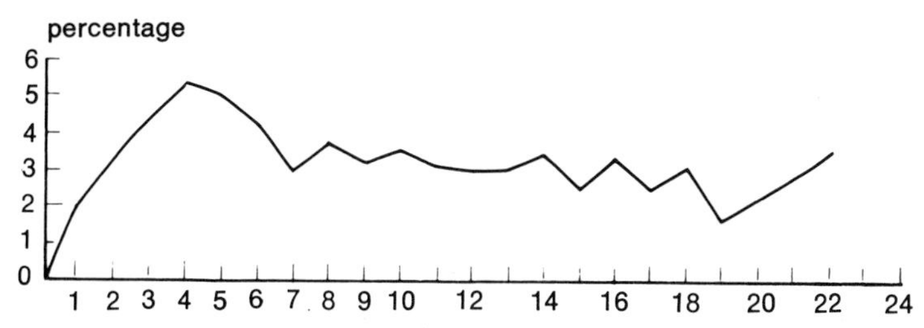

B. Proportion of total still free at the beginning of each monthly period arrested in that month

mean = .035 per month

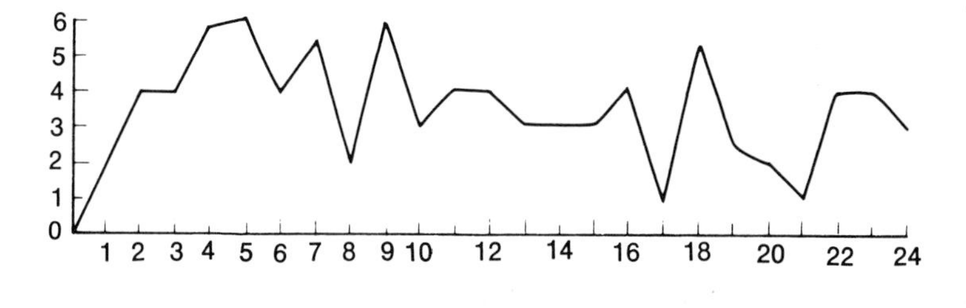

C. Proportion of those to be arrested within twenty-four months still free at the beginning of each monthly period arrested in that month

mean = .086 per month

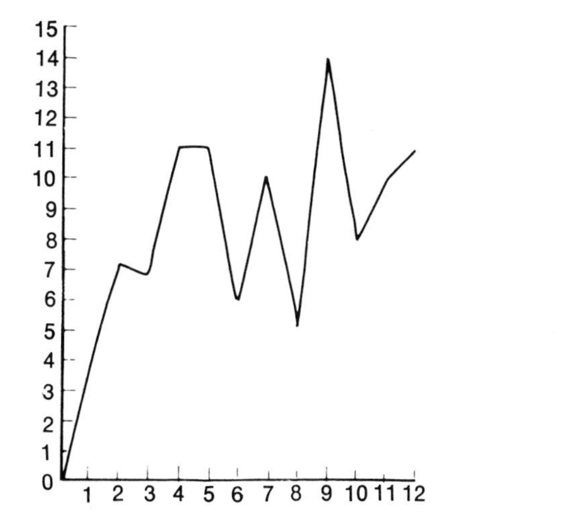

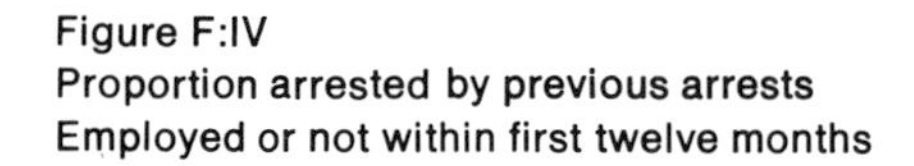

Figure F:IV
Proportion arrested by previous arrests
Employed or not within first twelve months

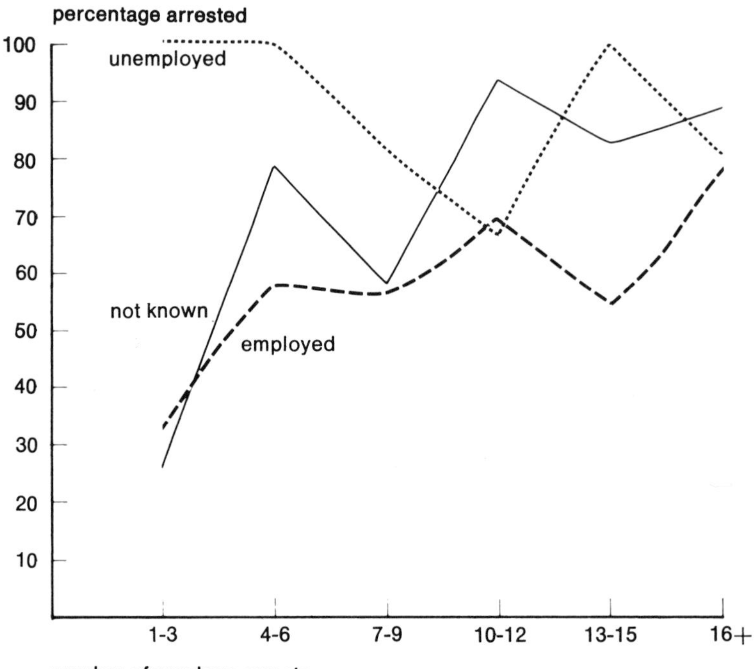

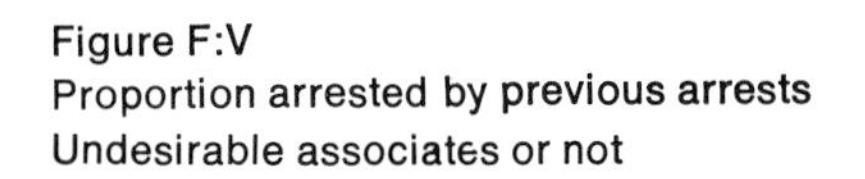

Figure F:V
Proportion arrested by previous arrests
Undesirable associates or not

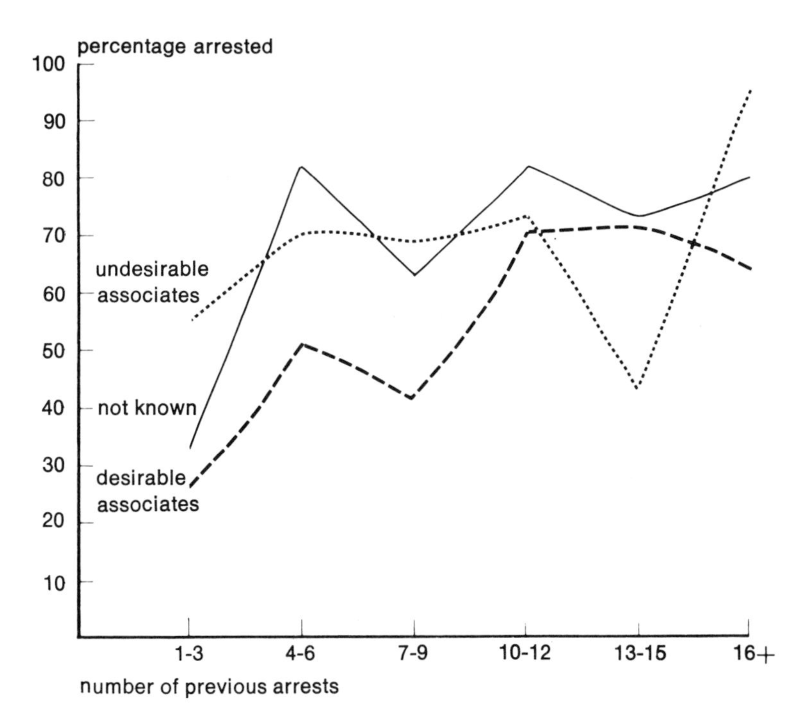

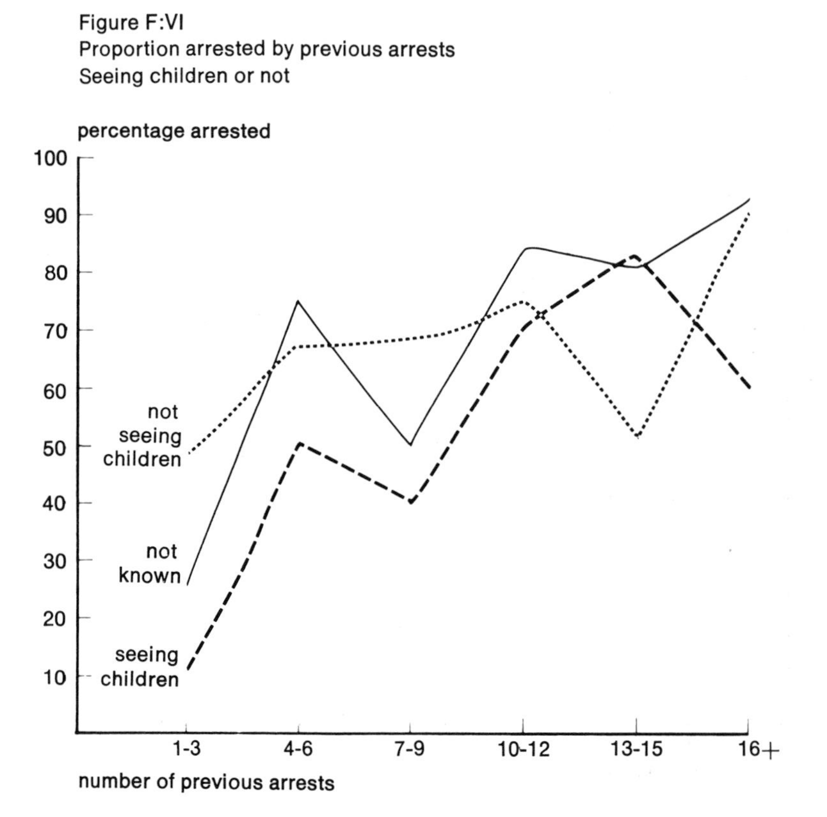

Figure F:VI
Proportion arrested by previous arrests
Seeing children or not

Figure F:VII
Proportion arrested by previous arrests
Fights or not

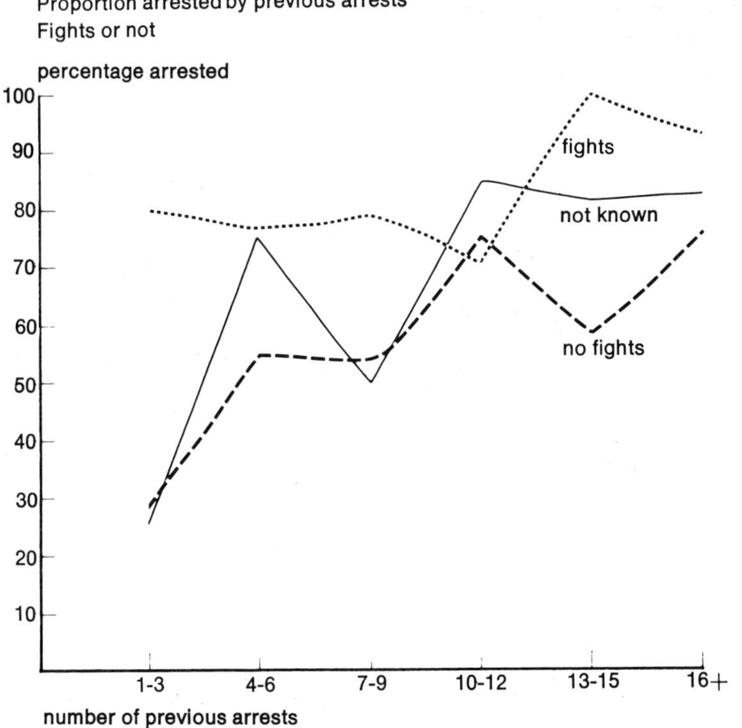

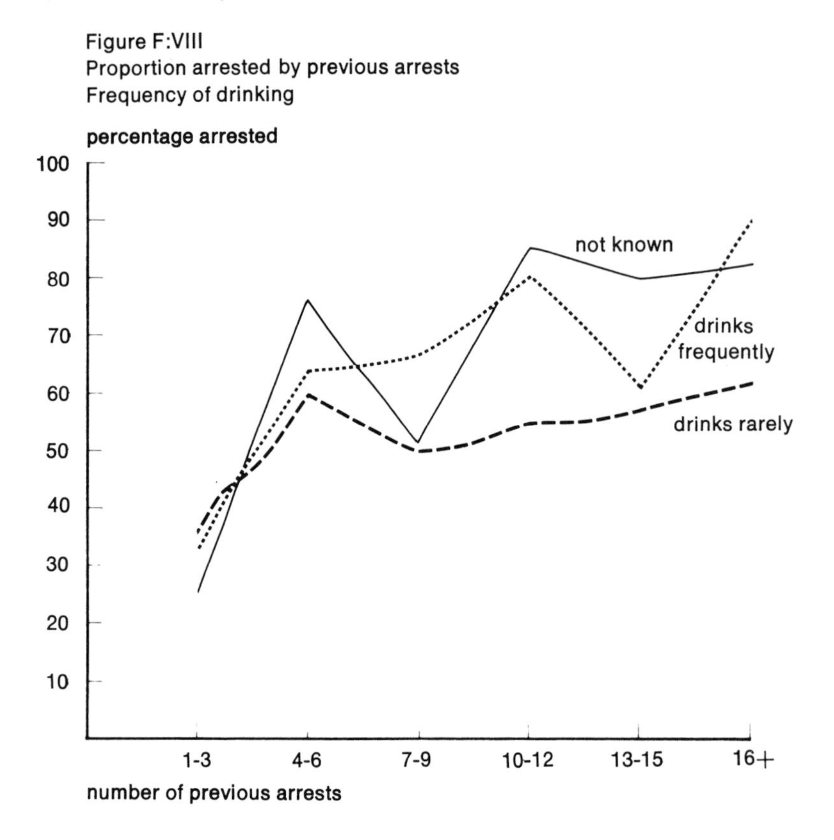

G PREDICTION EQUATIONS

In chapter 9, the analysis involving prediction equations was inevitably restricted to summarizing conclusions. This appendix presents certain equations which were selected to illustrate the findings, particularly the importance of individual variables, the extent of shrinkage on replication, and the over-all levels of prediction efficiency. No attempt has been made to discuss each individual table. However, the manner in which the prediction equations are presented is first explained.

EXPLANATION OF TABLES

In Table G.1, the prediction equation developed on the construction sample, against arrest within six months for combined dischargees and parolees, omitting background expectancy scores, is displayed. In the first column, the shorthand form for the variable name is set out; reform commitments, for instance, refers to the scaled number of previous reformatory commitments recorded on the prisoner's admission form at the time he was admitted through

Kingston Penitentiary before being released in 1968. The second column displays the regression coefficient which was finally indicated on the construction sample. The regression coefficients do not reflect the importance of a particular variable because some of the variables, such as drinking or not, are dichotomized; some are discrete, such as reformatory commitments; and some are continuous, such as the Jesness combination score. In the third column the significance value is displayed. This is the significance of the *t*-value associated with the particular regression coefficient and can be used to measure the statistical significance of the increase in information accounted for by including that particular variable. Thus, if an equation were developed omitting reformatory commitments, but including the other five variables, the increase in the proportion of variance, explained by adding reformatory commitments to that equation, would have a *t*-value of −4.020, and be likely to occur less than one time in a thousand.

At the bottom of each table the statistics calculated on the construction and validation sample, in both the limited and real prediction models, are displayed. A validated correlation of more than 0.40 is extremely rare in the criminological literature on samples of any size less than 1000. A recent study of probationers in the United Kingdom, on a sample marginally larger (construction 303, validation 379) than the present study, achieved validated values of about 0.25 for the correlation in predicting reconviction within twelve months (Simon, 1971).

The variables are presented in the tables in the order in which they were included in the equation: thus, for arrest within six months, reformatory commitments had the highest single correlation coefficient; when added to reformatory commitments, the Jesness combination score resulted in the largest increase in the multiple correlation coefficient; and so forth. The 'stopping rule' used for the development of these prediction equations was that the *t*-value for the regression coefficient should be significant at less than the 1 per cent level and the proportion of sum of squares reduced in a particular set should be larger than 0.01.

The reader interested in definitions and discussions of the statistics – mean cost rating, *J. D. t* – used to assess the prediction equations is referred to Simon (1971). These statistics have been presented for both the real and limited prediction modes, which were discussed in the text.

TABLE G.1

Prediction equation developed on construction sample (N = 128/204) against arrest within six months for dischargees and parolees combined, omitting background base expectancy scores

Variable	Regression coefficient	Significance value
Reform commitments	−0.069	0.001
Jesness combination score	−0.023	0.001
Employed or not	0.047	0.001
Got first job through Manpower	0.269	0.01
Drink or not	−0.146	0.01
Sees children or not	−0.152	0.01
Constant	1.984	

		Multiple correlation coefficient	Mean cost rating	*J*	*D*	*t*
Limited prediction	Construction	0.528	0.618	0.488	0.0	6.979
	Validation	0.207	0.247	0.274	0.167	2.576
Real prediction	Construction	0.383	0.471	0.333	0.0	5.891
	Validation	0.236	0.335	0.235	0.124	3.569

TABLE G.2

Prediction equation developed on construction sample (N = 204/204) against arrest within twelve months for dischargees and parolees combined, background data only

Variable	Regression coefficient	Significance value
Type of previous commitments to penal institution	−0.034	0.02
Age at release under 25 or not	0.292	0.001
Constant	1.370	

		Multiple correlation coefficient	Mean cost rating	*J*	*D*	*t*
Real prediction	Construction	0.303	0.351	0.384	0.0	4.525
	Validation	0.199	0.185	0.175	0.111	2.987
Limited prediction	Construction	0.393	0.442	0.333	0.0	4.876
	Validation	0.240	0.242	0.202	0.106	3.014

TABLE G.3

Prediction equation developed on construction sample (N = 128/204) against arrest within twelve months for dischargees and parolees combined, omitting background base expectancy scores

Variable	Regression coefficient	Significance value
Fights or not	0.313	0.001
Employed or not	0.069	0.001
Drinks or not	0.221	0.002
Sees children or not	−0.196	0.01
Constant	1.486	

		Multiple correlation coefficient	Mean cost rating	*J*	*D*	*t*
Limited prediction	Construction	0.495	0.532	0.374	0.0	6.388
	Validation	0.289	0.324	0.255	0.129	3.682
Real prediction	Construction	0.402	0.402	0.296	0.0	6.235
	Validation	0.276	0.291	0.221	0.102	4.229

TABLE G.4

Prediction equation developed on construction sample (N = 128/204) against arrest within twenty-four months for dischargees and parolees combined, omitting background base expectancy scores

Variable	Regression coefficient	Significance value
Undesirable associates	0.262	0.001
Fights or not	0.213	0.01
Penal record	−0.065	0.001
Age at release	0.258	0.001
Constant	0.553	

		Multiple correlation coefficient	Mean cost rating	*J*	*D*	*t*
Limited prediction	Construction	0.512	0.566	0.426	0.0	6.692
	Validation	0.326	0.323	0.254	0.070	4.206
Real prediction	Construction	0.413	0.458	0.311	0.0	6.451
	Validation	0.299	0.287	0.242	0.099	4.618

TABLE G.5

Comparison of regression coefficients on background data only against arrest within twelve months, arrest within twenty-four months, and conviction

Variable	Arrest 12 months: regression coefficient	Arrest 24 months: regression coefficient	Conviction 12 months: regression coefficient
Age at release under 25 or not	0.292	0.198	0.193
Type of previous commitments to penal institution	−0.034	−0.061	−0.050
Constant	1.370	1.169	1.564

TABLE G.6

Construction and validation multiple-correlation coefficients by characteristics of data base and arrest criteria for dischargees and parolees combined

	Arrest within 6 months		Arrest within 12 months		Arrest within 24 months	
	Construction	Validation	Construction	Validation	Construction	Validation
LIMITED PREDICTION						
Background data						
With age and penal record forced			0.398	0.240	0.408	0.316
With psychometric data forced			0.423	0.249	0.428	0.285
Background and post-release data						
Omitting BE	0.528	0.207	0.495	0.289	0.537	0.289
Including BE	0.448	0.217	0.511	0.236	0.512	0.326
REAL PREDICTION						
Background data						
With age and penal record forced			0.303	0.199	0.328	0.272
With psychometric data forced			0.344	0.221	0.358	0.266
Background and post-release data						
Omitting BE	0.383	0.236	0.402	0.276	0.424	0.290
Including BE	0.380	0.234	0.435	0.232	0.413	0.299

TABLE G.7

Prediction equation developed on construction sample (N = 82/101) against arrest within twenty-four months for parolees only, omitting base expectancy and including parole supervisor variables

Variable	Regression coefficient	Significance value
Reprimands	0.417	0.001
Financial standing	0.109	0.01
Type of previous commitments to penal institution	−0.019	0.01
Constant	0.492	

		Multiple correlation coefficient	Mean cost rating	*J*	*D*	*t*
Real prediction	Construction	0.393	0.447	0.344	0.0	4.254
	Validation	0.285	0.267	0.328	0.126	3.074
Limited prediction	Construction	0.477	0.525	0.382	0.0	4.852
	Validation	0.287	0.316	0.340	0.227	2.825

TABLE G.8

Prediction equation developed on construction sample (N = 110/204) against release from Kingston Penitentiary or not for dischargees and parolees combined, including both background and post-release information

Variable	Regression coefficient	Significance value
Offences against staff	−0.179	0.001
How long did money last after release	0.200	0.001
Admit year	0.107	0.001
Fights or not	0.220	0.001
Drinks rarely or regularly	0.215	0.001
Tries to avoid previous friends	−0.160	0.001
Intention ever changed or not	−0.126	0.01
Original offence against property	0.160	0.01
Constant	0.699	

		Multiple correlation coefficient	Mean cost rating	*J*	*D*	*t*
Real prediction	Construction	0.421	0.550	0.500	—	6.594
	Validation	0.282	0.351	0.349	0.131	4.325

TABLE G.9

Prediction equation developed on construction sample (N = 128/204) against written application for parole made during last sentence or not

Variable	Regression coefficient	Significance value
Pre-release perceived chances of post-release failure	0.076	0.01
Longest job held within 12 months	−0.035	0.01
Spend first night	−0.230	0.001
CPI combination score	−0.017	0.002
Debts	−0.170	0.001
Pay-off	−0.140	0.01
Fights or not	0.153	0.01
Constant	2.477	

		Multiple correlation coefficient	Mean cost rating	*J*	*D*	*t*
Limited prediction	Construction	0.544	0.771	0.705	0.0	6.585
	Validation	0.274	0.378	0.279	0.112	3.167
Real prediction	Construction	0.273	0.343	0.284	0.0	4.733
	Validation	0.160	0.227	0.177	0.073	2.988

TABLE G.10

Prediction equation developed on construction sample (N = 87/204) against parole granted or refused as final decision for persons making written applications for parole

Variable	Regression coefficient	Significance value
Pre-release perceived chances of post-release failure	−0.153	0.001
Longest job held within 12 months	0.060	0.001
Employed within 5 weeks	−0.256	0.001
Admission year	−0.084	0.001
CPI combination score	−0.172	0.002
Constant	2.753	

		Multiple correlation coefficient	Mean cost rating	*J*	*D*	*t*
Limited prediction	Construction	0.567	0.746	0.703	0.0	6.352
	Validation	0.431	0.590	0.531	0.089	4.799
Real prediction	Construction	0.506	0.608	0.496	0.0	7.047
	Validation	0.414	0.479	0.340	0.099	5.795

TABLE G.11

Prediction equation developed on construction sample (N = 133/204) against release as a parolee or dischargee

Variable	Regression coefficient	Significance value
Penal record	0.050	0.001
Drink problem before and after	−0.250	0.001
Yes/no guys in prison interested	0.202	0.01
Undesirable associates	0.048	0.01
Unemployed throughout first 5 weeks	−0.210	0.01
Could name a pay-off	0.167	0.01

		Multiple correlation coefficient	Mean cost rating	*J*	*D*	*t*
Real prediction	Construction	0.426	0.513	0.376	0.0	6.700
	Validation	0.376	0.445	0.368	0.080	5.977

TABLE G.12

Prediction equation developed on construction sample (N = 110/204) against fighting or not within five weeks for dischargees and parolees combined, background data only

Variable	Regression coefficient	Significance value
Age	0.24333	0.001
Release from Kingston Penitentiary	0.25781	0.001
CPI combination	0.02152	0.001
Applied for parole or not	0.25469	0.001
Constant	0.10548	

		Multiple correlation coefficient	Mean cost rating	*J*	*D*	*t*
Real prediction	Construction	0.339	0.402	0.325	—	5.873
	Validation	0.180	0.271	0.197	0.122	3.188

TABLE G.13

Equations used in analysis of variance

Criteria	Data base	Variables
Arrest within 12 months	Background only	Age/penal record
Arrest within 12 months	Background only including psychometric data	Age/penal record/Jesness combination score
Arrest within 12 months	Total data omitting background base expectancy	Fights or not/employed or not/drinks or not/sees children or not
Arrest within 6 months	Total data including background base expectancy	BE age/penal record/Jesness combination score/reform commitments/spent time in psychiatric unit in KP/drink with friends
Arrest within 12 months	Total data including background base expectancy	BE age/penal record/Jesness combination score/fights or not/employed or not
Arrest within 24 months	Total data including background base expectancy	BE age/penal record/Jesness combination score/undesirable associates/fights or not

TABLE G.14

Significant values for twenty-four month base expectancy (6), by parole selection variables

	Parolee/dischargee	Applied or not	Granted or not
vs 6 months	0.098	0.001	—
vs 12 months	0.006	0.001	—
vs 24 months	0.061	0.083	—

TABLE G.15

Probability of F-values associated with analysis of variance

	Parolee /dischargee			
	Limited prediction		Real prediction	
	Number significant at less than 0.05	Crucial* n = 155/219	Number significant at less than 0.05	Crucial* n = 219/219
vs 6 months	5/6	0.026	0/6	0.137
vs 12 months	6/6	0.006	5/6	0.012
vs 24 months	5/6	0.06	4/6	0.100
	Applied or not during last sentence			
	Limited prediction		Real prediction	
	Number significant at less than 0.05	Crucial* n = 155/219	Number significant at less than 0.05	Crucial* n = 219/219
vs 6 months	6/6	0.000	3/6	0.035
vs 12 months	6/6	0.000	5/6	0.017
vs 24 months	5/6	0.083	1/6	0.262
	Granted or not after application			
	Limited prediction		Real prediction	
	Number significant at less than 0.05	Crucial* n = 124/219	Number significant at less than 0.05	Crucial* n = 164/219
vs 6 months	0/6	—	0/6	—
vs 12 months	0/6	—	0/6	—
vs 24 months	0/6	—	0/6	—

* Crucial refers to the F-value in the analysis of variance using the post-release base expectancy score predicting that definition of re-arrest

TABLE G.16

Probability of F-values associated with analysis of variance, to test for differences associated with release form (maximum security)

	Limited prediction		Real prediction	
	Number significant at less than 0.05 (N = 155/219)	Range	Number significant at less than 0.05 (N = 219/219)	Range
vs 6 months	6/6	0.022–0.011	0/6	—
vs 12 months	1/4	0.000–0.083	0/6	—
vs 24 months	0/6	0.082–	0/6	—

TABLE G.17

Summary of analysis of variance for parolees only (N = 91/109)

Parolee base expectancy	Parole variable	*t*	Significance value
6 months	Contacts	1.577	0.112
	Reprimands	1.199	0.229
	Closeness	1.300	0.101
	Help with employment	−3.061	0.003
	Crime problem	−1.552	0.118
12 months	Contacts	—	—
	Reprimands	—	—
	Closeness	—	—
	Help with employment	−1.398	0.159
	Crime problem	—	—
24 months	Contacts	—	—
	Reprimands	—	—
	Closeness	1.467	0.140
	Help with employment	1.534	0.111
	Crime problem	—	—

Glossary

CASEWORK
A technique, or group of techniques, for dealing with disapproved conduct or situations by personal influence on individuals as distinct from coercion or material assistance (Walker, 1969, 216).

CHI-SQUARED TEST
A common statistical test for differences in distributions on a variable composed of discrete categories between two samples, such as parolees and dischargees. See Siegel (1956).

CPI
The California Psychological Inventory is a true/false questionnaire comprising 480 items with 19 standard scales designed to measure personality characteristics significant in the daily living and social interaction of normal persons. It differs from many existing tests in: (*a*) its emphasis on the positive and favourable aspects of personality as opposed to the morbid and pathological; (*b*) its development of scales to predict practical, meaningful, complex social outcomes of behaviour rather than abstract or 'undimensional traits.' See Gough (1956).

CONSTRUCTION SAMPLE
The group of persons on whom the predictors in the prediction model are determined so as to optimize the predictive efficiency.

CONTAINMENT MEASURE
A measure intended to prevent absolutely or reduce significantly the probability of an individual committing an offence by making it physically or practically difficult for him to do so. See also Walker (1969), 200.

DYNAMIC VARIABLE
A variable measuring some aspect of an ex-prisoner's situation that can change during the first twelve months from release. For instance, he can start as unemployed, but become employed later. A variable such as age or number of previous convictions cannot change.

INDEFINITE SENTENCE
A sentence of imprisonment which leaves the date of release to be decided by

the executive – usually the parole board or the parole board and the governor general – and which, in theory at least, lasts for the rest of the offender's life.

INDETERMINATE SENTENCE
A custodial sentence for which the maximum duration is not specified by the law or by the sentencer (Walker, 1969).

INDICTABLE OFFENCE
Under the Criminal Law of Canada, an offence is either indictable or punishable on summary conviction. Originally, an indictable offence could be tried in a higher court and was presumed to be more serious. However, many indictable offences can now be tried in provincial courts, or what used to be called 'Magistrates Courts' (Hogarth, 1971, 35–6). Technically, an indictable offence is one in which the charge must, or may, be tried before a jury.

INTERVENING VARIABLE
A variable measuring an apparently independent situation which is, in fact, related to a higher probability of arrest. For instance, it is an empirical fact that a person who is unemployed (drinks regularly, fights, has undesirable associates, or weak family ties) is more likely to be arrested within a defined period from release. 'Unemployment' is therefore an intervening variable.

NOMINAL SENTENCE
The sentence pronounced in court. Where a number of nominal sentences are consecutive, the nominal sentence is assumed to be the same as the aggregate of the consecutive sentences or the longer of the concurrent sentences. See Remission.

PREDICTION EQUATION
A way of combining a series of scores on variables (age, penal record) to explain variation in a criterion (arrest within six months, release on parole).

PRISONISATION
The 'taking on in greater or less degree of the folkways, mores, customs, and general culture of the penitentiary' (Clemmer, Rev. ed., 1965, 299–300). Part of the process involves an expectation that 'the environment should administer' to the prisoner. It may make the man 'characteristic of the penal community and probably so disrupt his personality that a happy adjustment in any community becomes next to impossible.'

RECIDIVIST
Strictly speaking, any offender who breaks the law again after penal disposition. The term is usually reserved, however, for 'multiple recidivists' who fail to respond to several sentences; those who have relapsed only once are called 'primary recidivists.'

REGRESSION
A statistical technique used to relate the rate of change taking place in one or more variables to the rate of change in a criterion variable. 'Stepwise multiple linear regression' is the main technique used in this book and refers to the development of the regression equation by locating that variable which maximizes the proportion of the criterion variance explained and in subsequent steps

by adding that one new variable which maximizes the proportion of the criterion variance explained. At each step the weights for the variables are computed. For fuller discussion see Snedecor and Cochran (1967).

REMISSION (EARNED)
A deduction from the nominal sentence (q.v.) of a maximum of three days per month spent in the penitentiary. In theory, the number of days awarded is based on the employment and disciplinary behaviour of the prisoner. In practice, earned remission is deducted for misbehaviour.

REMISSION (STATUTORY)
An automatic deduction of one-quarter of the nominal sentence (q.v.), in theory, deducted at the beginning of the sentence. If parole is granted, followed by parole revocation or parole forfeiture, the statutory remission on the original nominal sentence is no longer deducted. However, a new statutory remission is deducted from the nominal sentence, less the time actually spent in the penitentiary, less the earned remission from the time in the penitentiary. This results for parole revocation in an extra total time spent in the penitentiary equal to one-quarter of the time actually spent in the penitentiary before parole was granted. Calculations with respect to earned remission and credit of time spent in the local jail after parole suspension have varied in the Parole Act.

RETRIBUTION
The infliction of suffering on a person solely because of a past act and in accordance with a divinely or socially approved code. (Walker, 1969).

SATISFICING
A form of behaviour in which the subject, faced with a difficult problem to solve, prefers to sacrifice some of the rewards of the optimum solution in order to reduce the pains incurred in searching for it (Marris, 1964).

SHRINKAGE
The extent to which predictive efficiency is reduced when a prediction equation developed on a construction sample is tested on a validation sample.

'SIEVE' CRIMINAL JUSTICE SYSTEM
The funnel-shaped filtering process starting from offence occurring, reporting to police, police decision to respond, police decision to press for charges, prosecutor decision on charges, court decision on guilt, court decision on disposition, parole decision to release, parole and probation officer decision to recall. 'Sieve' refers in particular to the selective manner in which this process operates.

STATISTICAL SIGNIFICANCE
In most analyses in this book a difference was significant if it would have occurred less than one in a hundred times on the basis of chance alone. If two alternative hypotheses are suggested, e.g., parolees are the same as dischargees in terms of age; parolees differ from dischargees in terms of age, then we test these hypotheses in our sample. The level of significance is the probability that such a difference between parolees and dischargees occur (Siegel, 1956).

VALIDATION SAMPLE
The group of persons on whom the prediction model with the parameters estimated from the construction sample is tested and the degree of shrinkage in predictive efficiency established.

VARIANCE
The mean of squared individual scores less the mean of individual scores squared. It is a common statistic for measuring variation within one variable, and can be partitioned so that one can talk about the proportion of 'arrest' variance explained by age. For fuller discussion see Diamond (1959) and Snedecor and Cochran (1967).

Bibliography

Adams, S. 1961 'Interaction between individual interview therapy and treatment amenability in older youth authority wards' *Inquiries Concerning Kinds of Treatment for Kinds of Delinquents* Monograph no. 2, California Board of Corrections (Sacramento, Cal.)

Adams, S. 1967 'Some findings from correctional case-load research' *Federal Probation* 31, no. 4 (Dec.), 48–57

Adams, S. 1967a 'A cost effectiveness comparison of correctional treatments' A paper presented at the 17th annual meeting of the Society for the Study of Social Problems (San Francisco; Aug.)

Ali, Badr-El-Din M. 1966 'A comparative study of two types of parole violators' *Criminologica* 4, no. 3 (Nov.) 32–8

Allen, F.A. 1964 'Legal values and the rehabilitative ideal' *The Borderland of Criminal Justice* (Chicago: University of Chicago Press) 25–41

Andenaes, J. 1966 'The general preventive effects of punishment' *University of Pennsylvania Law Review* 114:7 (May) 949–83

Andrews, A.L. 1965 *Social Factors Affecting Recidivism* (Toronto: School of Social Work, University of Toronto)

Andry, R.G. 1960 *Delinquency and Parental Pathology* (London: Methuen)

'Archambault Report' 1938 Royal Commission to Investigate the Penal System of Canada *Report* (Ottawa: King's Printer)

Arluke, N.R. 1969 'A summary of parole rules – thirteen years later' *Crime and Delinquency* 15, no. 2, 267–74

Babst, D.V., D.M. Gottfredson, and K.B. Ballard 1968 'Comparison of multiple regression and configural analysis techniques for developing base expectancy tables' *Journal of Research in Crime and Delinquency* 5, no. 1 (Jan.) 72–80

Babst, D.V. and J.W. Mannering 1965 'Probation versus imprisonment for similar types of offenders' ibid. 2, no. 2 (July) 61–9

Babst, D.V. et al. 1971 'The uses of configural analysis in parole prediction' *Canadian Journal of Criminology and Corrections* 13, 200–8

Bailey, W.C. 1966 'Correctional outcome: an evaluation of 100 reports' *Journal of Criminal Law, Criminology and Police Science* 57, no. 2 (June) 153–60

Barnes, H.E. 1959 *New Horizons in Criminology* 3rd ed. (Englewood Cliffs, NJ: Prentice Hall)

Barry, Sir John Vincent William 1969 'Judicial sentencing or treatment tribunals?' reprinted from Sir John Vincent William Barry *The Courts and Criminal Punishment* (Wellington, New Zealand: A.R. Shearer, Government Printer) 38–41, 43–6, 62–3

Becker, H.S. 1953 'Becoming a marijuana user' *American Journal of Sociology* 59 (Nov.) 235–42

Binnie, S.W.S. 1972 'A study of inmates' views on parole conducted in Ontario reform institutions' Draft report (Toronto: University of Toronto)

Blackstock, H. 1967 *Bitter humor* (Toronto: Burns and MacEachern)

Blozan, C.F. and W.M. Mahoney 1968 *Cost Benefit Evaluation of Welfare Demonstration Projects: A Test Application to Juvenile Rehabilitation* (Bethesda, Md.: Department of Health, Education, and Welfare, Resource Management Corporation)

Boulanger, P. 1969 'Employment related activity for a group of parolees: an exploratory study of the initial post-release activity of a group of parolees in the Montreal area' MSW thesis McGill University (May)

Bowie, Douglas 1971 'Some aspects of parole in Canada' *Queen's Law Journal* 1, no. 2, 167–207

British Journal of Criminology 1973 special issue on parole, 13, no. 1 (Jan.)

Buckley, W.F. 1968 *Modern Systems Research for the Behavioral Scientist* (Chicago: Aldine)

California 1968 Probation Subsidy Program *Annual Progress Report* (Sacramento, Cal.)

Canada, Dominion Bureau of Statistics 1969 *Canada Year Book* (Ottawa: Queen's Printer)

Canada, Dominion Bureau of Statistics 1970 *Correctional Institution Statistics* 1970 (Ottawa)

Canada, Dominion Bureau of Statistics 1970–1 *Canada Year Book 1970–71* (Ottawa: Queen's Printer)

Canada 1969 Canadian Committee on Corrections *Report: Toward unity; criminal justice and corrections* (Ottawa: Queen's Printer)

Canada 1970 *Parole Act and the Parole Regulations: office consolidation* (Ottawa: Queen's Printer)

Canada 1971 The Standing Senate Committee on Legal and Constitutional Affairs *Examination of the parole system in Canada* 11–12

Canada 1972a Department of the Solicitor General *Parole recidivism study, as of June 1972* (Management Data Centre)

Canada 1972b The Standing Senate Committee on Legal and Constitutional Affairs *Examination of the parole system in Canada* 1–5, 7, 9–11, 13, 14

Carter, R.M. and L.T. Wilkins 1967 'Some factors in sentencing policy' *Journal of Criminal Law, Criminology and Police Science* 58, no. 4, 503–14

Carter, R.M. and L.T. Wilkins 1970 *Probation and Parole; Selected Readings* (New York: Wiley)

Chappel, D., et al. 1972 'Explorations in deterrence and criminal justice' *Criminal Law Bulletin* 8, no. 6 (July–Aug.) 514–38

Christie, N. 1971 'Scandinavian criminology facing the 1970's' *Scandinavian Studies in Criminology* (Oslo: E. Sem A/S-Halden) 140–5

Ciale, J. 1965 'Rate of success in institutional treatment' *Interdisciplinary Problems in Criminology: Papers of the American Society of Criminology 1964* edited by W.C. Reckless and C.L. Newman (Columbus, Ohio: Publication Service, College of Commerce and Administration, Ohio State University) 23–8

Ciale, J. et al. 1969 Unpublished progress reports (Department of Criminology, University of Montreal)

Cicourel, A.V. 1954 'Method and measurement in sociology' quoting J.P. Dean *Participant Observation in Interviewing* (Harrisburg, Penn.: The Stackfield Co.)

Clark, J.H. 1953 Additional application of AWOL recidivist scale. *Journal of Clinical Psychology* 9, 62–4

Clark, J.H. 1948 'Application of the MMPI in differentiating AWOL recidivists from non-recidivists' *Journal of Psychology* 26, 229–34

Clemmer, D. 1958 *The Prison Community* (New York: Holt, Rinehart and Winston)

Clinnard, M.R. and R. Quinney 1967 *Criminal Behavior Systems* (New York: Holt, Rinehart and Winston)

Cloward, R.A. et al. 1960 *Theoretical Studies in Social Organisation of the Prison* (New York: Social Science Research Council)

Cohen, F. 1967 *Legal norms in corrections* submission to the President's Commission on Law Enforcement and the Administration of Justice (Washington DC)

Cormier, B. 1965 'The family and delinquency' *Sciences de L'Homme: Contributions a L'Etude*, cahier 6, 83–117

Courtis, M. 1970 *Attitudes to crime and police in Toronto: a report on some survey findings* (Toronto: Centre of Criminology, University of Toronto)

Cressey, D.R. (ed.) 1958 *The Prison: Studies in Institutional Organisation and Change* (New York: Holt, Rinehart and Winston)

Cressey, D.R. and D.A. Ward 1969 *Delinquency, Crime and Social Process* (London: Harper and Row) 60–6

Criminal Justice Newsletter 1972 'Special Bulletin' (supplement to vol. 3, no. 2, 17 Jan.)

Cross, R. 1965 'Paradoxes in prison sentences' *Law Quarterly Review* 81, 205–22

Cross, R. 1970 'Sentencing in a rational society' *Criminal Law Review*, 4–15

Davies, M. 1967 *The Use of the Jesness Inventory on a Sample of British Probationers* (London: HMSO)

Davies, M. 1969 *Probationers and their Social Environment* (London: HMSO)

Davies, M. 1973 *An Index of Social Environment* Home Office Research Studies (London: HMSO)

Davies, M and I. Sinclair 1971 'Families, Hostels and Delinquents: An Attempt to Assess Cause and Effect' *British Journal of Criminology* 11, no. 3 (July) 213–29

Dawson, R.O. 1969 *Sentencing: the decision as to type, length and conditions of sentence* (Boston: Little Brown)

Dean, C.W. 1968 'New directions for parole prediction research' *Journal of Criminal Law, Criminology and Police Science* 59, no. 2, 214–18

Diamond, S. 1959 *Information and Error* (New York: Basic Books)

Eaton, J.W. 1962 *Stone Walls Do Not a Prison Make* (Springfield, Ill.: C.C. Thomas)

Edmison, J. Alex. 1965 Some aspects of nineteenth-century Canadian prisons. In W.T. McGrath (ed.), *Crime and its Treatment in Canada* (Toronto: Macmillan)

Empey, L.T. and S.G. Lubeck 1970 *The Silverlake Experiment* (Chicago: Aldine)

England, R.W., Jr. 1955 'A study of post-probation recidivism among five hundred federal offenders' *Federal Probation* 19 (Sept.) 10–16

England, R.W., Jr. 1956–7 'What is responsible for satisfactory probation and post-probation outcome?' *Journal of Criminal Law, Criminology and Police Science* 47, 675

Erikson, K.T. 1967 'Notes on the sociology of deviance' *The Other Side* edited by H.S. Becker (Toronto: Collier-Macmillan Canada) 9–21

'Fauteux Report' 1956 Committee to Inquire into the Principles and Procedures Followed in the Remission Service of the Department of Justice of Canada *Report* (Ottawa: Queen's Printer)

Feistman, E.G. 1966 *Comparative Analysis of the Willowbrook Harbour Intensive Supervision Program* Research report no. 28 (Los Angeles: County Probation Department, June)

Finestone, H. 1967 'Reformation and recidivism among Italian and Polish criminal offenders' *American Journal of Sociology* 72, no. 6 (May) 575–88

Folkard, S., S. Lyon, M.M. Carver, and E. O'Leary 1966 *Probation Research: A Preliminary Report, Home Office Studies in the Causes of Delinquency and the Treatment of Offenders* (London: HMSO)

Fox, R.G. 1971 'Temporary absence, work-release and community based corrections in Ontario' *Australian and New Zealand Journal of Criminology* 4, no. 1 (March) 46–61

Gallant, D.M. et al. 1968 'Enforced clinic treatment of paroled criminal alcoholics' *Quarterly Journal of Studies on Alcohol* 29, 77–84

Garfinkel, H. 1956 'Conditions of successful degradation ceremonies' *Amercian Journal of Sociology* 61 (March) 420–4

Gibbons, D.C. 1965 *Changing the Law Breaker* (Englewood Cliffs, NJ: Prentice Hall)

Glaser, D. 1964 *The Effectiveness of a Prison and Parole System* (Indianapolis: Bobbs-Merrill)

Glaser, D. et al. 1966 *The sentencing and parole process*, prepared for the

National Parole Institutes (Washington DC: US Department of Health, Education and Welfare)

Glaser, D. and J. Statton 1958 'Measuring inmate change in prison' Cressey (1958) 381–92

Glaser, D. and V. O'Leary 1966 *Personal characteristics and parole outcome*, prepared for the National Parole Institutes (Washington DC: US Department of Health, Education and Welfare)

Glueck, S. and E. Glueck 1930 *500 Criminal Careers* (New York: A.A. Knopf)

Glueck, S. and E. Glueck 1962 *Family Environment and Delinquency* (Boston: Houghton Mifflin)

Glueck, S. and E. Glueck 1968 *Delinquents and Non-Delinquents in Perspective* (Cambridge, Mass.: Harvard University Press)

Goffman, E. 1961 *Asylums: Essays on the Social Situation of Mental Patients and Other Inmates* (Chicago: Aldine)

Gordon, R.C. 1969 *Interviewing, Strategy, Techniques and Tactics* (Illinois: Dorsey Press)

Gottfredson, D.M. 1967 'Assessment of prediction methods in crime and delinquency' *Task Force Report: Juvenile Delinquency and Youth Crime*, President's Commission on Law Enforement and Administration of Justice (Washington: US Government Printing Office)

Gottfredson, D.M. and K.B. Ballard 1964 *'Association Analysis, Predictive Attribute Analysis and Parole Behavior', a paper presented at the Western Psychological Association meetings in Portland, Oregon (April)*

Gottfredson, D.M. and K.B. Ballard Jr. 1965 *The Validity of Two Parole Prediction Scales, an eight year follow-up study* (Vacaville, California: California Medical Facility)

Gottfredson, D.M. and K.B. Ballard 1966 *Offender Classification and Parole Prediction* (Sacramento, California: Institute for the Study of Crime and Delinquency

Gough, A.G. 1956 *Manual for the California Psychology Inventory* (Palo Alto, California: Consulting Psychologists' Press)

Gough, H.G., E.A. Wenk, and V.V. Rozynko 1965 'Parole outcome as predicted from the CPI, the MMPI, and a base expectancy table' *Journal of Abnormal Psychology* 70, no. 6 (1965), 432–41

Grant, J.D. and M.Q. Grant 1959 'A group dynamics approach to the treatment of non-conformists in the navy' *Annals of the American Academy of Political and Social Science* 322, 126–35

Great Britain 1969 *People in Prison*. Cmnd. 4214 (London: HMSO)

Great Britain 1969a *Report of the Parole Board for 1968* (London: HMSO) 7–13, 31–4, 25–7

Great Britain 1969b *The Sentence of the Court: a handbook for courts and the treatment of offenders* (London: HMSO)

Great Britain 1970 'non-custodial and semi-custodial penalties' *Report of the Advisory Council on the Penal System* (London: HMSO) 12–21, 51–6, 66–70

Great Britain 1970a 'Reparation by the offender' *Report of the Advisory Council on the Penal System* (London: HMSO)

Great Britain, Home Department 1971 *Report on the Work of the Prison Department* Cmnd. 4724 (London: HMSO, July)

Grygier, T., F. Blum, and O.R. Porebski 1971 'Decision and outcome studies and parole prediction' *Canadian Journal of Criminology and Corrections* 13, no. 2 (April) 133–46

Grygier, T. 1966 *Social Adjustment, Personality and Behavior in Training Schools in Ontario* (Toronto)

Guze, S.B., V.B. Tuason, P.D. Gatfield, *et al.* 1962 'Psychiatric illness and crime with particular reference to alcoholism: a study of 223 criminals' *Journal of Nervous and Mental Disease* 134, 512–21

Hadden, T. 1971 'Contract, tort and crime: the forms of legal thought' *Law Quarterly Review* 87 (April) 240–60

Hall, R.H. et al. 1966 *A Descriptive and Comparative Study of Recidivism in Pre-release Guidance Centre Releases* US Department of Justice Bureau of Prisons, Special Project on Work Release (Washington, DC)

Halmos, P. 1965 *Sociological Studies in the British Penal Services* (Keele: University of Keele)

Hann, R. 1972 'Decision making in the Canadian Criminal Courts: a simulation' a paper read at Operations Research Society of America, annual meeting (New Orleans: April)

Hann, Robert G. 1973 *Decision making in the Canadian Criminal Court system: a systems analysis* II (Toronto: Centre of Criminology, University of Toronto)

Harrington, J. and D. Devine (1967) 'The habitual criminal – a review of the jurisprudence' *McGill Law Journal* 13, no. 4, 632

Havel, J. 1965 *Special Intensive Parole Unit: Phase* IV *– The Parole Outcome Study* Research Report no. 13. California Department of Corrections (Sacramento, Cal.)

Havel, J. and E. Sulka 1962 *Special Intensive Parole Unit: Phase* III Research Report no. 3, California Department of Corrections (Sacramento, Cal.)

Hawkins, K.O. 1971 *Parole Selection: the Amercian Experience* unpublished PHD dissertation (Cambridge University)

Hawkins, K.O. 1971a *Parole: a Select bibliography with especial Reference to American Experience* Bibliographical Series no. 3 (Cambridge: The University Library)

Hayner, Norman S. 1958 'Sentencing by an administrative board' *Law and Contemporary Problems* 23, 477–94

Hays, P. 1964 *New Horizons in Psychiatry* (London: Cox and Wynn)

Herbert, J. 1968 *Fortune and Men's Eyes* (Chicago: Aldine)

Himelson, A.N. and P.T. Takagi 1963 *Parole Panel Studies: Report* A, Theory and Method with Comparison of Experimental and Control Subjects Research Report no. 7, California Department of Corrections (Sacramento, Cal.)

Hirschi, T. 1969 *Causes of Delinquency* (Berkeley, Cal.: University of California Press)

Hogarth, J. 1971 *Sentencing as a Human Process* (Toronto: University of Toronto Press)

Holt, N. and D. Miller 1972 *Explorations in Inmate-Family Relationships* Research Division, California Department of Corrections (Sacramento, Cal.: Jan.) 60–4

Hood, R.G. 1962 *Sentencing in Magistrates' Courts* (London: Stevens)
Hood, R.G. 1967 'Research on the effectiveness of punishments and treatments' *Collected Studies in Criminological Research*, vol 1 (Strasbourg: Council of Europe)
Hood, R.G. and R.F. Sparks 1970 *Key Issues in Criminology* (New York: McGraw-Hill)
Huffman, A.V. 1961 'Problems precipitated by homosexual approaches on youthful first offenders' *Journal of Social Therapy* 17, 216–22
Hugessen, J.K. 1973 Task Force on Release of Inmates *Report* (Ottawa: Information Canada) cat. no. JS92-673
Hunt, S.K. 1964 'The revocation decision: a study of probation and parole agents' discretion' unpublished MS dissertation (University of Wisconsin)
Hyman, H.H. 1954 *Interviewing in Social Research* (Chicago: University of Chicago Press)

Irwin, J. 1970 *The Felon* (Englewood Cliffs, NJ: Prentice Hall)
Irwin, J. and D.R. Cressey 1962 'Thieves, convicts and the inmate culture' *Social Problems* 10, no. 2, 142–55

James, L. 1971 *Prisoners' Perceptions of Parole* (Toronto: Centre of Criminology, University of Toronto)
Jeffery, C.R. 1971 *Crime Prevention Through Environmental Design* (London: Sage)
Jesness, C.F. n.d. *Preston Typology Study*. In press
Jesness, C.F. 1965 *The Fricot Ranch Study: Outcome with Small vs Large Living Groups in the Rehabilitation of Delinquents* Research Report no. 47, California Department of the Youth Authority (Sacramento, Cal.)
Jobson, K.B. 'Imprisonment' *Ottawa Law Review* 4, no. 2 (winter) 435–57
Johnson, B.M. 1961 *Parole Agent Job Analysis* Research Report no. 19, California Department of the Youth Authority (Sacramento, Cal.)
Johnston, N. 1970 *The Sociology of Punishment and Corrections*, 2nd ed. (New York: Wiley)

Klapmuts, Nora 1973 'Community Alternatives to Prison' *Crime and Delinquency Literature* 305–7 (National Council on Crime and Delinquency)
Klare, H.J. 1960 *Anatomy of a Prison* (London: Hutchinson)
Korn, R. 1965 Review of Glaser (1964) *American Sociological Review*, vol. 30 (Oct.)
Kroger, R. 1967 Personal communication

Landreville, P. 1967 *Expected Relapse Rates for Classes of Offenders* a paper delivered at the Canadian Congress of Corrections
Landreville, Pierre 1969, 'Prédiction de la gravité de l'agir délinquant' Thèse de doctorat (Montréal: École de criminologie, Université de Montréal)
Langlois, Robert 1972 *Analyse de la récidive sur une période d'épreuve de 10 ans* (Montréal: École de criminologie, Université de Montréal)
Laune, F.F. 1936 *Predicting Criminality* North Western University Studies in Social Sciences no. 1 (Chicago)
Lerman, P. 1968 'Evaluative studies of institutions for delinquents: implications for research and social policy' *Social Work* 13, no. 3 (July), 55–64

Léveillé, Yves 1968 'Qui Libère-t-on en libération conditionnelle' Thèse MA (Montréal: École de criminologie, Université de Montréal)
Léveillé, Yves 1970 'A qui accorde-t-on la libération conditionnelle?' *Canadian Journal of Criminology and Corrections* 12, 132–50
Lipsky, M. 1970 'Attrition in the legal process' *Law and Order Police Encounters* (Chicago: Aldine) 94
Lohman, J. et al. 1967 'The intensive supervision case-load' *The San Francisco Project: A Study of Federal Probation and Parole* Research Report no. 11 (Berkeley: School of Criminology, University of California)
Lohman, J.D. et al. 1966 'An afterview of supervision: research design' *The San Francisco Project* Research Report no. 10 (California: University of California, Dec.)
Lynch, M.L. 1967 Parole and the Habitual Criminal. *McGill Law Journal* 13, no. 4, 632

Mann, W.E. 1967 *Society Behind Bars; a Sociological Scrutiny of the Guelph Reformatory* (Toronto: Social Science Publishers)
Mannheim, H. and L.T. Wilkins 1955 *Prediction Methods in Relation to Borstal Training* (London HMSO)
Mannheim, H. 1965 *Comparative Criminology, a text book* (London: Routledge and Kegan Paul)
Marris, R. 1964 *The Economic Theory of 'Managerial' Capitalism* (London: Macmillan)
Martinson, R.M., G.G. Kassebaum, and D.A. Ward 1964 'A critique of research in parole' *Federal Probation* 28, no. 3, 34–8
Marx, G.L. 1969 *Counseling in Probation and Parole: A Research Report* (College Park, Md: University of Maryland)
Mathieson, T.E. 1965 *The Defences of the Weak: a Sociological Study of a Norwegian Correctional Insitution* (London: Tavistock Publications)
Menachem, A. 1971 *Patterns in Forcible Rape* (Chicago: University of Chicago Press)
Miles, A.P. 1964 *A Time Study of Wisconsin Probation and Parole Agents* (Madison: Wisconsin Division of Corrections)
Miller, F.P. 'Parole' *Crime and Its Treatment in Canada* edited by W.T. McGrath (Toronto; Macmillan of Canada) 326–83
Mohr, J.W., R.E. Turner, and M.B. Jerry 1965 *Pedophilia and Exhibitionism* (Toronto: University of Toronto Press)
Molof, M.J. 1970 *Statistical Prediction of Recidivism Among Female Parolees* Research Report no. 57, California Department of the Youth Authority (Sacramento, Cal.: Jan.)
Montreal, Canada 1970 *Montreal Star* (April 1)
Morris, N. 1967–8 'Psychiatry and the dangerous criminal' *Southern California Law Review* 41, 529–36
Morris, N. and G. Hawkins 1970 'Rehabilitation: rhetoric and reality' *Federal Probation* 34, no. 4 (Dec.) 9–17
Morris, Pauline 1965 *Prisoners and Their Families* (London: Allen and Unwin)
Morris, T.P. and P. Morris 1963 *Pentonville: A Sociological Study of an English Prison* (London: Routledge and Kegan Paul)
Mott, J. 1969 *The Jesness Inventory: Application to Approved School Boys*

Home Office Studies in the Cause of Delinquency in the Treatment of Offenders, no. 13 (London: HMSO)

McEachern, A.W. (ed.) 1968 'The juvenile probation system' *American Behavioral Scientist* 11, no. 3 (Jan.-Feb. 1968)

McEachern, A.W. and M. Taylor 1966 *The Disposition of Delinquents* Project Report no. 2 (Los Angeles: Youth Studies Centre, University of Southern California)

McGee, R.A. 1967 *The Organisation of State Correctional Services in the Control and Treatment of Crime and Delinquency* (Sacramento, Cal.)

McGrath, W.T. (ed.) 1965 *Crime and Its Treatment in Canada* (Toronto: Macmillan of Canada)

McGrath, W.T. 1968 *Report of the Alberta Penology Study* (Edmonton)

MacGregor, J.F. and M.E. Fowler 1965 'Work time demands on parole agents: a work sample study unpublished rough draft (California Department of Corrections)

Macnaughton-Smith, P. 1970 *What Is Crime and Why Do We Fight It?* (Toronto: Centre of Criminology, University of Toronto) 1970

Macnaughton-Smith, P. 1973 *'Permission to be Slightly Free'*, unpublished study of the granting, refusing, and withdrawing of parole in Canadian penitentiaries (Toronto: Centre of Criminology)

National Council on Crime and Delinquency 1972 *Parole Decision-making* (February) Report no. 1 'The utilization of experience in parole decision-making – a progress report' Report no. 2 'Developing a data base for parole decision-making' Report no. 3 'Parole decision-making coding manual' Report no. 4 'The problem of overlap in experience table construction' Report no. 5 'Summarizing experience for parole decision-making' Report no. 6 'Do experience tables matter?' Report no. 7 'The operational use of an experience table' Report no. 8 'Paroling policy feedback' Report no. 9 'Information selection and use in parole decision-making' Report no. 10 'Use of an information retrieval system for parole decision-making'

National Probation and Parole Institutes 1970 'Uniform Parole Reports' *Newsletter* (Davis, California: Aug.-Sept.)

Newsletter 1970 *Uniform Parole Reports of the National Probation and Parole Institutes* (Davis, Cal.: Nov.)

Newsletter 1971 *Uniform Parole Reports of the National Probation and Parole Institutes* (Davis, Cal.: Aug.)

Newspaper Enterprise Association, Inc 1968 *The World Almanac and Book of Facts*

Ohlin, L.E. and R.A. Lawrence 1952 'A comparison of alternative methods of parole prediction' *American Sociological Review* 17, 268–72

Ottawa, Canada 1960 'Parole Act parole regulations' *Canada Gazette* part II vol. 94 (Ottawa: Queen's Printer, 8 June)

Ottawa, Canada 1963 *Annual report of the National Parole Board* (31 Dec.)

Ottawa, Canada 1970 Canadian Bureau of Statistics *Correctional Insitution Statistics, 1970* (Ottawa: Queen's Printer)

Ottawa, Canada 1971 *The Standing Senate Committee on Legal and Constitutional Affairs Evidence* no. 11 (Dec. 15) 5–7

Ottawa, Canada *Bill C-2* sections 57, 58, and 72, House of Commons of Canada (Ottawa: Queen's Printer)

Ottawa, Canada 1972a J. Ciale 'Brief presented to *Eighth Proceedings on the Examination of the Parole System in Canada* Senate of Canada *Legal and Constitutional Affairs* no. 7 (27 April)

'Ouimet Report' 1969 *Toward Unity: Criminal justice and corrections* Report of Canadian Committee on Corrections, Chairman Roger Ouimet

Packer, H.L. 1968 *The Limits of the Criminal Sanction* (California: Stanford University Press) 292–5

Panton, J.H. 1959 'Inmate personality differences related to recidivism, age and race as measured by the MMPI' *Journal of Correctional Psychology* 4, no. 1 (spring) 28–35

Panton, J.H. 'Use of the MMPI as an index to successful parole' *Journal of Criminal Law, Criminology and Police Science* 53 no. 4 (Dec.) 484–8

Paradis, Georges, André Beaulne, René Blain, Gérard Héroux 1972 *Image de la libération conditionnelle par les détenus et ex-détenus de Montréal métropolitan* 1 et 2 (Montréal: École de criminologie, Université de Montréal, mai, août)

Parker, T. 1963 *The Unknown Citizen* (London: Hutchinson)

Parker, T. 1967 *A Man of Good Abilities* (London: Hutchinson)

Parker, T. and R.H. Allerton 1962 *The Courage of His Convictions* (London: Hutchinson)

Polsky, H. 1962 *Cottage Six* (New York: Russell Sage Foundation)

Price, Professor R.R. 1970 'Mentally disordered and dangerous persons under the criminal law' *Canadian Journal of Corrections* 12, 241–64

Radzinowicz, L. and M.E. Wolfgang 1971 *Crime and Justice* (New York: Basic Books)

Reiss, A.J., Jr. 1971 *The Police and the Public* (New Haven: Yale University Press) 102–20

Richardson, R.B. 1964 *A Pilot Investigation of Parole Follow-up Criteria*, Research Report no. 9, California Department of Corrections

Robison, J. 1967 *Two Years on Continuous Parole* Bay Area Research Unit paper (March)

Robison, J. 1971 *By the Standard of His Rehabilitation; information, decision and outcome in terminations from parole: the implementation of Penal Code Section 2943* Research Report no. 39, California Department of Corrections (Sacramento, Cal.)

Robison, J. n.d. '2943 PC decision making study – a preliminary analysis' unpublished paper, California Department of Corrections, Bay Area Research Unit

Robison, James and Paul Takagi 1968 *Case decisions in a state parole system* Research Report no. 31, California Department of Corrections (Sacramento, Cal.)

Robison, J. et al. 1969 *It's Time to Stop Counting* California Prison, Parole and Probation System, technical supplement no. 2 (April)

Robison, J. et al. 1969a 'A review and new findings: offender classification, sentencing, disposition, supervisor intensity, violation rate' Final Report *The San*

Francisco Project: a Study of Federal Probation and Parole (Berkeley: School of Criminology, University of California)

Robison, J. and G. Smith 1971 'The effectiveness of correctional programs' *Crime and Delinquency* 17, no. 1 (Jan.)

Saleebey, G. 1971 'Five years of probation subsidy' *California Youth Authority Quarterly* 24, no. 3 (fall) 3–15

Sarbin, T.R. 1967 'The dangerous individual: an outcome of social identity transformations' *British Journal of Criminology* 7, no. 3, 285–95

Sawyer, J. 1966 'Measurement and prediction, clinical and statistical' *Psychological Bulletin* 66, no. 3, 178–200

Schwartz, R.D. and J.H. Skolnick 1962 'Two studies of legal stigma' *Social Problems* 10, 133–8

Shearing, C.D. 1968 'Work adjustment measure' and 'Parole integration draft schedules' unpublished drafts; also 'Offenders, after-care agencies and the labour market: an exploratory case study unpublished MA dissertation (Toronto: University of Toronto)

Sheppard, C. 1971 'The violent offender: let's examine the taboo' *Federal Probation* (Dec.) 12–19

Siegel, S. 1956 *Nonparametric Statistics: for the Behavioral Sciences* (Toronto: McGraw-Hill)

Simon, F.H. 1971 *Prediction Methods in Criminology; Including a Prediction Study of Young Men on Probation* Home Office Research Studies no. 7 (London: HMSO)

Skolnick, J.H. 1960 'Towards a developmental theory of parole' *American Sociological Review* 25, no. 4, 542–9

Smelser, N. 1962 *Theory of Collective Behaviour* (London: Free Press)

Smigel, E.O. and H.L. Ross 1970 *Crime Against Bureaucracy* (New York: Van Nostrand Reinhold)

Smith, G.W. and L.T. Wilkins 1968 'Sound an alarm: the problem of bias' *Journal of Research in Crime and Delinquency* 5, no. 2, 115–201

Snedecor, G.W., and W.G. Cochran 1967 *Statistical Methods*, 6th ed. (Ames, Iowa: Iowa State University Press)

Sparks, R.F. 1968 'Research on probation, parole and measures of after-care' *Collected Studies in Criminological Research* vol. 3 (Strasbourg: Council of Europe)

Sparks, R.F. 1971 'The use of suspended sentences' *Criminal Law Review* (July) 384–401

Sparks, R.F. 1972 *Local Prisons in the English Prison System* (London: Heinemann)

Stafford-Clark, D. 1963 *Psychiatry To-day* (Harmondsworth: Penguin)

Sternberg, D. 1963 'Synanon House – a consideration of its implications for American correction' *Journal of Criminal Law, Criminology and Police Science* 54, no. 4 (Dec.) 447–55

Stockdale, E. 1967 *The Court and the Offender* (London: Gollancz)

Strathy, D.A. 1961 'The expectations of the parole supervision experience held by penitentiary inmates prior to their release on parole' unpublished MSW thesis (Toronto: University of Toronto)

Street, D., et al. 1966 *Organisation for Treatment: A Comparative Study of Institutions for Delinquents* (New York: Free Press)

Street, T.G. 1968 *Minutes of the House of Commons Standing Committee on Justice and Legal Affairs* (Ottawa: Nov., Dec.)

Street, T.G. 1971 'Canada's parole system' *A Presentation to the Sub-Committee of the Standing Senate Committee on Legal and Constitutional Affairs* (Dec.)

Studt, Elliot 1967 *The Re-entry of the Offender into Society* JD Publication no. 9002 (Washington, DC: US Department of Health, Education and Welfare, Welfare Administration, Offices of Juvenile Delinquency and Youth Development)

Studt, Elliot 1970 'Parolees and agents in interaction' unpublished draft (Berkeley: Centre for the Study of Law and Society, University of California)

Studt, Elliot 1971 *People in the Parole Action System: their tasks and dilemmas* report of the Parole Action Study MR-163 (Los Angeles: Institute of Government and Public Affairs, University of California)

Studt, Elliot 1972 *Surveillance and Service in Parole* report of the Parole Action Study MR-166 (Los Angeles: Institute of Government and Public Affairs, University of California)

Sturup, G.K. 1968 *Treating the 'Untreatable': chronic criminals at Herstedvester* (Baltimore: Johns Hopkins Press)

Sutherland, E.H. and D.R. Cressey 1964 *Delinquency, Crime and Differential Association* (The Hague: M. Nijhoff)

Sutherland, E.H. and D.R. Cressey 1970 *Principles of Criminology*, 8th ed. (Philadelphia: Lippincott)

Sykes, G.M. 1958 *The Society of Captives* (Princeton, NJ: Princeton University Press)

Sykes, G.M. and D. Matza 1957 'Techniques of neutralization: a theory of delinquency' *American Sociological Review* 22 (Dec.) 664–70

Takagi, P.T. 1965 *Parole Panel Studies, Report C, Criminal Types and Parole Prediction and Attitude Change on Parole* Research Report no. 14, California Department of Corrections (Sacramento, Cal.)

Takagi, P.T. 1967 'Evaluation systems and adaptations in a formal organization: a case study of a parole agency' unpublished PHD dissertation (Stanford University)

Takagi, P.T. 1969 'The effect of parole agents' judgements on recidivism rates' *Psychiatry* 32, no. 2 (1969) 192–9

Takagi, P.T. and J. Robison 1968 *Case Decisions in a State Parole System* Research Report no. 31, California Department of Corrections (Sacramento, Cal.)

Takagi, P.T. and J. Robison 1969 'The parole violator: an organizational reject' Journal of Research in Crime and Delinquency 6, no. 1, 78–86

Tappan, Paul W. 1960 *Crime, Justice, and Corrections* (Toronto: McGraw-Hill)

Thomas, D.A. 1970 *Principles of Sentencing* (London: Heinemann) xlix.

Thomas, D.A. 1963 'Stating reasons for decisions' reprint of 'Sentencing – the case for reasoned decisions' *Criminal Law Review* (April) 243–53

Time Magazine 1971 (18 Jan.) 42–7

Tompkins, D.C. 1972 *The Prison and The Prisoner* Public Policy Bibliographies: 1 (Berkeley: Institute of Governmental Studies, University of California)

Toronto, Canada 1970 *Toronto Star* (18 June)

Toronto, Canada 1971 *Globe and Mail* (16 Feb.)

Truax, C.B., and R.R. Carkhuff 1967 *Toward Effective Counselling and Psychotherapy: Training and Practice* (Chicago: Aldine)

USA 1961 *Special Intensive Parole Unit: Phase IV – High Base Expectancy Study* Research Report no. 10 California Department of Corrections (Sacramento, Cal.)

USA 1965 Space General Corporation California *A Study of Prevention and Control of Crime and Delinquency* Final Report PCCD-7 (California Youth and Adult Correction Agency)

USA 1967 Joint Commission on Correctional Manpower and Training *Research in Correctional Rehabilitation: report of a seminar* (Washington)

USA 1967a President's Commission on Law Enforcement and Administration of Justice *Task Force Report: Science and Technology* Insitute for Defense Analyses (Washington, DC: US Government Printing Office)

USA 1967b US President's Commission on Law Enforcement and Administration of Justice *Task Force Report: Corrections* (Washington, DC: US Government Printing Office)

USA 1967c US President's Commission on Law Enforcement and Administration of Justice *The Challenge of Crime in a Free Society* (Washington, DC: US Government Printing Office)

USA 1967d Bureau of the Census *Estimates of the Total Population of the United States and Armed Forces Abroad* (Washington, DC: US Government Printing Office, July)

USA 1970 National Commission on the Causes and Prevention of Violence 'International Comparisons' *Task Force Report: Causes of Violence, 1970*

USA 1972 House of Representatives *Hearings on H.R. 13118 To Improve and Revise the Procedures and Structure of the Federal and State Parole Systems* Corrections Federal and State Parole Systems, Part VII-A, Serial no. 15 (Washington, DC: US Government Printing Office)

Vichert, B.W. and W. Zahnd 1965 'Parole: low and high risk parolees' *Canadian Journal of Corrections* 7, no. 1 (Jan.) 39–48

Wald, A. 1945 'Statistical Decision Functions which Minimize the Maximum Risk' *Annals of Mathematics* 46, 265–80

Walker, N. 1969 *Sentencing in a Rational Society* (London: Penguin)

Waller, J.I. 1971 'The helping and the square: a brief consideration of the ex-prisoner's portayal of himself and others important to him' unpublished addendum to THIS STUDY (Centre of Criminology, University of Toronto, Oct.)

Ward, D.A. 1967 'Evaluation of correctional treatment: some implications of negative findings' *Law Enforement Science and Technology* edited by S.A. Yefsky (New York: Thompson Book Co.) 201–14

Wechsler, H. 1968 'Principles of sentencing under the model penal code' reprint of 'Codification of criminal law in the United States: the model penal code' *Columbia Law Review* 68, no. 8 (Dec.) 1450–6

Weeks, H. Ashley 1958 'The Highfields Project and its success' *Youthful Offenders at Highfields* (Ann Arbor: University of Michigan Press) 1–2, 3–5, 7–10, 20–4, 118–28

West, D.J. (ed.) 1972 *The Future of Parole; commentaries on systems in Britain and* USA (London: Duckworth)

Wheeler, S. 1961 'Socialization in correctional communities' *American Sociological Review* 26, no. 5, 697–712

Wilkins, L.T. 1969 *Evaluation of Penal Measures* (New York: Random House)

Willcock, H.D. 1967 'Deterrents and incentives to crime amongst youths aged 15 to 21 years' unpublished report prepared for the Home Office by the Social Survey

Wilson, J.Q. 1968 'The Patrolman' *Varieties of Police Behaviour* (Cambridge: Harvard University Press) 16–18

Wolff, H.G. 'The relation between the courts and the National Parole Board' *University of Toronto Law Journal* 19 (1969)

Zalba, S.R. 1967 'Work release – a two-pronged effort' *Crime and Delinquency* 13, no. 4 (Oct.) 506–12

Zimring, F.E. 1971 *Perspectives on Deterrence* Crime and delinquency issues: a monograph series, Public Health Service Publication no. 2056 (Washington, DC: US Government Printing Office, Jan.)

Zimring, F.E. and G. Hawkins 1967 'Deterrence and marginal groups' *Journal of Research in Crime and Delinquency* 5, no. 2, 100–14

Zimring, F.E. and G.J. Hawkins 1973 *Deterrence, the legal threat in crime control* (Chicago: University of Chicago Press)

Index